# THE MARCO POLO EXPEDITION

Portrait of a Uighur girl, near Kashgar, Xinjiang.

# THE MARCO POLO EXPEDITION

## A Journey Along the Silk Road

### RICHARD B. FISHER

*Photography by Tom Ang*

HODDER AND STOUGHTON
LONDON   SYDNEY   AUCKLAND   TORONTO

All photographs are by Tom Ang, except the one of him on page 16 which is by Paul Crook.

British Library Cataloguing in Publication Data

Fisher, Richard
    The Marco Polo Expedition.
    1. Asia. Description & travel
    I. Title   II. Ang, Tom
    915'.04' 428

    ISBN-340-41606-8

Published by Hodder and Stoughton,
a division of Hodder and Stoughton Ltd,
Mill Road, Dunton Green, Sevenoaks, Kent TN13 2YE
Editorial Office: 47 Bedford Square, London WC1B 3DP.

Book designed by Trevor Spooner

Photoset by Rowland Phototypesetting Ltd,
Bury St Edmunds, Suffolk
Printed and bound in Great Britain by
Butler and Tanner Ltd, Frome, Somerset

To the source of love without whom
this wonderful journey would have
been improbable and the last incredible
years impossible.

The photographs are for Ros.

# CONTENTS

Emperors and kings, dukes and marquises, counts, knights, and townsfolk and all people who wish to know the various races of men and the peculiarities of the various regions of the world, take this book and have it read to you. Here you will find all the great wonders and curiosities of Greater Armenia and Persia, of the Tartars and of India, and of many other territories.

Marco Polo, *The Travels*

History is full of men who saw cities, and went to them, and found them shrunk to villages or destroyed centuries before or not built yet. And the last sort were the luckiest.

Alasdair Gray, *Lanark: A Life in Four Books*

# PERSONNEL OF THE MARCO POLO EXPEDITION

British:    Richard B. Fisher, Expedition leader
            Tom Ang, Expedition photographer
            Don Baker, Arabic and Islamic art and architecture
            Geoff Clarke, Medical officer
            Paul Crook, Chinese language and history

Soviet:     Yuri Petrovich Badenkov, Deputy Director, Institute of
                Geography, USSR Academy of Sciences
            Dmitri Borisovich Oreshkin, Liaison officer and publicist
            Olga Ivanovna Omelchenko, Translator and interpreter
            Natalia Borisovna Steglik, Translator and interpreter
            Anatoly Nikolaevich Bobrovich, Stills photographer
            Boris Lvovich Antsiferov, TV cameraman, Central TV,
                Moscow
            Valery Dmitrievich Chekushin, Driver
            Gennady Ivanovich Kozlov, Driver
            Artiom Yurievich Badenkov, Dogsbody

Chinese:    Liu Guanjian, Deputy Manager of the Mountain Scientific
                Expedition Advisory Service and Liaison officer
            Shen Peng, Driver
            Zheng Yupei, Physician and nutritionist
            Hu Youquan, Journalist
            Liu Ziai, Driver
            Xiao Wang, Liu Guanjian's fiancée

The imam of the main mosque, Lanzhou, Gansu.

# Marco Polo and Other Preliminaries
## December 1983–April 1987

Until we reached the Soviet Union, our van was never left entirely unattended. The roof rack carried valuable spares, wheels, tyres and camping equipment, chained or strapped in place but detachable given time and determination. Even in Soviet central Asia, despite the assurances of our Russian colleagues that nothing would be disturbed, I at least was sceptical.

Nevertheless, in Samarkand it was left for two hours one warm and sunny morning locked but alone on a busy pavement near the entrance to the bazaar and in front of the mosque of Timur's favourite wife, Bibi Qanum. Our party, three Britons, two Muscovites, our seasoned local guide and a Samarkand city official, had walked back 250 metres to explore the symbolic city centre, the Registan. When we returned, the van was surrounded by a buzzing, shifting crowd of brightly-dressed women, men in shirt sleeves wearing square-blocked Uzbek hats and six or eight children, mostly small boys. They were peering in the windows, examining the large red jack chained to the bumper and twirling the air-conditioning fan in front of the radiator. The fan-twirling we stopped at once, but nothing else had been touched. Mainly, both adults and children were reading aloud to each other the names painted in black on the white van.

On the near side of the body were the names of our commercial sponsors. On the far side a list of our academic sponsors appeared, with the Institute of Geography, USSR Academy of Sciences in Russian as well as English. The Institute of Geology, Academia Sinica, similarly had been painted in Chinese. Both rear mudguards carried the words: "Scouts: UNESCO Silk Road Project" with the bold black letters, UNESCO, especially prominent. On both doors, our Islington sign painter had reproduced the expedition logo, mountains beside desert in a lozenge with the words, Marco Polo Expedition, in a band separating them. Beneath, the name had been repeated in Turkish, Farsi, Chinese, Uigher and Russian.

Three twelve-year-old boys pointed to the Russian in deep discussion.

"They are telling each other the story of Marco Polo," said Ludmilla, our local guide.

"What are they saying?"

"That he was an Italian, they think, who went all the way to China on camels a long time ago, more or less. The blond boy says he was European, not Italian."

"I wonder if they have heard of UNESCO?"

She asked them, pointing to the letters. One nodded uncertainly, but all three backed away. Ludmilla put the question to an old man. He smiled and waved his hand dismissively.

"I think they may have heard of it," she reported, "but I wouldn't like to press them to say what it is."

In a small town called Silvan in southern Anatolia I observed very much the same thing. We had parked near the entrance to a five-hundred-year-old, much-restored mosque, and the usual crowd had gathered. I had come back to the van so that my colleague, who had stayed behind on temporary guard, could appreciate the building. The boys in the crowd certainly recognised Marco Polo. In fact, along our route his name was universally familiar, far better known than the prestigious international organisation, UNESCO, or the respective Academies of Science. Such fame reflects the human appreciation of adventure.

The majority of the great travel writer's admirers probably did not know that he had left Venice on *his* great journey in 1271. The Mongol invasions of central Asia that began with the wild explosion of Genghis Khan from the eastern Siberian homeland at the beginning of the century had by this time finally guttered out. The nomad conquerors had for the most part been sucked into the sedentary cities they had sacked, settling in to the enjoyment of their spoils. They had become Muslim, the religion of the peoples whom they now governed. After the middle of the thirteenth century, political and military conditions once again permitted trade across central Asia between Europe and China.

Marco Polo's father and uncle had first taken advantage of these conditions during the previous decade, but not without experiences of war between Berke, Khan of the Mongol Blue Horde in south Russia, and Hulegu, first of the Il-Khanid Mongol rulers of Persia. This conflict cut off their return route and forced them to remain in "the large and splendid city called Bukhara" for three years. Although Marco does not report these details, I think you can assume they made a living through trade in one of the greatest bazaars in central Asia.

While they were staying there, said the son and nephew, "there came an envoy from Hulagu . . . on the way to the Great Khan of all the Tartars, whose name was Kubilai. He lived at the ends of the earth in an east-north-easterly direction . . . he said to them: 'Sirs, if you will trust me, I can offer you an opportunity of great profit and great honour.'"

Niccolo and Maffeo Polo agreed to trust the envoy and accompanied him to China. Kubilai Khan learned from the brothers about the power of the Catholic Church and asked them to convey letters to the Pope requesting instruction in the teachings of Christianity. With these letters they returned to Venice in 1269. "There Messer Niccolo learnt that his wife was dead, and there was left to him a son of fifteen, whose name was Marco."

It was sensible for the father and uncle to take the boy with them when they returned to the court of Kubilai Khan. He would learn not only the fine points of trade but where goods could be bought cheaply and where resold at a higher price. First, however, they had to await the election of a new Pope following the death of Clement IV. For two years they remained in Venice but then decided they could not postpone their return any longer. The party sailed for Acre, a Christian Crusader enclave on the coast of what is now Israel. There they obtained the backing of an eminent Papal legate, Tedaldo Visconti, to whom they explained their mission. They sailed on to Ayas, a port in the north-eastern Mediterranean armpit of Turkey which has literally disappeared. At Ayas, however, a courier brought them news that none other than Visconti had been elected as Pope Gregory X. Now, with full diplomatic status and accompanied by two missionaries appointed by the new prelate, they continued their epic journey.

Lacking the stamina or the stomach of the Polos, the missionaries soon asked to be left behind. Niccolo, Maffeo and young Marco travelled through eastern Turkey, probably to the former Armenian capital at Ani, into north-western Iran at Tabrīz, south through western Iran and Iraq, along the Gulf to Hormuz and thence north to the Afghan city of Balkh. During this difficult part of the journey through the eastern Iranian desert, Marco fell ill and almost died. He might have caught malaria. When the party could move again, they travelled as far as the Pamirs in the north-eastern tail of what is now Afghanistan, the Wakhan. Marco reported that the clean air gradually produced a cure, but a year passed before they could carry on. From the high mountains they descended into the great desert of western China, the Taklimakan, made their way around its southern rim and thence to the summer court of Kubilai Khan north of his new capital at Khan-balik, now Beijing. The journey had taken three years.

Twenty-one years later, the three men again reached Venice. According to the famous book by Marco, most of those years had been spent in the service of the Chinese court. He reported that, with his father and uncle, he had participated as an engineer in the battle of Xiang Yang Fou. Although Chinese sources say that foreign engineers did participate in the battle, it took place in 1273 at which time Marco was recovering from near-fatal illness in Afghanistan. Marco also describes his governorship of a Chinese city, but the annals of the dynasty, the Yuan, founded by Kubilai Khan, contain no record of any such name amongst those who are listed as incumbents of the post.

Probably in part because of the wealth with which he returned to Venice, Marco Polo became a captain commanding a ship in the city's navy. In 1298, he was captured by Genoese forces and imprisoned in the enemy city. He shared his captivity with one Rustichello of Pisa, a professional writer of romances. Rustichello may even have met the Polos at Acre twenty-five years before; he had travelled there with the future Pope Gregory X in the suite of King Edward I of England. In any case, the writer, along with others of Marco Polo's fellow prisoners, had probably heard the wonderful travellers' tales Polo told. He may have recognised in them a new kind of romance because there is no doubt that Rustichello became Marco's amanuensis. It was he who wrote Marco Polo's *Travels*, despite the fact that Marco was certainly literate, enjoyed reliving his adventures and had plenty of time in prison to do the job himself. It has been widely accepted that what Marco saw, he described faithfully and accurately, but that hearsay accounts are filled with errors and naïve superstitions. No doubt the Genoese imprisonment fostered some of the grander flights of fantasy.

Rustichello deserved whatever rewards he received. To his readers, it all seemed like fiction. Marco Polo, aged seventeen, enjoyed the favours of a chieftain's wife as part of the hospitality of central Asia. Marco Polo suffered delirium from the heat and thirst of a terrible desert. Marco Polo travelled in state to the far corners of distant China on diplomatic missions for the Emperor. These are the very stuff of romance, whether they are true or not.

Of course, Marco Polo travelled with merchants who paid their way by trading goods. The only other reason for travel in the thirteenth century was religion. Two Jesuit monks, Giovanni di Piano Carpini and Guillaume de Roubrouck, made the hard and perilous journey to the Mongol capital at Karakorum, another city that has disappeared, in 1245 and 1253 respectively, to convert the Great Khan to Christianity and make an alliance with him against the Muslims. Despite the relative tolerance of the Mongols for all religions, the Jesuits failed on both counts, though there had been a time a few years earlier when one of the Mongol Khans had tried to interest the papacy in an alliance. Both men wrote reports of their journeys for their patrons. They are shorter, less colourful and probably more factual than the *Travels*. On the other hand, no other merchants left written records of their experiences.

The trading routes followed by the Polos were part of an intricate network of roads and tracks that carried caravans across the great Eurasian land mass. Everywhere towns were linked by such routes. If a series of towns provided rich enough markets, merchants travelled from one to the next making local trade into something akin to international exchange. In the case of valuable goods like horses, precious stones and silk, the major centres of demand were separated by thousands of miles from the sources of supply. Thus the Silk Road, a generic term for trading routes first applied in the last century, referred to a route for caravans that travelled from silk-producing areas in China to Constantinople, Venice or even Paris. The same route might also be used for local trade, and it might equally be used by merchants carrying paper or carved wood. Like the world's airline networks today, the Silk Road was a cat's-cradle of highways along which an individual merchant followed the thread that served his commercial needs. Thus, Niccolo and Maffeo Polo went to China the first time via Bukhara and Samarkand. On their return journey with Marco, they travelled only two or three hundred miles further south, but below the great Oxus River, the Greek name for Amudar'ya.

Though the merchant's selection of a route depended principally on a commercial judgment about the market for his goods, politics and war inevitably played a role in the decision he made. Thus, Niccolo and Maffeo travelled to Bukhara partly because they could not return to Constantinople at that time.

The Marco Polo Expedition lacked the commercial motive entirely. We could select freely amongst Silk Roads those highways that led through the most beautiful scenery to the most exciting historical monuments and archaeological discoveries. Originally, I defined the Silk Road in terms of Bukhara, Samarkand and the southern route around the Taklimakan Desert followed by Marco Polo. That route had the merit of avoiding Afghanistan, closed to all travel except by the rare intrepid loner since the Soviet invasion in 1976.

We might have landed in Asia near the site of Acre, but it was sadly impractical to drive north through the Lebanon, and ancient Ayas no longer survives. Therefore I selected Antakya as our starting point, ancient Antioch, despite the harsh historical fact that the Christian Crusaders finally lost the fortified city to the Saracens in 1268, three years before Marco Polo left Venice. It is the nearest Turkish city to Syria and the Levant.

Our route led across northern Iran through Tabrīz, Tehrān, Samnun, Dāmghān and the site of Nishapur to Mashhad. The original proposal to enter the Soviet Union at Sarakhs, the ancient former capital of the province of Khorāsan, was modified at the request of the Soviet authorities, but in any event, politics and one of those unforeseeable diplomatic crises between Britain and Iran not only forcibly changed our plan but almost destroyed the expedition.

Yet even this near-disaster produced a traveller's bonus. Thrown back into Turkey, we had to pass through Kars in order to enter the Soviet Union. It gave us an opportunity to see the scattered magnificence of Ani which had not been on our original route.

One more disappointment remained. Two days before we left London, our Chinese hosts wrote to say that the military authorities had withdrawn their approval of the southern route around the Taklimakan. We were left with the northern route, but it, too, had been part of the Silk Road. Cities like Kumul, Turfan and the neighbouring ruins and Kucha had also been centres of trade and civilisation for centuries.

Though we bowed to political necessity, most of the alternative routes brought their own prizes, just as they had done for the Polos. Of course, our objectives were not commercial, but we, too, prospered along those Silk Roads we followed.

I was, and continue to be, interested by central Asian historical geography, a phrase that includes archaeological remains, major architectural monuments and written records. In particular, I am fascinated by caravanserais, also called hans, particularly if they are in cities. They are basically motels, places where travelling merchants could rest and refresh themselves, their servants and their animals. Caravanserais, literally palaces for caravans, also provided facilities for exchanging goods and animals and buying food. Usually, they were two storeys high with rooms including cooking facilities built around one or more open courtyards. Not surprisingly in these semi-arid regions, they were located near a fresh water supply. Most contained a mosque. In Persia, after the Mongol conquest, the caravanserais became staging posts for the official mail service. In China, beyond the Great Wall, they were combined with garrisons. Often they were constructed and maintained by a local ruler who recognised that they brought taxable goods into his domain. Their common purpose dictated a common architectural layout which is remarkably consistent.

I have a doctoral degree in American history which helps to explain this focus of interest. When the expedition took place, I was sixty-eight and had lived in London for more than twenty years. After the statutory five-year residence in Britain, I applied for and eventually obtained British nationality. In practice, becoming a British citizen means only that I carry a British passport and can vote. You do not have to be a citizen of this or any other country to be subject to its taxes, income or poll. Being a native of the United

Richard B. Fisher          Tom Ang

States, I am familiar with the American revolutionary slogan, "No taxation without representation."

To my own surprise, I awakened only a decade ago to the realisation that I had never actually read Marco Polo's *Travels*. The omission was rapidly put right and it made an immense impression on me. At about the same time, the yearning to do something different before it was too late began to grow in me as it does in so many of us when advancing age loosens the sense of responsibility. I thought of the Silk Road which no one had crossed for 400 years, never by automobile. I was not satisfied by the expensive and restricted package tours to the Soviet Union and China that provided occasional bezaz. Being a little old for individual adventures and too poor to buy the help of experienced travellers, I determined to collect two or three friends with special interests and fit them together with my newly-discovered, Polo-inspired awareness of the Eurasian Silk routes.

During the middle of 1983, I mooted the idea to Tom Ang, a photographer whose work I have admired since he first showed me examples when we were beginner students of Chinese at the Polytechnic of Central London. Half a dozen years ago we had talked about writing and directing a TV documentary on Marco Polo's journey and soon learned that we were not the first to come up with the idea. Indeed, television viewers of the world have since been subjected to two series: an Italian romance, loosely based on the *Travels*, but with more sex than sense or scenery, and a serious-minded Sino-Japanese

Don Baker

Paul Crook

Geoff Clarke

production about the Silk Road which is arguably even worse television. The expedition seemed to us both to offer a viable alternative.

Tom was just over thirty, born in Singapore of Chinese parents but educated in England. With a young family to support, his time for speculative ventures had to be limited, but he enthusiastically accepted the responsibility when the time came for obtaining the expensive camera equipment he would need. Even at the early stages, he suggested that we attempt to do holography. He also proposed the use of photogrammetry, a technique that we abandoned finally only very late in our preparations. Tom felt that having now become the Associate Editor of *Photography* magazine, for which he wished to write monthly reports during the journey, he had enough on his plate already.

Don Baker was an even earlier and much more sceptical recruit. Don was about fifty and had his own established business as a private conservator working for dealers and institutions as well as private collectors. Shortly before we talked about the expedition, when he was nearing completion of a course in paper conservation at what was then the Camberwell College of Art and Design, he had undertaken a required major practical project involving restoration and protection of two sheets from a tenth-century Qurân. The work had commercial as well as academic interest because he began to specialise in Islamic books and manuscripts. He also began to study Arabic and the history and culture of Islam. In 1983, he was employed by UNESCO to design and set up a brand-new conservation department in the King Faisal

Centre for Research and Islamic Studies in Riyadh. He trained the original conservation staff and was asked to return a year later to repeat the training programme for a new group.

Apart from the fact that we have been friends for many years, therefore, Don was able to contribute expert knowledge of the architecture and the social and religious customs that have dominated the Silk Road since the Arab conquest of central Asia beginning in the eighth century. From the outset, it was agreed that because he has a one-man business to run, he would travel with us only as far as Samarkand which meant about two months. Unfortunately, because of Iranian bad faith he was forced to leave us just before we finally entered the Soviet Union and missed the riches of Turkmenistan and Uzbekistan.

The fourth member of the expedition chronologically and the youngest by a few months was Paul Crook. He had been my teacher at the polytechnic after Tom had left the course. Paul was born in Beijing where he went to school until he was seventeen. His mother is Canadian and his father English. The Crooks have worked at the Foreign Languages Institute in the Chinese capital for the better part of forty years. Both were imprisoned for several years by the Cultural Revolution, though in separate prisons and without knowledge of the whereabouts or well-being of the other. Paul, who was fifteen at the time, discovered his mother's location quite by accident when he saw her standing in the window of an Institute building that he passed every day during his bicycle ride to school. After their release and eventual rehabilitation by the Chinese authorities, including a personal apology from the long-serving Prime Minister, Zhou Enlai, Mr and Mrs Crook stayed on, teaching and travelling as before. Like his two older brothers, Paul left to complete his education.

Some time after he and I had discussed the expedition, he was employed by the Chinese section of the BBC External Services. He thought he could obtain leave to do the second half of the journey, meeting us in Samarkand just before Don went home. Apart from his knowledge of Chinese history, customs and practices, he is bilingual, an inestimable asset. The BBC also commissioned him to make tape recordings which he could use for programmes on the External Service. Paul flew to Samarkand on June 22nd where he was met by our Russian hosts, as planned. During the next three weeks, he represented the Marco Polo Expedition in the Soviet Union, giving speeches of thanks on our behalf to officials of collective farms and local factories – and receiving generous gifts like an Uzbek coat that happened to fit him. Paul is six feet four.

The fifth member of the expedition, Geoff Clarke, joined us a year and a half later as the nominee of the Imperial Cancer Research Fund, his employer until his recent retirement. It came about as part of a complicated sequence of events aimed at obtaining the travel permits we needed.

Some travellers are young enough or feckless enough to travel alone across the world's troubled surface without documents and often disguised. Perhaps the greatest of these is Peter Fleming, but the most recent is Nick Danziger. (The books they wrote about their adventures are listed in the Bibliography.) If you want to travel as a small, independent unit as the Polos did, you must face problems that took me four years to solve.

In December 1983, I took the first formal steps towards realising the expedition by writing letters to the Turkish, Iranian, Soviet and Chinese Embassies in London. The Turkish authorities welcomed our plans and showered us with expensive travel brochures in full colour. The Iranians assured me that we could have two-week transit visas any time, and that we could enter the Soviet Union at any point approved by the Soviet authorities. As far as Iran was concerned, they said, all border points with the Soviet Union were open. Now, their assurance provokes a hollow laugh.

In February 1987, after the Chinese and Soviet authorities had at last opened their borders to us, I applied to the Iranian Consulate for visas. The application form asks where you intend to leave Iran and whether the country on the other side of the border has given you permission to enter at that point. I answered the first by entering the name of the Iranian border post at Bājgirān and the second with a yes.

"That border is closed," said the Iranian visa clerk.

"But you told me three years ago that we would be allowed to enter the Soviet Union at any crossing point approved by them."

"Maybe, but the border is now closed. We can send your applications to Tehrān to ask for special permission, but it will take time, perhaps six to eight weeks."

I thanked him. He had offered to apply for us to the Foreign Ministry, the highest authority, I thought. But I explained that we had to leave London by May 1st in order to keep our schedule in Iran and the Soviet Union.

There had been no reply by April 1st. On that date, I went to Paris to attend the first meeting of the Task Force for the as yet unofficial UNESCO Silk Road Project. I had heard about this extraordinary project during my first visit to Moscow in connection with the expedition the previous December. My hosts at the Institute of Geography of the USSR Academy of Sciences knew of rumours, but it was my earlier contact at the Soviet National Commission for UNESCO, Sergei Klockov, who knew details. He had already been involved in formulating the proposal for what was then seen as a three-year field and academic study of the Silk Road. The field work would require fleets of vehicles to travel the branching trade routes as well as a journey by sea from the Chinese coast via India, following approximately Marco Polo's homeward voyage. Major seminars were to be held in Xi'an, Ashkhabad and other cities. The project was to open with an exhibition and seminar on the Silk Road in Nara during October 1988. The man in charge, Klockov told me, was Eiji Hattori, chief of the Promotions Department of the UNESCO Secretariat. It was Hattori's baby. "Phone him. He will be very pleased to talk to you."

Mr Hattori was enthusiastic. He came to London in March to meet the members of the Marco Polo Expedition. The Silk Road Project, he explained, had not yet obtained the necessary formal approval of the UNESCO Council. Indeed, the project was not to be put before the Council until November 1987, but meanwhile, preliminary planning would continue within the Secretariat. The April meeting was to be a step forward in the co-operation between UNESCO employees like Hattori and central Asian scholars and interested people like ourselves. At the meeting, I was asked to describe the route we expected to follow. It was then proposed that the expedition might be willing to report on practical aspects of driving along the Silk Road, such matters as road surfaces, the availability of petrol and parts and resources available to scholars, such as permission to take photographs. The UNESCO connection added a new dimension to our objectives. In addition to my interest in historical geography, we were to act as scouts.

Of more immediate importance to me was the fact that our difficulties in obtaining Iranian visas now concerned the UNESCO planners. Mr Hattori introduced me to the permanent Iranian delegate to UNESCO, His Excellency Dr Feiz. This charming and helpful gentleman offered to enlist the Iranian National Commission for UNESCO in Tehrān which is a part of the Ministry of Foreign Affairs. Despite his efforts, however, May 1st approached with no Iranian visas in sight. "Go on to Istanbul," suggested a Consular official in London. "We know of the intervention of Dr Feiz, and the visas will no doubt be waiting for you there."

Before we proceed to Istanbul, I must return to the Soviet and Chinese authorities, the Imperial Cancer Research Fund and our third expedition objective. My first letters to the Soviet and Chinese Cultural Attachés in London had produced exactly similar results. Both commended me to the London offices of their respective tourist organisations, Intourist and the China International Travel Service (CITS). Despite differences in tone reflecting underlying national characteristics, Intourist and CITS have much in common. Both are monolithic monopolies desperately in need of perestroika. Both own a chain of hotels designed exclusively for foreigners and control directly all group travel not organised for academic, scientific or aesthetic purposes by the relevant ministries and academies. Neither Intourist nor CITS care a toss about the wishes or comforts of their thousands of customers whom they see as dirty, demanding but profitable cattle. To restrict the vagaries of their customers, both organisations post dozens of rules and regulations which their employees disregard as the need arises, but which the tourist overlooks at great peril to his or her meals, onward flights and chances to wash in hot water. Neither Intourist nor CITS, both of which I approached in London and in Moscow and Beijing respectively, could help the Marco Polo Expedition.

An immense amount of correspondence ensued as I sought bodies in the USSR and China that would sponsor us. Sponsorship means that your objectives have official approval. The route that the expedition wishes to follow will be arranged with the respective local authorities and with national organisations such as the military. Your food and accommodation are arranged in advance, and in China the costs for these and all related services are negotiated by the sponsor. Above all, facilities for the achievement of your objectives are supposed to be laid on by the sponsor.

We were not sportsmen, merchants, teachers or nuclear physicists. Our interests were fundamentally academic and aesthetic. Nevertheless, at the suggestion of the then Chinese Cultural Attaché, Zhou Erliu, I had applied to the China Sports Service Company in Beijing. Mr Zhou said that, despite its name, the company organises special tours for people with non-sporting objectives. I wrote to them on August 8th, 1984. To my delight and astonishment, I received a reply dated August 22nd bearing the company seal in lieu of a signature and reading as follows:

Dear Sir,

Thank you for your copy letter dated August 8, 1984 to Mr Zhou Erliu.

We are interested in your proposed significant journey across the ancient silk road from Antakya in Turkey to Beijing. In order to make this project realize, we have to make much preparation. We regret to tell you that we can hardly decide the dates to carry it out. However we would like to keep in contact with you and will inform you once conditions become mature.

Our best wishes

You can decide whether we were naïve, guilty of wishful thinking, or both, but we were over the moon. Almost without effort, I had found Chinese hosts who would organise our travel. Now if I could crack the Russian nut, we would be underway in May 1985, the date originally planned for our departure.

For the next six months, my correspondence with China dealt with planning details. For example, Paul discovered a new book in Chinese about the Silk Road by Chen Liang, an historian who works as a city official in Lanzhou. We wrote to ask some questions about the route. Mr Chen's detailed reply led directly to a side journey to Lanzhou during my trip to Beijing in January 1986. Meanwhile, the China Sports Service Company remained silent. At the end of March 1985 I wrote to them saying that I had not written before because of their request but pointing out that if we were going to enter China that summer, I must apply for visas very soon. Again their response was immediate but this time soul-destroying: they could find no record of any correspondence with us. Despite some fancy footwork with telex and facsimile transmissions, the location and use of which requires the same kind of research as finding a telephone in a Kirgiz village, they could discover no correspondence. What is more, the China Sports Service Company now felt that they were not appropriate sponsors for the Marco Polo Expedition!

My correspondence with possible sponsors in the Soviet Union followed more predictable lines. (Appendix II gives a chronological account of all correspondence about sponsorship.) First, the Soviet Union of Writers and then the Union of Journalists replied by recommending Intourist. I then applied to the All-Union Geographical Society and, simultaneously, to the Institute of Geography of the USSR Academy of Sciences. Both the President of the Society and the octogenarian Director of the Institute who retired later that year, 1985, wrote polite replies directing me to Intourist. At the same time, I had written to Sergei Klockov of the Soviet National Commission for UNESCO who had helped one or two Britons complete cultural projects in European Soviet regions closed to tourism. Although Klockov tried very hard to be helpful, suggesting contacts in the Academy of Sciences and at UNESCO in Moscow, the expedition raised diverse problems with local authorities, Customs and the military that he was not in a position to resolve.

However, Klockov also suggested that I write to the then Secretary-General of UNESCO, His Excellency Mr A. M. M'Bow. Mr M'Bow promptly offered us UNESCO patronage if we could obtain the support of the National Commissions in the countries through which we planned to drive. Only the Turkish National Commission responded positively at that stage. Not even the Soviet National Commission would support us until we had a Soviet sponsor. The same applied in China, and Iranian support was not forthcoming until we were appointed scouts for UNESCO two years later. Obviously, the National Commissions are unable to lead the pack. I should add, though, that in what must have been one of its last official acts, the UK National Commission for UNESCO not only gave us formal support but wrote on our behalf to their Turkish, Iranian, Soviet and Chinese counterparts.

Klockov finally urged that I follow up an approach I had made to Central TV, Moscow, at the end of 1984 at the suggestion of the veteran organiser of expeditions and travel writer, Tim Severin. Central TV had obtained permission for Severin to land on the Black Sea coast of the Georgian Soviet Republic when he was organising *The Jason Voyage*. They had arranged his brief stay in exchange for film rights to the landing. My first and later replies from Central TV were unhelpful, but there was to be a happy sequel.

Despite these setbacks, I remained convinced that the academic approach, probably through the Academy of Sciences, was the most suitable and most likely to succeed eventually. Under existing cultural exchange agreements between Britain and the Soviet Union, the Royal Society is responsible for exchanges with the Academy of Sciences, each giving special consideration to projects supported by the other. The same is true of the Chinese Academy of Sciences and the Chinese Academy of Medical Sciences, a separate body under the Ministry of Public Health. I had asked the Royal Society to recommend the Marco Polo Expedition, but none of us are scientists. My request had been addressed to the Secretary, John Deverill, for the then Foreign Secretary of the Society, Sir Arnold Burgen. Mr Deverill, a former RAF pilot who approves of enterprise and challenge, explained that we needed a legitimate scientific objective if the Royal Society was to support us. In the middle of 1985, he phoned me to suggest such an objective: Dr Charles O'Neill of the Imperial Cancer Research Fund had a theory that oesophageal cancer, unusually common in north-western China and north-eastern Iran, might also have a high incidence across the interlinking, semi-arid region. His etiological hypothesis implicated silicon fibres of a specific size found in the seed coverings of certain grasses known to contaminate accidentally cereals harvested in this region. If we were to collect epidemiological data and samples of the relevant cereals, we would be performing legitimate scientific research. However, we would also have to add Geoff Clarke to our group because he had participated in oesophageal-cancer research for the ICRF in both Iran and China. In anticipation of Royal Society support, my three colleagues agreed to take on the third expedition objective and its fifth member.

Thereupon, Sir Arnold Burgen wrote to the Scientific Secretary of the USSR Academy of Sciences, Professor G. K. Skryabin, and to the Presidents of the Chinese Academy of Medical Sciences, Professor Gu Fangzhou, and of the Academy of Sciences, then Professor Lu Jiashi. Professor Skryabin replied that the Academy of Sciences had already explained their inability to help the Marco Polo Expedition. He recommended that we apply to the All-Union Oncological Institute. I did but received no reply.

On the other hand, the Chinese responded positively to the Royal Society initiative. The Academy of Medical Sciences invited me to come to Beijing to discuss the project. They agreed to sponsor the expedition, and their parent body, the Ministry of Public Health, accepted the task of organising the medical side of our journey. It was a great leap forward, indeed, but left unanswered all the questions about entering China from the Soviet Union, visiting sites of historical and cultural interest, accommodation and other such fundamentals.

Meanwhile, a favourable letter from Professor Lu Jiashi reached me on December 31st, 1985, the day before I flew to Beijing. Professor Lu recommended the Mountain Scientific Expedition Advisory Service, a commercial tour-planning organisation set up by the Institute of Geology of the Academy of Sciences. The Beijing trip gave me the opportunity to meet Mr Zheng Xilan, the manager of the new service. Most of our two four-hour discussions dealt with personnel and costs. It looked as though they would fill all the lacunae left by the medical authorities. Events proved otherwise, but I returned smugly with the Chinese puzzle solved.

That left the Soviets. I had recently seen a wonderful, romantic, British-made movie called *Letter to Breshnev*. Thinking "what the hell", I wrote to Mikhail Gorbachov. I described who we were, our objectives and my previous correspondence with the Soviet authorities, and asked for his assistance.

That was in March 1986, and the story almost ended there. In May, I had a heart attack. Then during the first week of September, the Science section of the Soviet Embassy phoned one morning. Was I still interested in driving across Soviet central Asia? They had had an enquiry from the Academy of Sciences! Soon afterwards, Dr Y. P. Badenkov, Deputy Director of the Institute of Geography, invited me to come to Moscow to discuss the project. We arranged to meet during the first week of December, but not before the Embassy had rung again to hurry me along if possible. The shoe had definitely changed feet.

One warm winter day with a broken sky and no standing snow, I walked with Dmitri Oreshkin, candidate member of the Institute, publicist, liaison with the Marco Polo Expedition and now my friend, from the Institute car parked beside the gleaming National Hotel to the Intourist foreign exchange office where I could buy rubles. Dmitri had met me at the Sheremetievo airport the day before.

"The Academy of Sciences is to be your host because word has come down from the very highest authority," he said.

"You mean that my letter to Mr Gorbachov has produced results?" I asked. I was more surprised to be told so openly, I think, than by the fact itself.

"From the very highest authority," Dmitri replied. His careful, precise English came a little faster as he repeated the phrase. "If I were you," he added with a little smile, "I would write a thank-you letter."

"Note," I said, bemused and pedantic. "Thank-you note."

Both my original letter to the Soviet leader and the thank-you note are reproduced in Appendix I. There was no direct reply to either.

# Chapter I

# ISTANBUL

We fixed departure from Highbury Fields, north London at 8.00 a.m., Friday, May 1st. Paul Crook decided to accompany us as far as Dover so all five members of the expedition had arrived to pack the van by 7.00 a.m. Within five minutes, we had learned lesson one: dry runs save time. Like most salutary experiences, it came too late because there was only one first packing. Yet the fact is that almost a month went by before we got it right. At first, the opinion seemed to prevail that what counted was preventing rattles: enamelled cups against enamelled plates, for example. Don Baker did the cooking while he was with us because he had no driving licence. It took him extra hungry minutes at the end of the day to track down the bread which had been used to separate aluminium pot from steel pan, and finally I realised that cooking equipment had to be packed together, regardless of noise, and similar dispositions applied to dried vegetables or camera film. Thereafter, packing became easier if not much faster.

On that first morning, a dry, cool spring day, we waved goodbye to the small group of relatives, waifs and well-wishers at about 8.15. The drive to Dover was auspicious, only our second day out in the vehicle which drove easily and unremarkably. P. F. Foley, who had sold us the car as an export vehicle, free of VAT, had asked that we collect the Customs form from his shipping agent, tucked away in a cul-de-sac surrounded by motorways near the docks. When the 1.00 p.m. ferry to Ostend cleared Dover harbour, the adventure had positively begun.

Four hours later, it seemed to have ended. At Ostend, Customs identified us from the ship's manifest and asked to see our document. It was called a T2L and meant that we intended to sell our car in the first EEC country we entered, i.e., Belgium. We had a choice, however: pay the Belgian VAT, a staggering 25 per cent on cars, or return to Dover for the document that would allow us to export from the EEC itself, a T2 form. There was a certain irony in being pipped at the post by the new European free trade area, as we have quite mistakenly come to think of the Community, rather than by the Iranians or the Chinese, but such refined observation occurred to none of us at that moment. Customs were closed for the May Day Bank Holiday. We had no alternative but to spend the night in Ostend, not in itself a hardship, and to return the next day to Dover.

The car could not be removed from the Dover docks because it had legally been exported from Britain – unless we wanted to pay British VAT. It took all day Saturday, and the intervention of a number of people, to get the T2L replaced with a T2. The latter requires a guarantor prepared to put up the value of the vehicle, including tax, against failure to export it from the EEC. Finally, recognising that their shipping agents had been the immediate if not the ultimate cause of our difficulties, Foley agreed to act as guarantor. This philosophical distinction between immediate and ultimate cause, akin to the problem of who started the First World War, failed to hold my attention then or later, and I am merely grateful to Foley for guaranteeing the T2 form as required. In the event, it cost him nothing, but he could not be sure of that at the time.

Once bitten, as the saying goes, twice shy. Was the T2 really enough? It carried no weight in Yugoslavia, separating Austria which co-operates in such matters, though it is not a Community member, from Greece which is. Nor would the T2 help us in Turkey or Iran. After the blow to the purse as well as the morale dealt by that return journey from Ostend, I began to distrust my own research. Sorting out travel documents and insurance for an export vehicle that we intended to drive to its destination on the other side of Asia raised controversy as well as complications. In addition, it seemed probable that our photographic and holographic equipment, to say nothing of the BBC tape recorders, might raise eyebrows somewhere, and they had to be insured. I phoned first the London Chamber of Commerce and the Road Haulage Association. They gave diametrically opposing advice on a commercial-goods transit document called a Carnet ATA. I begged the latter to phone the former and the Chamber of Commerce prevailed: for the Marco Polo Expedition, the Carnet ATA was inappropriate.

Nevertheless, Tom knew a girl who knew all about these things because she was in the business of providing documentation for international expeditions as well as trade. Yes, we must consult her. Like the man with a bad chest pain, how under stress one puts one's faith in experts.

She was an expert: knowing, plausible and costly — but wrong. She began with a Carnet du Passage, a document issued by the Chamber of Commerce for transit vehicles carrying goods of commercial value. It required a guarantor of four times the value of our van, about £60,000. That is, if the car was wrecked or involved in an accident of any kind, insurance cover would be assured. But this was a Bank Holiday Saturday. Even assuming we could eventually find someone able and willing to guarantee such a sum, the task would take days if not weeks. She then suggested that a Carnet ATA would cover our photographic and holographic equipment. This is a list, certified by the London Chamber of Commerce, and duplicated a number of times equal to all Customs posts through which we would travel, both into and out of the respective countries, in and out for each country. As I had learned, it was not meant to cover non-commercial goods which would be returned to the UK. It had nothing to do with the van, it was not recognised in the USSR and China and ours listed only our photographic equipment, omitting sound recorders, for example. The Carnet ATA says on its formal, yellow, board, A4, know-all-men-by-these-presents cover, Iran is among the nations that does recognise its validity. Our expert reasoned that, apart from Yugoslavia and Turkey, our real problem was going to be Iranian Customs. The Carnet ATA might distract their attention from the car itself. I agreed. She even drove to Dover after office hours to bring the completed document. It cost £600 plus her room and board. The Iranians refused to glance at it.

Chastened but wiser, we thought, we embarked again. By some fluke, the weather that long weekend was superb: all three of our crossings were smooth and restful. We camped that first night, May 6th, beside a pond full of ducks and their ducklings near Bruges. The main course at dinner was superb Belgian tinned cassoulet bought at a supermarket beside the inner harbour at Ostend. Our unfamiliarity with the camping equipment showed but did not prevent a good night's sleep on foreign ground.

We drove straight through to Istanbul, camping in official campsites, clean, well-appointed and usually very pretty, and halting only for Customs and the occasional purchase of food. Even motorways afford views of changing scenery, at least if you are not driving, and we kept fairly rigorously to two-hour "watches". Towards Munich, Don noticed that some of the village churches had onion domes, often pink and grey. Every village had its maypole in a central square. We saw storks nesting occasionally. From Salzburg, the road ploughed through spectacular Alpine scenery, emerging from a mountain wall suddenly into the lush flat land of northern Yugoslavia. Near Niš we began to see mosques in the villages, small, square, undecorated buildings with minarets. The further south we drove, the more common vineyards became. The road into Greece passes through a wild, desolate countryside on the Yugoslav side and then enters almost at once the urban sprawl around Thessaloníki. Had our campsite that night not been beside the sky-blue sea at Kaválla, the stark outline of Thásos offshore, I might have doubted the classical romance of Macedonia.

Parked beside us with a decent interval of perhaps five metres was a German-built campervan. Like people of all ages everywhere we went, a boy of about eleven from the van was attracted by the lists of sponsors on the sides of our car and especially by the words, "The Marco Polo Expedition", beneath the logo in six languages: Turkish, Iranian, Russian, Uigher, Chinese and English. He offered to help with the cooking or the laundry in progress, and he seemed to have some disability affecting his face and speech muscles. His mother, displaying that extra sense born of experience with her child, called him away amidst our protests that he was no trouble.

"He has homework to do," explained Rebecca in unmitigated Australian accents. "Come on, now, Paul. Before supper."

"It must be hard, getting him to stick at it."

"Not really. He's very bright and enjoys lessons, but of course you were something new."

"Travelling must mean there's always something new."

"Often. We stay put when we like a place. We've been here a week already. Both of them understood there would be school work. Paul has a younger brother, Martin. He and Peter, my husband, should be back soon. Martin finds it even harder to do his schoolwork, but all the more reason not to let it slide. I'm not sure whether it's good or bad, but I was a school teacher back home."

"You should be way ahead, except that it's always harder to teach your own. Have you been away long, then?"

"We left Melbourne last October, about six months ago," she said. "We had friends in Hamburg. They bought the camper for us." She looked beyond us to a tall, bearded man walking with a boy by his side. "It's Peter and Martin."

We introduced ourselves. Rebecca sent Martin into the camper with instructions to "get to work for half an hour like Paul. Then we'll have supper. These people are the real travellers," she said to Peter.

We explained our objectives, already able to command practised brevity. "Our problems are all likely to be external, Customs, breakdowns. You have the real encumbrances. Where are you heading?"

Peter said, "We thought about Turkey, but decided to stick to Europe this time. We've taken a year. I got fed up with my job; social work can lack clear goals, and you feel short on accomplishment. Becky felt the same. We decided we needed a break, a look around, for a year. Then we'll go home and decide where to go from there. Naturally, the boys had to come too. What they lose in formal schooling, we figure they gain in all sorts of ways."

We had a very similar conversation at the Ishak Paşa Serai campsite with a Danish couple who also had their two young sons with them. Both of them were school teachers. We met other couples without children, and single men on motorbikes who were travelling not just for a holiday but for career, perhaps life restructuring. That was interesting at the time, but perhaps because I have completed my own journey, another facet of these pleasant, intelligent people now catches the light. We met no more drifters after Turkey, although in Erzurum my colleagues spent hours with three British and Dutch couples who had driven together through Iran to Pakistan and back. They only emphasise the rarity of these golden few thrown up by our highly-productive civilisation with the money to live out the dream that you can go as you please, be whatever you fancy. Nor does it take much money. Far more important is the personal decision to go. Yet these Australians, Danes, Britons, Dutch, Germans, French have in common not just the will, but their apperception of a secure world.

Seven hundred years ago, people travelled with one or both of two motives. Either they were traders buying cheap and selling dear in the next valley, or their mission related to the next life. Their motives were clear. No one had any false notions about order or personal security.

How could the Turks, or the Iranians, Turkmens, Uzbeks, Uighers or even the Han Chinese we lived amongst appreciate our perception of certainty that reason and law govern all things? Without that quality, they must have thought us wealthy and therefore mad. If you have money, you are mad to make yourself uncomfortable. Surely, the only security is amongst one's own, just as the only certainty can be found in the other world. But how much is that changing, I wonder, as material conditions improve? How much does our very presence, Western travellers illuminating our faith in order, help to bring about change?


We drove into Istanbul during peak-hour traffic. It made Paris, Rome and particularly London look like models of well-ordered, fast-moving motor travel. The main road from the west becomes an eight-lane highway as it approaches the metropolis. In the bumper-to-bumper agglomeration of lorries, vans, buses, cars and motor bicycles, lane discipline is a myth, pedestrian crossing occurs at random and in any numbers and there is a demonstrable relationship between increasing numbers of horn presses and declining numbers of accelerator presses. One senses that this life-threatening chaos, which in fact kills very few, harks back to nomads on horses galloping in great numbers along well-defined routes. For Westerners with centuries of settlement in their genes, driving in Istanbul is best avoided.

Though the historical significance of this exciting and beautiful middle-eastern city as a trading centre can scarcely be overemphasised, it was still, if only just, under Byzantine domination when the Polos travelled and more friendly to Genoa than to Venice. In the spirit of our expedition, Istanbul should have been only a rest stop. But Istanbul was the last place where we could hope to obtain Iranian visas. We waited there for seven absorbing days.

Each of us followed our own bent. We met at six or six thirty each evening in the bar of the Hotel Klodfarer, just above the Sultan Ahmet Mosque, room with shower about £8 a night, and dined together. Otherwise, I had not escaped the thralldom of a guided tour to impose one on my associates. Tom got up several mornings at dawn to take photographs in the early light. Don explored the new Museum of Islamic Art and Culture in what was the palace of Ibrahim Paşa beside the Hippodrome when he was not showing me the city he remembered from one earlier visit. I spent part of each day at the Iranian Consulate, near the hotel, and the rest seeing for myself.

On the first day, after a frustrating two hours at the Consulate, I walked down a steep, broad, curving road to the Golden Horn. Despite the boats in the harbour in front of me, the fishermen on the quay, the Galata Bridge to the left, my first impression was of noisy traffic, busy crowds and the realisation that my perception of the famous waterway owed more to a map memory than to direct sensory intake, a little like the blind man who sees the elephant by reputation.

All this changed when I went to the Topkapi Serai the next day. The builders of the palace put it on the southern corner where the Golden Horn enters the Bosphorus. The crowded hills of Istanbul as well as the great river separating Europe and Asia to the north and the narrowing sleeve twisting inland to the north-west must brighten the dullest eye and unleash the most sodden imagination. On Sunday, the day before we finally left Istanbul, Iranian visas stamped in passports, Don and I took the ferry boat that travels up the Bosphorus, with one exception touching at the European villages. In brilliant sunshine on a clear May day, we cruised past the medieval-looking Dolmabahçe Palace, built in 1852, where Atatürk died, beneath the great suspension road bridge followed by a second under construction. At the fishing village of Kaviçi, we got off for lunch at a restaurant built, it seemed, for the view of a ruined fortress wall on the opposite Asian hilltop. The natural scenery of Istanbul is on a par with San Francisco and Sydney.

The difference is in the buildings, of course. There are three sorts that stand out from the mass: a few Byzantine buildings, Islamic buildings and the bazaar. Of the Byzantine buildings, most people see Haghia Sophia, situated almost surprisingly between the Topkapi above it and the Sultan Ahmet Mosque. Haghia Sophia is now a very empty museum as though the secular government had compromised with both its Islamic population and the tourists of Christian Europe by restoring the church but leaving it without special attractions.

We observed an upsurge of Islamic fundamentalism no doubt influenced by the revolution next door. In front of the campus of Istanbul University, students were demonstrating against the exclusion of women who wore a chador. Don speculated on what their attitude would be, if the fundamentalists took power, towards the admission of women who did not cover their heads.

The main structure of Haghia Sophia is ancient, enormous and cold. On the mezzanine are the mosaics. For me, their beauty is diminished by the hugeness of the structure surrounding them, unlike the Ravenna mosaics, for example, which totally dominate the interior walls of their churches, like some bit of half-hidden fresco in Padua compared to Michelangelo's Last Judgment. In the south-east corner of the mezzanine, however, you can see a trompe l'oeil window which must be fairly modern and none the less surprising there.

Much more reminiscent of the specifically Byzantine city are two small churches to the west on the ridge along the Golden Horn. They were part of Don's guided tour. The Church of Theotokos Pammakaristos contains beautiful frescoes, the most striking of which surrounds the interior of the dome. It is a small building, built in the twelfth century and now attached to a structure against which it seems to lean. There is a newly-cultivated garden around two sides including the entrance, and the lady who controls both church and garden admitted us at the stated price though it was Thursday and the opening hours are 12.00 to 1.30 p.m. on Friday and Saturday. Perhaps on those days the money goes to the state whereas at other times it helps the woman to buy seed.

Further west near the city walls, facing a nicely rebuilt public square with shops, stands the Kariye Cami, the Church of St Saviour in Chora. It was built in the eleventh century, but the magnificent mosaics and frescoes which decorate its walls were made about 300 years later. Nowhere else in Istanbul can you find such a beautiful series of Byzantine religious paintings.

After leaving the Kariye Cami, we continued uphill to the ramparts that bind the city to the sea. The great Theodosian walls reaching seventeen kilometres from the Sea of Marmara to the Golden Horn were originally constructed during the fifth century. Gaping holes emphasise their height and thickness. We were approaching these impressive if soulless remains down a fairly steep hill with well-kept blocks of flats on both sides, children playing in the street and little traffic in the hot afternoon. At pavement level, a wide window ledge, barred on the street side, gave access to a kitchen. In the corner of the ledge leaning against a pillow lay a smiling pudgy baby playing with his feet. I hastily focused the camera and took the picture, whereupon three small girls ran from behind me into the flat calling, no doubt, "Mummy, Mummy, the man took a picture of Mehmet." Suddenly, an informally dressed woman stood by the window. After a quick glance at her happy, silent infant, she smiled, addressed me and disappeared. Within fifteen seconds, she reappeared on the pavement, a business card and pencil in hand. She scribbled some words and handed me the card with her name and address.

"I'll be happy to send you a print, but it will be at least four months," I said, holding up four fingers. She did seem to understand and, in any case, I have now sent her the picture.

Despite its walls and churches Byzantium crumbled away. In 1453 the Ottoman Turk, Mehmet the Conqueror, entered Constantinople through the Edirne Gate near where I photographed little Mehmet, if that is his name.

The Topkapi Serai was begun only six years later, expanded by many of the Sultans who lived and reigned from the palace and abandoned only in the last century. Now it is a great museum consisting of the private libraries and collections of the Sultans, but the principal feature of the Topkapi is neither the artefacts nor the buildings. One of the most beautiful natural settings in the world has been exploited to build a palace in a garden, that ideal of the semi-arid Muslim regions. Even the coachloads of school children whom we saw swarming and shattering the peace underline the green restfulness sought by the Sultans' architects.

Below the Topkapi on your left as you face the Golden Horn is the Archaeological Museum, a vast pile full of treasures much in need of better and more selective display. Within the L made by the museum buildings stands the Çinili Köşk, the Tiled Kiosk, with a handsome columnar tiled façade in the Persian manner built about the same time as the Topkapi. Appropriately, it now houses a beautiful collection of tiles, principally examples of Iznik art.

Behind the Topkapi and Haghia Sophia soars the Mosque of Sultan Ahmet I, better known because of the tiles that cover the huge interior as the Blue Mosque. We arrived at our hotel above the mosque in the late afternoon and almost the first sight I noticed were the six minarets surrounding the rising waves of the Sultan Ahmet domes. When the lights with which they are outlined came on in the evening, the magical effect of this mammoth building becomes undeniable. Certainly it twinkled and almost seemed to fly. For the end of Ramadan and the tourists in general, the mosque had organised a son et lumière in different languages on different evenings. It paled before the building itself.

Beside the Sultan Ahmet Mosque are remains of the Roman city, principally the Hippodrome or Circus. At the far end a street leads down to the left and on the right are the curved foundations of the Circus itself, ramshackle buildings extruded as if by pressure against them like a Piranesi etching.

Continue along this street as I did under Don's guidance, and you come to a treasure of Istanbul, the tiny Sokollu Mehmet Paşa Cami. Completed in 1572, it was designed by one of the world's architectural geniuses, Sinan. The decoration of this "perfect" mosque is enriched by polychrome Iznik tiles with no prevailing colour despite the use of green and white marble for some of the main structural supports.

I saw two more mosques designed by Sinan. The Rüstem Paşa Cami is down in the spice market near the Galata Bridge. What one sees is inseparable from what one smells. It, too, is a small mosque. You enter from a twisted street that I would have trouble finding now, climbing some steps into the courtyard. Rüstem Paşa was Vizier to the great Süleyman the Magnificent. Like that of Sokollu Mehmet Paşa, this mosque is notable for its beautiful tiles used everywhere on the interior and even on the façade of the porch.

For about fifty years during the middle of the sixteenth century, Sinan held the office of Architect of the Abode of Felicity in the Imperial court. In our words, he was Clerk of the Works and the senior engineer of Constantinople. He was buried at the age of ninety-seven in a small tomb just at the entrance to the great courtyard surrounding perhaps his masterpiece, the Süleymaniye.

The Süleymaniye is a complex containing madrasas, colleges for the teaching of Islam, now used as the library and archives, a caravanserai and museum and the tombs of the donor, Süleyman the Magnificent, and his wife, Roxelana, treated today as shrines. This enormous Friday Mosque, an Islamic cathedral in size and importance, has both grandeur and restfulness which are strikingly different from Western religious architecture where grandeur is more often associated with excitement, like Lincoln Cathedral or Winchester. Even badly behaved western European tourists who insist on walking into areas marked clearly as enclosures for prayer, cameras blazing, cannot diminish the quiet.

For 400 years, the bazaar must have remained largely unchanged except in the detail of who owns what shop. It is a vast warren beginning with the spice market down near the Golden Horn and climbing slowly up the hill. There is an enormous closed market near the top, now showing signs of expensive tourist tat and trendy Western gear. Dotted through the ancient streets, internal as well as external, are the remains of hans, caravanserais where visiting merchants once lived and exchanged their wares. Among the most striking of these ancient hotels is the Zincirli Han, built in the sixteenth century. Its courtyard is surrounded by a double arcade, two storeys which are still vaguely pink and ochre.

The trouble with word descriptions is that they omit the other senses. Of course smell is scarcely restricted to the spice market. In this book, vision is enriched by the photographs. But there is no way of giving you the direct experience of the muezzin's call. In a village in eastern Turkey or a Chinese city like Lanzhou, the call has an effect even on infidels. The first time I heard it was in Istanbul where the voice was amplified by electricity, and the same call was repeated, out of synchronisation, presumably according to the clocks of individual mosques throughout the city. The same thing happened later in Ankara, but never in Tehrān. Especially at four in the morning when the city was quiet, the sung ritual call to prayer, repeated at all the points of the compass, reminded you that Islam is a world religion.

# Chapter 2

# ANTIOCH

With our passports bearing visas from the Islamic Republic of Iran, we left Istanbul during the early afternoon of Monday, May 18th. Three weeks later under less relaxed circumstances we discovered that, for unknown reasons, my visa was good for two weeks beginning June 1st, 1987, whereas my colleagues each had visas for four weeks.

That first night we camped on a hilltop high above a blue reservoir where people were rowing small boats. Our site was dry and rocky, but covered with tiny wild flowers in every basic colour, small grape hyacinths, little red poppies, yellow flowers that looked like daisies and unidentifiable white flowers. We slept quietly amongst them about 100 yards off the highway twenty-five kilometres north of Kütahya, once second only to Iznik as a source of ceramic tiles.

Western Anatolia, through which our road lay, bustled and thrived. Farms and orchards seemed well watered and prosperous though the people are shabby and farm machinery seldom seen. Lorries and trucks carry most of the local goods, and they show both age and wear. Urban buildings look jerry-built, but the towns are crowded and seem to be expanding. Akşehir, reputedly the home of the popular scoundrel and teller of tales, Nasr ud-din Hodya, typically gives the raw impression of a frontier town in the western USA or the Australian outback.

Konya was our first large city after Istanbul. Like every other Turkish town, the first kilometres of the main road after it enters the built-up area become a linked fabrication of potholes. Within an outer fringe of expanding dilapidation, however, Konya is laid out around its monuments and a central park occupying what may once have been a citadel. At the park entrance, the Alâeddin Cami was closed so that we saw little but the outer walls of the largest Selcuk mosque in the city.

The Selcuks ruled parts of Anatolia, Syria, Iraq, Iran and what is now Soviet Turkmenistan and Uzbekistan during the eleventh and twelfth centuries. A branch of the ruling dynasty known as the Selcuks of Rum with their capital at Konya continued to dominate Anatolia for a further 150 years.

The principal monument, the Mevlana Tekke, owes much of its brilliantly tiled external beauty to later Ottoman rulers, but this tomb of two religious leaders, father and son, became a shrine soon after the son's death in 1273 and remains a shrine today and a museum.

Konya contains more monuments than we had time to pause for after our delayed departure from Istanbul. Fortunately, we did stop to admire the Ince Minare Madrasa, the seminary with the Slender Minaret. In 1901, the minaret was struck by lightning and is roughly half its original height. With its unobtrusive glazed brick decoration amidst geometrically-designed courses of plain brick, the remaining entrance gate and tower is a marvellous example of late Selcuk architecture. It was a short afternoon in Konya and for the first time, very hot.

For 200 kilometres, past Ereğli, the land lay flat, cultivated with cereals for the most part. Villages could be seen in the distance and mountains on the far horizon, but there were neither hills nor trees nearby. Finally, we hid behind the railway embankment that parallelled the road and made a comfortable, remarkably quiet camp. Trains were very rare, and we were awakened at 4.30 a.m. by the muezzin from the distant village calling without electricity in the silent dawn.

The next day, May 20th, we crossed the Taurus Mountains and passed the Cilician Gates, through which had marched Alexander the Great, Pompey and almost every Arab, Turkish and Armenian conqueror, on a four-lane highway. Adana, a huge Mediterranean up-river port and manufacturing city, straggled on for miles. About noon, very near the site of Ayas, our road turned south and, just for a moment, left the present behind. To our left on a crag straight out of Sir Walter Scott stood the Crusader castle of Toprakkale. Actually it was built by the Byzantines before the Crusaders launched their dubious adventures and captured and destroyed by the Mamluks in the thirteenth century. Below Iskenderun, we found a perfect place for lunch beside a stream pouring into the sea, from which we were separated by a railway embankment. No trains ran along this disfigurement during the two hours we were there, and the stream was very shallow, swift and warm enough to make possible a discreet bathe and some laundry.

Having decided as a gesture to Marco Polo's first Asian landfall at Acre to reach the sea again as close to the Syrian border as possible, we stopped in Antakya only long enough to obtain a local map from the Tourist Information Centre. It showed twenty-eight kilometres to Samandaği, the new resort town of Antakya. It did not show that the road is largely under construction, and that after a core village of working peasants, the resort is a ghost town before it ever lived. Fronting a rolling sea and wide sand beaches stood a series of unfinished, one- and two-storey hotels. Their owners and apparently sole occupiers were naturally avid for any breath of custom. We were perhaps not unique but certainly very welcome. When the road is finished in a year or two, those who have managed to hold on to their property should benefit. Despite the wind, the situation is magnificent. To the south beyond the Orontes, the uninhabited mountains fall directly into the sea. On the top of one are said to be two ruined churches dedicated to St Symeon Stylites the Younger who emulated the Elder of that name, dweller on columns near Antioch until his death in 459. To the north across a fan-shaped plain, another spur cuts off all land connection with the hinterland.

We left our luxury apartments-to-be at a reasonably early hour for the drive back to Antakya. What little remains of ancient Antioch sits like bristles in a worn-out brush across the rim of mountains against which the city is built. The so-called Water Gate through the quondam city walls is itself well up the hillside and very hard to find with the poor map provided by Tourist Information. A path led from the gate up towards fortifications which

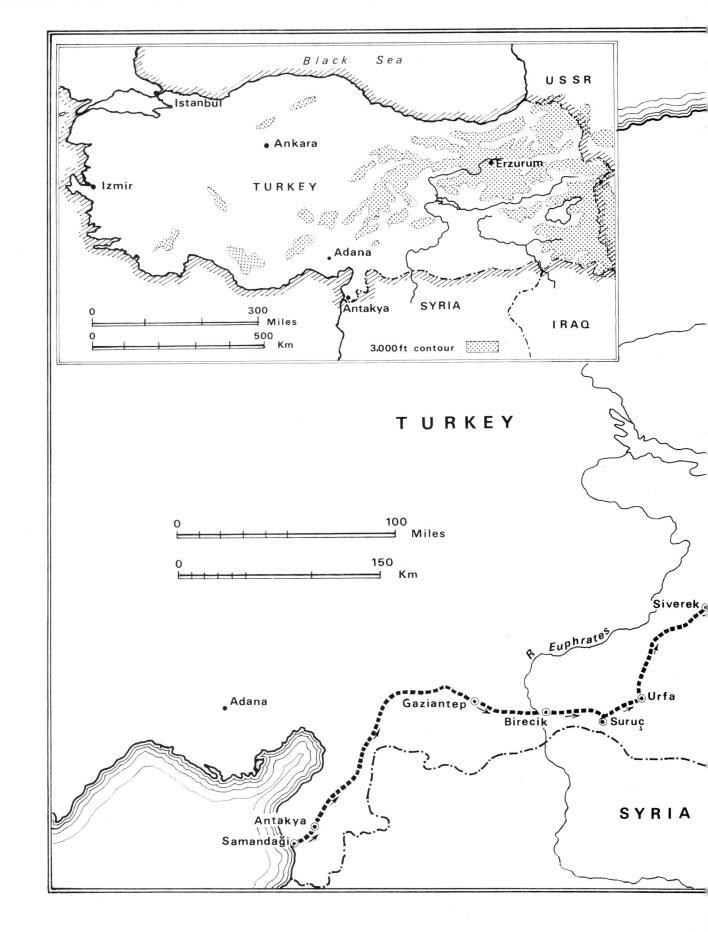

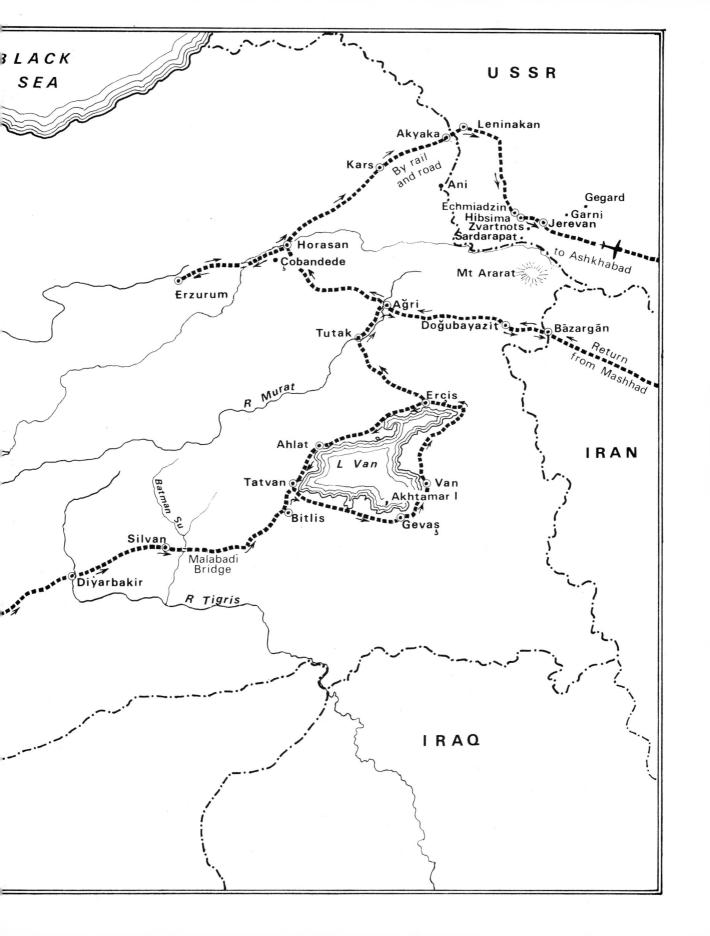

required more expert knowledge than we had to identify. The view was marvellous over Antakya, a thriving, jerry-built city in a cup surrounding the river, but distracted the imagination from filling in details of the Norman capital in the twelfth century.

Near the main bridge in the town centre stands an excellent Archaeological Museum with a display of coins organised chronologically by ruling power from the earliest days of the city to the present. The coin room in Antakya also houses small sculptures of domestic animals made during the Byzantine age by unknown artists.

In another room, we found an exhibition of pictures by local school children. The remarkable aspect of this display was our self-appointed guide, a lad of twelve or so whose English was superb. "I will show you around," he announced when we unwarily appeared, "and explain to you who we are, and what we are doing." Sweeping aside those classmates who inadvertently crossed our paths, he proceeded to do just that: school, class, ages and names of each of the artists. He made it clear that the exhibition had a theme, peace and international goodwill. Few of the individual contributions matched our guide's linguistic ability and enthusiasm, but the presence of the exhibition itself speaks well, I think, for both the museum and school authorities.

Due to my overestimate of the time needed to reach the Iranian border on June 1st, we left Antakya that same morning. On the trip north, we followed the only route beside the swampy lake behind Antakya as far as the branch at the castle of Bağras and this time, instead of the sea road, took the inner route close to the Syrian border. To our left, the narrow valley floor before the mountains was heavily cultivated and dotted with villages. We stopped for a bread and cheese lunch beneath a mulberry tree at the fork where a road ran back to one of them. A rivulet rushed down the hillside to flow beneath the tree, but before reaching it, earthworks caused the waters to divide, a major portion running off beneath the branch road into irrigation channels through the fields. Yet another division forced part of the water to flow into a cistern-like structure dug into the side of a hill. It was uncovered and had high, partially manmade walls, but only on the hill side. The air was hot and very quiet except when people from the village came along in a donkey cart, greeting us in a friendly, offhand way.

To the right of the road, the east, the band of cultivation where it existed at all was very narrow. Then a scrubby desert extended into low arid brown hills along the Syrian border. After rejoining the main road between Adana and Gaziantep, we drove for miles across a fertile plain. About four in the afternoon, the road crossed the Euphrates (Turkish: Firat) to a cliff-top town called Birecik, once the head of navigation. During our journey we were to cross the Tigris (Turkish: Dick), the Amudar'ya (Greek: Oxus) and the Syrdar'ya (Greek: Jaxartes), but the wide, slow Euphrates was the first and, therefore, the most exciting.

Near a village called Suruç on a side road that headed into Syria, we camped in an orchard of very junior, unripe pomegranates. We had plenty of room to drive the car into a space between the first two rows of trees and were busily making camp when visitors began to arrive. Inasmuch as we were trespassing, there was the possibility that the landowners might be possessive, requesting a fee, if not actually unfriendly. We could but smile and make questioning gestures; none of us knew Turkish. Amongst the four men and four boys who eventually assembled were certainly the owners of the orchard, but we paid our way very simply, by providing them with entertainment for an hour or so. Don's cookery and our very basic arrangements to eat fascinated our hosts. One of them seemed totally unaware that he had expropriated one of our four chairs so that Tom had to make do with a nearby rock. They commented on our manners and no doubt our morals, laughed and discussed our equipment, without seeming in the least to be rude. After the elders had observed the show and smoked a cigarette or two, they politely said goodnight and, ordering the boys to follow, went back to their homes in the gathering dusk.

Urfa, called Sanliurfa on the road signs, is a huge sprawling city with a population well over a million. Its central tree-lined streets contain good shops with an air of prosperity, but as in most other large Asian cities, monuments are unmarked.

The citadel, set on top of a high rocky outcrop south-west of the old town, alone signals the city's ancient history. The citadel area may first have been fortified in the Bronze Age, but the city entered history named Edessa by veterans of the armies led by Alexander the Great. Edessa it remained as a Byzantine stronghold, when it was captured by the Selcuks, as a Crusader state and after it was recaptured by the Selcuks in 1146. Beginning with the two Hellenistic columns in the topmost keep, known locally as the Throne of Nimrod, the citadel shows some signs of most of these occupations, like the huge granite foundation blocks covered with parts of Arabic inscriptions. Surrounding the outer moat today is a higgledy-piggledy straggle of houses, one or at most two storeys, clad in dirty white lath and plaster and occupied by dozens of children and an appropriate number of adults. Women are infrequently seen and usually completely covered, although their costumes and yashmaks tend to be colourful. Down the middle of the dusty, unpaved streets run steel water pipes above and below each other, turning to the right or left as though each had been installed privately and without regard to the others by the householder benefiting from it. Surrounded by this mass of housing but totally unreachable from it, except possibly by small adventuresome boys, the citadel seemed completely irrelevant to me.

Even from the standpoint of the modern city below, the judgment can be sustained. Urfa is the Turkish name of the place, used continuously since the seventeenth century. With the exception of the Ulu Cami built by the original Selcuk rulers, of which a minaret and courtyard remain, the centre of religious life is a new Friday Mosque constructed near to the sacred spring that gushes from the base of the citadel into a small pond called the Pool of Abraham. Canals filled with carp link that pool with two others, surrounded by oleander- and rose-filled gardens. To the west of the principal pool stand the remains of the thirteenth-century Makham al-Khalil Madrasa, and to the north, the lovely seventeenth-century Abdürrahman Madrasa. This complex attracts pilgrims as well as tourists from Turkey and other parts of the Islamic

Beachcombers, Samandaği, Turkey.

Selling mackerel near the Galata Bridge, Istanbul.

Watching passers-by at a tea shop in Erzurum.

The museum-keeper's daughters at Van.

A visitor at the Topkapi Serai, Istanbul.

Kurdish guide at Akhtamar Island, Lake Van.

world, while the citadel remains largely unclimbed excepting by Westerners like my three colleagues.

Again, we rushed on too quickly, but sightseeing in rising midday temperatures is at best inefficient and at worst unwise. The rolling south-eastern Anatolian plain is widely cultivated with grasses adapted to semi-arid conditions. Flocks of variegated sheep tended by boys or old men added to the food supplies. Beside another village grazed a flock of dromedaries. We had just passed a man dressed in black, except for a red burnous, riding a black horse leading a black pony with a white muzzle. A group of brightly-dressed women were pounding their laundry on rocks beside a stream just outside their village. The villages are built of mudbrick in an architecture that could be found in north Africa and south-west Arizona.

Near a small town called Siverek, the road descended into a valley where there were marks of two more parallel roads. One consisted of newly-turned earth and could be part of the oil pipeline to Iran. The other had a bridge with Byzantine arches across the little stream.

Later in the afternoon we passed just north of Diyarbakir and crossed the second historic river, the Tigris. A dirt road turned off upstream just after the bridge, and we found a well-sheltered piece of disused gravel pit in which to camp. Don and I set off to walk what seemed at most 500 metres to the banks of the river, but it was probably further and became progressively more swampy as we advanced. The next morning we returned to Diyarbakir.

The eastern light accentuated the detail of the huge basalt wall still surrounding the ancient city which has of course flowed beyond it. Very few cities retain their walls, but even fewer look more or less intact as you climb towards them from the Tigris River bridge. Inside the fitted constructions of hewn dark blocks, the scale is awe-inspiring despite the evident decay. The floors have fallen away inside one huge watch tower which stinks of age and human faeces, but the masonry walls and circular stairs remain.

Diyarbakir is the city's Arabic name, adopted when the Byzantine town was allotted to the Beni Bakr clan after the conquest in 639. Now a thriving metropolis of about 350,000, the authorities are restoring the 400-year-old Deliller Han, the ancient caravanserai inside the Mardin Gate, probably as a museum. Alternating courses of marble and basalt masonry give an unusual width to the usual two-storey courtyard. New oak doors have been hung on the cells that may once have housed kitchens or stables. It is a handsome monument but lacks the bustle and reality of the Hasan Paşa Han on the central square. Built at about the same time, the Hasan Paşa Han is the carpet bazaar and may have been for centuries.

On the opposite side of the square is the Ulu Cami, the first Selcuk Great Mosque in Anatolia, built at the end of the eleventh century. Perhaps the most astonishing aspect of the mosque are the walls of the huge central courtyard. They carry bas-relief sculptures of classical columns repeated in two-tiered columned arcades at either end. Along with the square campanile-like minaret, they look as though the structure might have originally been a church. A common enough history for buildings further west, it is just not the case, but the architect must have been influenced by decorative elements from the Byzantine past.

The Isak Paşa Serai, Doğubayazit, Turkey, an unroofed arcade separating two courtyards.

Al Aman Hani between Bitlis and Tatvan, Turkey, the base of what was a huge series of two-storey chambers, looking west through the central enclosed avenue.

A decorative ironwork gate near the north end of the Galata Bridge, Istanbul.

We bought sausages, a cheddar-like dry cheese, yoghurt, olives, a spinachy vegetable and dried pulses before leaving Diyarbakir. The rolling plain continued with the cultivation of cereals and grasses. Many petrol stations, each with a clutch of tankers and lorries parked in front, a shop selling cold drinks, possibly a restaurant – these are today's caravanserais.

The town of Silvan contains a wonderful Ulu Cami begun probably in the twelfth century in the place of an even older mosque, but added to by later dynasties until a restoration as recently as 1913 which also considerably enlarged the structure. In fact, part of the building was closed during the summer of 1987 for reconstruction. Inside the original dome and around the thirteenth-century mihrab or niche indicating the direction of Mecca, are curious stone carvings. The whole has an effect of great elegance and dignity much enhanced by the storks nesting near the dome of the roof. Almost the entire male population, it seemed, gathered around our vehicle. One elder manage to control the more inquisitive boys. In Silvan and every other town, they were especially attracted to the air-conditioning fan in the radiator because it could be twirled by busy fingers.

A few kilometres past Silvan the road crosses the Batman Su, one of many tributaries of the Tigris. Just to the south stands the Malabadi Bridge. The huge central arch, although reconstructed like other parts of the bridge, contains much of the original Selcuk stonework.

We had pulled off the road just before the bridge and were immediately approached by eight or ten children, aged perhaps six to twelve, most of them girls, itself unusual. They had fossils, picked up locally we gathered, and quite genuine to the amateur eye, which they were trying to sell. No doubt the price was negotiable. They were badly dressed, and some might have been hungry, but their begging included cigarettes. Throughout the eastern Turkish countryside, men and boys using gestures begged by the roadside for cigarettes or matches. Some of them offered bundles of a rhubarb-like vegetable for sale. Other boys dashed with bravado into the road intending to slow us down to improve their chances. Tourists are not foreign to the region, and we could not distinguish between real need and a primitive form of exploitation, not least because none of us smoked. About this time, we began to buy kilogramme plastic bags of wrapped Turkish sweets, partly so that we had little gifts where something seemed appropriate. Very shortly, we were to gain real pleasure from this small exchange.

Meanwhile, the road was definitely climbing into mountain country. We approached Bitlis through a gorge worn by a rushing stream, the land mostly bare, purple and green in colour. Bitlis itself stands in a canyon formed by two streams. The citadel lours over the ribbon town. The Ulu Cami is a plain structure despite being another of the oldest Selcuk Great Mosques, *restored* about 1150. The date of its construction has been lost in time.

We had now reached the snow line with drifts in sheltered places melting slowly in the warmer midday temperatures. The road to Lake Van runs through the Güzel Dere, the Beautiful Valley. It is treeless and windswept but cultivated and looking quite green with the mountains to the south still snow-covered. Soon after Bitlis, below the road level on the north sits the first of two caravanserais. Bapşin Han is said by T. A. Sinclair in his remarkable survey of the buildings of eastern Turkey to be Ottoman though its squat, square look is much earlier. The main entrance, a handsome pointed arch, is completely blocked, and the walls are otherwise solid.

A little further on towards the head of the valley and just south of the road lie the partly ruined remains of one of the largest caravanserais in Anatolia, built in the sixteenth century. Al Aman Hani is being carefully restored by the Turkish authorities with tan stones that match the original structure but are dressed differently so the new work can be easily identified. To the east of the main block was a large courtyard that provided some protection for the vehicle and its occupants against the wind. Don had to take the Optimus cookers into a deep window ledge in order to keep up their heat. Even he felt he had overreached himself in the circumstances by creating his usual three-course meal. Cooking took much longer, and we were hungry. At last, we ate our meal in the northernmost of the great covered areas that had once provided individual shelters, bedrooms in effect, and cooking facilities for the merchants. Opposite the window lay a drift of snow. A sketch floorplan that I made at the time may help to explain the immense excitement we felt in that place.

AL AMAN HANI

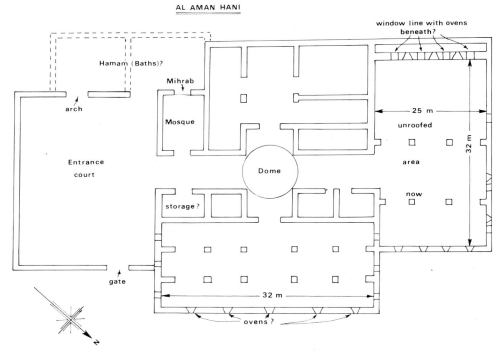

The ancient structure provided unique accommodation for the night. Two of us slept in the car, as usual. The other two put up the tents on the western side of the same huge covered area in which we had our meals. During the night, they heard bats and tracked them the next morning to the southern part of the main block hanging from the curved brick roof of what may have been stables. Before our late 10.00 a.m. departure, we sketched and photographed, explored and discussed the uses of the shapes and spaces. Just to the left of the main entrance arch inside the main east-west corridor is a door to a small room. The mihrab unmistakably identified the room as a mosque.

The road descends a little into Tatvan because you can see the sweep of Lake Van from five kilometres away. Despite the wind where we were, the morning was misty so that the horizon faded in the near distance, and the lake looked unruffled. Tatvan, at the south-western end of Turkey's biggest lake, has a harbour formed by an extensive mole. As it came in sight, we could see the ferry boat from the town of Van approaching. The wide main street of Tatvan displays the same unfinished, Wild West quality we now found so familiar.

To the east, the road climbs into the mountains south of the lake losing sight of it entirely. It follows a rushing river, descends into a heavily-cultivated valley and climbs again through green and snowy mountain scenery. When at last it returned to the lake shore, the mist had lifted so that we could see the mountains to the north-west and west across the bright blue water.

Almost immediately a roadside sign in English as well as Turkish told us that we were about to reach Akhtamar. Around the curve, nearer than one imagined across the blue lake, stood the green-tinged brown island, but only as the road approached the lonely quay was it possible to distinguish the small, earth-coloured church. Akhtamar could properly be called one of the reasons for our journey, not because the Polos had come that way although they may have, but for Don and me especially because this ancient Armenian church in so good a state of repair is an architectural miracle.

The little boat carried fifteen passengers and ran, we were told, regularly when that number had gone aboard. We took bread, cheese and our water bottles and hurried to make up the number. The wind had dropped, and the twenty-minute crossing was smooth and warm. The island anchorage consists of two huge boulders on the north-east, and on the way up the hill, a tall lugubrious ticket seller intercepted us. He turned out also to be one of the ferry boat "captains", and a Kurd, he assured us.

To be a Kurd in eastern Turkey can be somewhat iffy. Stories persist about tourists robbed by Kurds, or worse, and the Turks, like the Iraqis and the Iranians, are forever at war with them. Later, we heard news of a horrific village massacre allegedly by Kurds. The news broke the day after the European Parliament passed a resolution condemning Turkish genocide against the Armenians seventy years before during the First World War. The Kurds we met, like the ticket seller at Akhtamar, behaved with the most dignified courtesy.

A grove of mulberry trees at the top of the hill shades three or four half-tree-trunk picnic tables and benches. While we were there, a party of German tourists arrived, quietly enough, with a vast picnic lunch which their guides unpacked and arranged on the tables while the travellers took photographs.

Beside this glade and slightly below it stands the Church of the Holy Cross. Built between 915 and 922 by a powerful King, Gagik, it stood beside his castle which crowned the western end of the island. Today, nothing at all remains of the castle, but the little cruciform church with its later additions miraculously looks as though it had been finished fifty years ago. The main walls are covered with sculptured friezes. Religious figures appear amongst them, especially near the entrance and the windows, but animals, flowers and plants predominate. The squat dome is supported by a frieze around its short barrel vault.

Inside, the pale, weathered frescoes tell parts of the bible story. The dome supported by the four corner pillars seems extraordinarily high, perhaps because the internal dimensions of the church are no more than fifteen metres by ten including the bays.

Across the well-paved, two-lane highway from the quay stands a roadside café. We camped that night in a prepared site behind the café along with Austrian and Belgian campervans and German motorcyclists with their small geodesic tents. Almost immediately to the east of the site near Gevaş stands the pretty fourteenth-century tomb of a princess. The field smelled of artemesia, and a hoopoe called from the very top of the cut stone roof.

The citadel at Van can be seen stretching inland from the lake shore before any other signs of a town appear. Indeed, the frontier feeling is fully justified by the fact that the present town grew up on the plain east of the citadel about 1930. Prior to that, no city at all had existed since the bombardment of the old town in the plain south of the citadel by Turkish forces seeking to expel the Armenian population which had barricaded itself into one of the walled quarters. The area is now a lumpy grassed precinct, the only visible remains being two Ottoman mosques. Van, along with much of eastern Turkey, was occupied briefly by the Russians in 1917 after the Revolution, and the Armenians evacuated when the Russian troops left.

The citadel itself may once have touched the lake shore at its western edge which now stands a kilometre or more inland. The new land has been utilised to build fish farms. The main path leads up to the oldest Urartian inscriptions and various tombs cut into the rock, dating from the eighth and ninth centuries. Above them, the central fortresses may have been very ancient, though the present structure is basically Urartian. Various systems of walls have been built along the citadel, most recently by the Ottomans. Van was a fortress on the Persian frontier even more than it was a trading centre.

It is now a tourist town with an airport. There are excavations and other ruins in the plain to the east which have also supplied artefacts for the local museum. This is approached from a dusty, unpaved street through a small garden full of sculptured stones which may be mainly Urartian and trees which provided shade for a pleasant bread and cheese lunch. This was the first time we came across the curious division characteristic of other eastern Turkish and Iranian museums. Exhibitions on the ground floor are labelled archaeological and extend from earliest time to the Islamic conquest. On the second floor, entirely devoted to aspects of Islamic culture in the region, the exhibits are called ethnography.

The unusual feature of Van from our standpoint was a street, or rather a long, dusty plaza with alleys extending off it, where the local motor repair industry concentrated on the northern edge of the town. We had two problems with our car: the horn honked occasionally, and we had discovered a water leak near the radiator. The local Tourist Information Centre told us that on this street we could find a Land Rover repair shop. Not so, but we did find a shack or stall, the young owner of which insisted he could help. With his few words of Turkish and many gestures, Tom tried to explain our problems. Then, with the Turkish mechanic on his knees to watch, I lay down on the ground beneath the vehicle to indicate the water leak. None could be seen.

"Turn on the motor," I called. Tom did. Still no water. It ran for several minutes while I peered anxiously into the entrails. No sign of a leak.

Meanwhile, Tom had indicated the horn housing at the top of the radiator as the probable source of that trouble and pressed the horn button. It worked. He turned off the engine. Still the horn worked. On again, and the hooter hooted faithfully. Never before had I witnessed a car responding to a garage like a man with a toothache to a dentist. Our Turkish friends, for we now had an interested gathering of six or eight, seemed to accept our apologies and must have thought us even more unbalanced than most tourists as we drove out of their warren towards the lake and the road north. I should add that the wonderful horn failed completely a few days later and had to be replaced. As to the water leak, it disappeared, though the car displayed a persistent and incurable tendency to overheat.

We camped that night about forty kilometres north of Van in front of an empty two-room house and a carefully-tended, irrigated orchard of mixed fruit and shade trees. Beside one of the irrigation canals in the shade grew a magnificent wild orchid. A stream ran into the lake under the main road just behind the orchard. Boys from the village inspected us, followed in good time by a few of their elders. As usual, they seemed moved by curiosity rather than concern about our trespass.

Just before Erciş we stopped near a stream with a rapids and a waterfall that wound about to run into the lake in the distance. The land was rolling and green, though uncultivated, and in the quiet air, the snow-capped mountains to the west seemed very near.

From Erciş, the circumnavigation of Lake Van requires that you turn south on a road which is, according to the map, worryingly secondary. In fact, it turned out to be newly paved and at least as wide as the main road. So that Tom could photograph, we turned away from the lake towards the mountains and a mud-walled village where the principal products were sheep and small boys. We did see one or two girls, but they passed the throng around us furtively, their faces averted though not veiled. Despite the efforts of one or two elders to control them, the boys so plagued Tom, trying to inspect his equipment or to pose in the way of his camera, that he could do very little.

Another aspect of village life on the north shore of Lake Van still lacks an authoritative explanation. Five hundred years ago, Ahlat was an important trading centre on the main road between Persia and Mesopotamia with the population of a city. Today it is a straggling village with a remarkable necropolis. The Ottoman fort, built near the lake shore in the sixteenth century, after the town had already died, now contains a school and was not open. It being lunch time, we parked on the grassy verge between a full irrigation channel and the narrow dirt road across from the black basalt fortress wall. As usual, local people gathered to inspect us. Lunch consisted of bread and cheese. When we had finished and stowed the uneaten food, I used my hand to scrape the crumbs and a cheese end into the dust behind the car. Two men in our audience, heavy with disapproval, came forward and collected every visible crumb of bread and the bit of cheese. Because they held the debris and seemed to hesitate, I offered the plastic sack we carried for rubbish into which they emptied their hands, carefully brushing in the crumbs. I apologised by saying something like sorry, for what exactly I was not sure, and the older man replied with a clear reference to Allah. Had Allah's will, in this instance, to do with waste, littering or some local prohibition?

The huge cemetery runs north from the lake to the west of the present village. Scattered through it were pink-stone kümbets or mausoleums of different sizes and states of repair. The earliest were built in the twelfth century. By far the largest was the Ulu Kümbet which stands alone between the road and the lake, but the most ornate, the Bayindir Türbesi, was built in 1477 for a local Karakoyunlu chieftain. In addition to the mausoleums, the graveyard contained hundreds of gravestones which also cover the era of the town's eminence, from the early thirteenth to the fifteenth century. The small museum by the road contained a few artefacts which may have come from the graves, and small boys offered coins for sale. Across the road was an unidentified modern building which certainly looked like a prison.

At Tatvan, we finished circumnavigating the most beautiful lake we saw during the summer. Its extreme saltiness must make it unpleasant for swimming but deepens its colour in the sun, adding to the jewelled effect of the snow-capped peaks north-west and south. In such a setting, the remains of a millenium point back to the birth of civilisation.


From Erciş, the road runs north-west, climbing. Near a village called Tutak, it crosses the Murat River which it then follows to the intersection with the main east-west highway between Ankara and Tehrān, certainly part of one of the great trading routes called the Silk Road. The Murat flows eastward towards Ararat. Below Ağri, this river runs through a narrow valley cultivated here and there near villages. After Ağri, it is the centre of a fertile plain.

We reached our final stopping point in Turkey, Doğubayazit, on May 28th, three days before we could cross the border. The town itself has no charms, though there are tourist hotels, carpet shops and groceries for campers like ourselves aplenty. The attractions are Mount Ararat, best seen from the Turkish side a few kilometres east of the town, the Isak Paşa Serai and for some, the near possibility of entering Iran. Sporadic camping signs led us along the road south from the town toward the Isak Paşa Serai. The magical fairy palace perched on the edge of the cliff 1,700 metres above the valley floor looked wholly isolated and unapproachable, but the road climbed steeply toward Camelot. It wound through a ruined village, beside a cemetery into an open area in front of the walls. There an unmetalled track turned sharply right and climbed another 100 metres to a small levelled area with a low white house at the far end. Near the house, inhabited by the caretaker, his female relatives and children, geese, dogs and cats, was a primitive privy with breeze block walls topped by mudbrick but no roof. Water could be obtained from the first courtyard of the serai below. The campsite was usually full. The relative silence and the view over the palace, the ancient Silk Road, the valley and town beneath and the constantly changing sky made it unique.

Isak Paşa was an official of the Ottoman Empire, probably with administrative responsibilities elsewhere, who chose to build his palace in the dominion of a part of his family, a hillside town called Bayazit, now in ruins, and uninhabited excepting for two or three peasant houses. Considering that the main east-west road, the Silk Road proper, then ran through Bayazit, past the site of the palace, up a canyon guarded on the opposite side by a citadel which dates back at least to eighth-century Urartian times, there is a possibility that the Paşa was also something of a highwayman, levying tolls legally or otherwise on the commerce that passed by.

The serai was completed about 1784 and actually inhabited for little more than a generation though it served later as a barracks for the Ottoman army. Its main axis is east-west with the west end built up on retaining walls from the cliff. No one knows who designed it, but it was meant to be a dwelling, not a fortified place. There are rooms that might have been used for purposes of state. Its architectural design is eclectic, drawing from the Selcuk as well as the Ottoman past, and the effect is exuberant, full of pleasure. Every arch and many of the windows are decorated with versions of the tree of life. Animals and plants abound. The public rooms along the second courtyard include what may have been a courtroom to adjudicate local cases and a large mosque. The mimbar, or pulpit, seems to be trying to climb into the wall. The mihrab itself is relatively plain, but there are still signs of frescoes in the dome and on the arcade that separated the women's balcony. Just outside the mosque in the courtyard where it would have been faced by the congregation stands a slender, carved kümbet which is in fact only the shelter for a staircase leading down into what was intended to be the family tomb. Only one Paşa, Mahmut, the last to use the whole palace, seems to have been buried there around 1800.

The domestic quarters occupy the western end of the palace. There was a harem of course, and the kitchen can easily be identified by the soot-blackened walls and ceiling. Window ledges and doorways are plain but carefully fitted, suggesting that luxury was meant to be comfortable.

There is a pretty square Ottoman mosque across the canyon just beneath the citadel. From the serai, the most spectacular remain is a window which must have been part of an altar high in the rock cliff. Urartian bas-relief carvings of preparations for a sacrifice cover the posts and lintel. To the right is a figure of a man, possibly a priest; to the left, a thinner figure often identified as a woman but probably an acolyte or assistant. The deer on the lintel is the sacrifice. The nearer one climbs to the window, the harder it is to identify the figures because of the angles from which they must be seen.

Further up the valley is another cemetery containing a tomb from the last century which has become a shrine. Beside it, within the cemetery walls, is the outline of a mosque from which a muezzin called during our stay. The end of May 1987 was also the end of Ramadan followed by the three-day holiday of Bayram. At first, the cemetery was a place of worship, but on the second day it seemed to become the place for picnics and family outings. Most of the people came by coach or lorry up the steep road beside the Isak Paşa Serai, but there were also a few families living further up the ravine in the mountains.

After two days of domestic chores and exploration, we spent our last full day in Turkey, according to plans and expectations, exploring the valley further east towards the border. We had been told that in the hills opposite Ararat there was a new excavation looking for remains of Noah's Ark. Fifteen kilometres east of Doğubayazit, we left the main road and began climbing. Perhaps 1,000 metres higher, between two villages at either end of a ridge, we stopped. Either we had taken the wrong turning somewhere, or the new excavations were yet another myth. Almost immediately, a handful of village lads followed by two older men approached and offered us tea. There seemed no good reason to refuse genuine hospitality, and shortly a boy appeared bearing a large tray, glasses, sugar and a tea pot. Now our bag of Turkish sweets took on a life beyond our occasional desire. There were some twelve boys, aged about two to sixteen, and six or seven adults – all men. They accepted the sweets with dignified thanks, and we enjoyed a very pleasant tea party without words for half an hour or so.

Close to the border lies another of the tourist attractions of Doğubayazit, a meteor crater reputed to be second only to one in Arizona. It is deep, round, lined with vegetation, and two coachloads of Austrians appeared laden with cameras in the ten minutes we spent there.

# Chapter 3

# TEHRĀN
## تهران

We made a misty departure from the Isak Paşa Serai at half past seven on the morning of June 1st and nerved ourselves for a difficult frontier. Although it took eleven and a half hours to cross, the border at Bāzargān raised only one serious problem, the black market, which I had not anticipated. The fact that we had no automobile insurance in Iran because it is a war zone never arose.

Turkish Customs required two hours to shuffle the Carnet ATA from official to official. I then drove the car through the adjacent Iranian guard post while Tom, Don and Geoff walked through the door separating Turkish from Iranian border police. Once our passports and currency declarations had been stamped, we drove down a hill into a huge dusty version of the Dover docks full of lorries in queues, some of them looking as though they might have been there for months. To the left where the entry port levelled out, we followed signs in Farsi, Turkish and English to the one-storey, modern Customs building. I was sent to see the Director of Customs while my colleagues emptied the car and Tom selected camera equipment that could be sealed against use within Iran, leaving free equipment he would need, a standard procedure unaltered by the Carnet ATA which the inspectors refused even to examine.

In a nearby four-storey office block, I found the Director's office on the top floor. The ground floor housed Customs for coach travellers, mostly Iranians. There was also a cafeteria, menu fixe as well as prix fixe, we later discovered. The offices were gloomy but otherwise undistinguished. Women were employed, but they wore headscarves, and male and female employees were segregated each to their own rooms. Whether they ever actually met or somehow passed papers through slots in the wall, I could not determine. The Director's factotum asked me politely in English to wait. Without exception, these people were polite and a surprisingly large proportion spoke passable English.

The Director, a small neat man with a friendly manner, asked what route we wished to follow in Iran. I explained that we had planned to drive to Tehrān via Tabrīz and Qazvīn and then directly west to Mashhad. From Mashhad, we proposed to drive north-west to the Iranian border crossing at Bājgirān to the Soviet village of Chowdan. I did not explain that it was exactly this route that Lord Curzon had followed, albeit in the opposite direction, a century before.

"That border is closed," said the Director, informatively.

"Yes, we know. That is why the Iranian National Commission for UNESCO, our hosts in Iran, specially arranged our visas with the Ministry of Foreign Affairs."

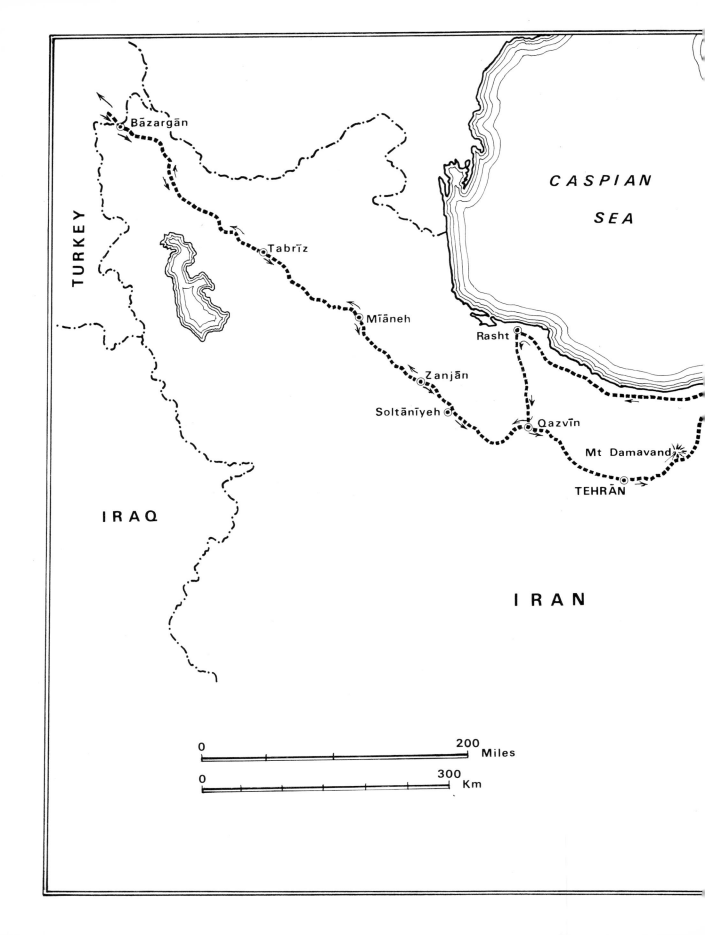

USSR

● Ashkhabad

Bājgirān

Gonbad-e Kāvūs

Abshar
Gulestan
(National Parks)

Qūchān

Minudasht

ābol Sar

Gorgān

Mashhad

Bābol

USSR

Caspian
Sea

0        300    Miles
0        400    Km

USSR

Tehrān

IRAN

AFGHANISTAN

IRAQ

6 000 ft contour

"You may go where you please, but only for two weeks."

"The Soviet authorities expect us to enter the Soviet Union on June 10th," I said.

"You must be accompanied by a Customs policeman during your stay in Iran."

This was information I had received in London from the Oxford Silk Road Expedition of 1986, three men who had followed the lorry route across Iran to Pakistan and crossed much of China by train. "That is perfectly agreeable. How do we arrange it?"

"I will give you a note that you will take to the Customs police." He wrote briefly on a note pad and handed the sheet to me. "My secretary will direct you. You will have to pay in advance for the expenses of this man, of course."

"Certainly. Can you tell me approximately what the charge will be, please?"

"About £100 in your money."

I thanked him, and we shook hands as he wished me a safe journey. On the way to the police station, I passed a branch of the Bank of Iran and exchanged £300 at the legal rate of 117 riyals to the pound sterling.

At the police station, I was given a glass of tea and offered the communal rock sugar bowl. Several candidates appeared to present themselves, but it emerged that each of them had other duties preventing their assignment to us. Only the man in charge, a cheerful thirty-five-year-old named Hassan, could make himself available, it seemed, his only inhibition being unofficial: his two children were scheduled to take their school exams on or about June 12th, an event for which Hassan most earnestly wished to be at home. Naturally, I accepted him as our minder with thanks, regretting only that his English was considerably less adequate than that of one or two colleagues, and that whereas to a man they were slender, even small, Hassan was decidedly stout. This potential difficulty in our crowded vehicle was solved by accepting Hassan's permanent occupancy of the right-hand front seat. Although the rest of us had breaks when we drove, Don was exiled to the uncomfortable rear seat during our Iranian journey. It appeared in time also that Hassan was partially sighted, partially illiterate or dyslexic; he seemed unable to read road signs whether they were written in English, Turkish or Farsi. He proudly showed us his loaded issue pistol when he joined us for the journey at the end of the day, though he stowed it in his hand luggage immediately. It was removed only when revolutionary guards at the roadside checkpoints demanded to see it.

Hassan was our living laissez-passer. He carried his own papers, of course, our official pass and, most of the time, our passports. Roadblocks near the frontiers occurred about every ten kilometres, less frequently elsewhere. Though we later learned incontrovertibly that some of the posts at least maintained telephone communications with each other, we saw no evidence that they informed each other that an ostentatiously British vehicle painted white and covered with signs had just passed that way. The median time for a stop was about five minutes, and Hassan had to leave the car to show his and our papers to an unseen official in a command post. Occasionally, we were waved through. Somewhat more often, the checks took much longer, the longest and most nerve-racking lasting two hours at a Caspian resort town called Bābol Sar. On that occasion, the armed men consisted of uniformed police mixed with bearded, unsmiling revolutionary guards. The latter consistently detained us longer. Once, Tom was ordered to enter the command post with Hassan. I had been driving, he was not carrying a camera at the time and the choice seemed totally arbitrary. It was not a happy fifteen minutes.

At Bāzargān, however, Hassan, having assigned himself to us, took me back to an office manned by several of his colleagues. I was handed a bill covering Hassan's salary for fifteen days, his expenses and bonus for the special duty. Half the sum would go to him and half to the state. The total was 90,000 riyals, roughly £900. The Customs police and Hassan advised me to change money on the black market where I would get about 900 riyals per pound. I explained that our role as scouts for UNESCO made illegal dealing most difficult, and I asked to see the Director of Customs again.

Accompanied by Hassan, I returned to the Director's office.

"Forgive me for troubling you, but you estimated the cost for our guard at £100. I have been given a bill for almost £900."

"But surely you understand that my estimate is based on the black market rate of exchange," he said. "I cannot advise you, of course."

As we left the building, I gave Hassan cash and travellers' cheques amounting to £265. We walked together out of the main guard post of the compound. Hassan and the armed guard exchanged greetings. We turned left towards some low warehouse-like buildings, and as we did so, a young man detached himself from a group lounging against sewer pipes waiting to be installed along the main road. He and Hassan talked briefly, and Hassan asked me to wait near the pipes. He and the young man disappeared around the warehouse. About five minutes later, Hassan reappeared alone, motioned me to join him, and we re-entered the main guard post. We returned to the car, now being reloaded, and Hassan handed me just over 238,000 riyals. I took the bill for his services to the bank, and paid 90,000 riyals to the same clerk who had changed my £300 legally for about 35,000 riyals three hours before. He received the 90,000 riyals angrily, it being all too obvious how I had come by it, and I recalled then having been told how the Oxford group under similar circumstances had hastened to leave Bāzargān as quickly as possible. I realised I had placed us irretrievably on the wrong side of the law and in Hassan's stubby-fingered hands.

It was quite dark when the five of us finally drove out through the main guard post, Hassan exchanging farewells with the same guard. Iranian time is half an hour later than Turkish time; north of the border in the Soviet Union, local time is one and a half hours later still and the daylight hours make a bit more sense.

Hassan took us to the Sahra Hotel and went home to spend the night with his wife. He returned at 8.00 a.m. for our departure. We had gone about ten kilometres when I realised that I had left our passports with the hotel manager. It was the first and only time, but in Iran of all places.

The morning was bright and sunny, the road excellent. Mountains made jagged by lava flows are red-brown and dry, but there are many mudbrick villages surrounded by trees and areas of cultivation. The first rice paddies appeared about fifty kilometres beyond the border. On such an ancient highway, one gets the feeling that armies may advance from either direction.

Marco Polo visited Tabrīz twice, on the outward and the return journey, and called it "the most splendid city in the province".

> The people of Tabrīz live by trade and industry; for cloth of gold and silver is woven here in great quantity and of great value . . . It is also a market for precious stones, which are found here in great abundance. It is a city where good profits are made by travelling merchants. The inhabitants are a mixed lot and good for very little . . . The city is entirely surrounded by attractive orchards, full of excellent fruit.

Now, it is vast, dusty and laid out on a grid, though how much of this pattern has been imposed more recently, I cannot say. As in all central Asian cities, entrance is through a wasteland of ribbon development. The heavy traffic was noisy and uncontrolled, a foretaste of Tehrān. As to the inhabitants, the evidence of our eyes supported the first of Marco's observations though not the second. In our brief experience, they were helpful and normally curious.

We parked beside deep run-off channels on the side of a main street in order to see the Blue Mosque, and to buy food and supplies for camping. Built in 1465, almost two centuries after Marco Polo's visit, the Blue Mosque has been much restored. Tiles on the entrance iwan or arch, are still ruinous, but the interior polychrome tile mosaics are in better repair and exquisitely beautiful. These mosaics are said to reflect Persian influences whereas the building itself is Karakoyunlu.

The shops we found were busy and well stocked, but with little variety or interest. The large, flat Iranian loaves are delicious and hard to buy because they seem to be in short supply. Queues form when the new bread is due, and you have to know the right time. We were lucky in Tabrīz, but seldom thereafter, a situation which was exacerbated because our minder preferred the sweetened breads that can be bought in bakeries any time. Incidentally, the flat loaf cost about 300 riyals, roughly 30p at the black market rate of exchange but at the legal rate, £2.75!

We camped well off the road near a stream in a rocky valley some twenty kilometres west of Mīāneh. It began disastrously. Either Hassan had not understood my statement that we camped as often as we could, or he had not believed me. He was very disgruntled, and pouted in a folding chair. Unfortunately, the weather had changed too: instead of the sun and heat of Tabrīz, a wind blew mist and all the valley dust directly at us. By moving from the open area near the stream to trees closer to the edge of the valley, we much improved matters, and after an hour or so, the wind dropped completely. Don rushed to make a cup of tea, first of course for Hassan, but because we all needed it. Dinner included rice so that there would be plenty for Hassan to eat, and that night the one-man tent and my little radio became his for the duration of our stay in his country. He was cosseted and catered to in recognition of his importance to us, demonstrated unmistakably at the police checkpoints on the first day. His failure in the end to get us across the border annoyed him as much as it frightened us simply because it delayed his return home.

We got up on the morning of June 3rd at about 4.45 a.m. The sun was rising directly behind the wall of jagged rocks closing off the valley. Our side was in absolute black darkness with the penumbra of light flooding the sky behind, so that the ridge seemed to saw the horizon. As the sun rose, the light descended on our side of the ridge and spread slowly down the valley, throwing the rocks in the stream bed into relief. The gullies of dusty sand remained for a time in shadow outlining the lighted rocks. Opposite us on the dry hillsides, the sun picked out the white and grey lines between the reddish rock and occasional patches of green. Such a sunrise emphasised the remarkable beauty of the site we had fretted over the night before.

The choice was fortunate in another way, too. Five kilometres further east, signs in Turkish and English announced that we had entered a no-stopping zone for foreigners. It included the town of Mīāneh and continued beyond through a spectacular valley for about forty kilometres. A railway had joined the road there, undoubtedly of strategic importance. Just before the last road bridge in the no-stopping zone stands a disused bridge that could be Ottoman or even Selcuk. Across the top it had a carriageway, beneath which were three arched passageways, possibly footways, also supported by the three great arches. The two outer arches appeared to be whole, but the central arch had fallen away.

Irrigation and cultivation increased as the highway began to emerge from the mountains into a vast plain. Perhaps fifty kilometres past Zanjān to the right, a large blue-domed structure dominated the flat landscape. This is Soltānīyeh, the tomb that was meant to form a centrepiece for the new capital of Uljāytū, a collateral descendant of Genghis Khan who governed Persia from 1304 to 1317. Though the city never grew from the village that still stands there, the Khan was buried in his magnificent tomb, over fifty metres high and with a dome covered in blue tiles. The building, including the tiled dome, is now being restored. There are other tombs nearby. The Chelebi Oghlu Tomb dating from about 1330 has been well restored along with the madrasa and mosque behind it. The eight arched panels on the tomb itself are faced with patterns of ordinary flat brick and punched brick plugs. The colour is always tan though there are said to be signs that some faience once decorated the façade.

After the friction the night before and the no-stopping zone, the wonders of Soltānīyeh recalled the normal excitements and the reasons for our journey. At Chelebi Oghlu, a scholarly young man associated with the restoration offered us information about the site. I felt the gloom had lifted.

Between Qazvīn and Tehrān there is a four-lane motorway, built of course by the corrupt and oppressive government of the Shah. Throughout Iran, the roads we travelled were much the best of our journey. We saw many more private cars in Iran than in Turkey and possibly Greece, not to mention the USSR and China. Petrol was cheaper than anywhere else in Asia, about the same price as in Britain.

At Qazvīn, we had the motorway almost to ourselves, but traffic gradually increased as we approached the capital. By the time we reached a turn-off that Hassan thought might be suitable, it had achieved that state of chaos we had last seen in Istanbul with the difference that we seemed to stand still much longer in Tehrān. The afternoon had become still and very hot as though a thunderstorm was imminent. None came despite the black sky to the north where we had seen snow-capped mountains as we entered the city. The noise and press of cars, lorries and buses, added to our guide's uncertainty, distracted all of us from the trees and flowers lining the roads and the fountains playing in a small park forming a traffic island at almost every major intersection.

Hassan said he had selected a hotel for us, but first I wanted the advice of the National Commission for UNESCO or possibly even the British Consulate. Since public telephones could only be found at the main Post Office, there would also be a chance to collect mail from poste restante. We parked opposite the Post Office but walked a quarter mile across a large square to the multi-storey office block containing the phones on the ground floor. Every window on approximately the twelfth floor was filled with a photograph of the Ayatollah. The offices up there must have been a bit gloomy even in the sunshine.

Neither the National Commission nor the Consulate answered. The next morning, I learned that the National Commission was open each day until about 1.00 p.m., and also got the correct phone number for the Consulate from the hotel. The telephone exchange had given me a number for the Swedish Embassy to which the British Embassy building nominally belongs. But that afternoon, I learned only how to make a phone call. The pay phone took 1 riyal when the party answered, very much like the old system in London. Nor had there been any post resting.

Tom, who was driving, had to follow Hassan's uncertain directions which finally brought us to the Hotel Bostan, previously the Versailles, on a main street in the north central area of Tehrān. We were discussing accommodation with the ageing clerk when a young managerial type appeared and abruptly stated that there were no rooms. They suggested another hotel around the corner, much smaller, and again we were told they were full. The number of keys hanging beside room numbers made this seem unlikely, but we could hardly argue. I felt like a black man trying to find a New York hotel room in the 1950s. The third attempt was at the Hotel Damavand, previously the Victoria, near the Bostan. An urbane and helpful clerk looked us over but then produced a suite into which a third bed could easily be fitted and a single room, both with baths, plenty of hot water and air-conditioning. There was even a lock-up car park beside the hotel. Luxury indeed, fortunately, in light of discoveries about to be made.

Hassan would be staying with a brother, Cyrus, who was in business in Tehrān and spoke excellent English. We did our best to explain that we hoped to visit UNESCO the next day and possibly to make other appointments in Tehrān. Although I am unsure whether Hassan knew what UNESCO is, his brother no doubt told him. He agreed that he would phone us the next day about 6.00 p.m. Our itinerary called for one day in Tehrān, plus a second day devoted to a side trip to nearby Rey, a former capital, and Veramin.

When we met for dinner, Geoff had managed to phone his wife in Cambridge. She told him about the arrest of an Iranian diplomat for shoplifting in Manchester a week or so earlier. She had not yet heard of the incident in

The Isak Paşa Serai, Doğubayazit, from the south-west.

Looking up into the dome of the Church of the Holy Cross on Akhtamar Island, Lake Van, showing the remains of frescoes on columns and ceilings.

The Church of the Holy Cross, with the mountainous shores of Lake Van beyond to the south.

which the British Consul's car was stopped near Tehrān, and he had been beaten up while his wife watched, because it happened either on that day, June 3rd, or the day before.

On the morning of June 4th, I phoned the National Commission principally to arrange a courtesy call. The acting secretary, Mr Afkhani, welcomed us to Tehrān, and asked that we visit the Commission later in the morning when the Director, Mr Saduq, would also be available. The hotel switchboard then phoned the British Consulate. The Vice-Consul, Simon Wilson, asked what we knew about the present diplomatic situation. When we explained the extent of our ignorance, he asked us to come to the Consulate after our visit to the UNESCO offices but added that, because of the crisis, he would get a message to us at the National Commission about the best time.

Street maps of Tehrān seemed unavailable, and no one relished the prospect of driving anyway so we took a taxi to the Iranian National Commission for UNESCO on an upper floor of an office block almost due south of the hotel towards the centre of town. Mr Afkhani welcomed us warmly, and we were soon joined by Mr Saduq. We were served small bowls of rose water ice, absolutely delicious and perfectly designed to satisfy. They asked how they could help us. I had corresponded with a Mr Pourjavadi, the Director of the Iranian Universities Press and a friend of Dr Feiz, the Iranian Ambassador to UNESCO. The UNESCO office arranged for us to meet Mr Pourjavadi two days later on Saturday at eleven. The call from Mr Wilson came through, and we were given the message that we would be welcome at the Consulate an hour later. UNESCO gave us directions. Not a word was said about the diplomatic situation. Mr Afkhani suggested that we might be interested to see the Iran-Bostan Museum, and arranged for us to be shown around that afternoon. We understood that because of Don's professional interest in paper conservation, we would be introduced to the museum's Director and head of conservation.

As we left the offices and waited for the lift, a well-dressed woman asked for our help. She said that UNESCO were supposed to be getting her out of the country but had let her down. She knew we were English. We urged that she talk again to the people whom we had left. Fortunately, the lift arrived.

No taxis to be seen despite heavy traffic. We started to walk towards Ferdowsi Square, the intersection with the street on which the British Embassy stands. The Consulate was still housed in the Embassy although the Ambassador had been recalled and his staff expelled during some previous crisis. We had walked perhaps a quarter of a mile and paused because someone had spotted a taxi. A private car driven by a man in his thirties stopped on the pavement in front of us. The passenger, a man of about the same age, asked where we were going and offered to drive us as far as Ferdowsi Square. Gratefully, the four of us squeezed in. The passenger said they were in business, but it was very difficult. We gathered it was some sort of import-export business. The government imposed too many regulations, looked over their shoulders constantly, he said. They wanted freedom to get on with their work. Unlike the woman at the lift, these people seemed genuine enough. Nevertheless, we expressed no more than polite good wishes for their business activities, and thanked them with complete sincerity for their kindness.

Mr Wilson was short with blond hair. His grey suit trousers and respectable black shoes provided only a backdrop for a lime green shirt with a white collar and a darker green tie covered by white polka dots two or three centimetres off centre. The next time we met, he was wearing white shorts and a football jersey and looked anything but cool. He explained that he had been burning classified papers in case of imminent expulsion. He and his colleagues were extremely informative and helpful, then and later.

Mr Wilson told us about the attack on the Consul and about the even more astonishing acceptance of responsibility by the Iranian government. He believed that the next move would be expulsion of Iranian diplomats in London and anticipated tit-for-tat expulsions of Britons from Tehrān. Although there had been no threats against British citizens, the barest facts had so far been made known by the Iranian press. The calm could be shattered any time with actual incitements against Britons. He strongly recommended that we leave the country as soon as possible.

We explained that our Soviet visas allowed us entry on June 10th. Mr Wilson said that the Soviet Embassy knew all about the situation and was sympathetic. It was nearby, furthermore, and he thought we should walk round there and try to see the Consul to arrange earlier entry if possible. He would attempt to telephone them. Meanwhile, he suggested then and both by phone and during our second call at the Consulate on Saturday that we keep a low profile. In particular, we were urged to stay off the streets the next day, Friday, because the Muslim Sabbath provided an opportunity for official incitement if there was to be any. He urged us to listen to the radio and was genuinely distressed when I explained that our radio picked up only local broadcasts and was on permanent loan to our minder for the duration of our visit to Iran.

We shook hands with thanks. Around the corner at the Soviet Embassy gate, we rang the bell and asked in English to speak to the Consul. While the guard sent for a colleague who could understand us, we were visited by two well-armed Iranian policemen from across the street. They had seen me hand our passports to the Soviet guard and did not know our nationality. Soon, a Soviet official appeared and said the Embassy was closed until Saturday. He told us to phone the Embassy to make an appointment with the Consul.

We found a taxi that took us back through the gathering heat and traffic to the hotel. The second-floor dining room was large, artificially illuminated even at noon, heavily furnished but clean. The food was adequate and the waiters polite. It was expensive by our exchange standards, but in the circumstances, we ate all our meals there.

A duty officer at the Soviet Embassy made an appointment for us to see the Consul at noon on Saturday. Our taxi driver had never heard of the Iran-Bostan Museum though he knew the Imam Khomeini Avenue! He stopped at a military post near the Majlis, but not even the commandant could give him directions. Fortunately, a young man came along who understood French. He provided the necessary information. About three kilometres east of the guard post along the broad, tree-lined street, the building is set well to the north of the road behind gardens. It seemed to have a new façade and new displays and may have been recently reopened.

Indeed, it is a superb museum, a wonderful collection beautifully displayed. As in Turkey, the ground floor takes you up to the Hijra, the Prophet's flight to Mecca which marks the start of the Muslim era, and the first floor, to the present. The head of the Cultural Department of the National Commission for UNESCO met us as planned. His role as guide was obviated by labels in English as well as Farsi on most displays, but he stuck by us. Carvings and sculpture, especially of animals, from Persepolis and the Sassanian era dominate the ground floor. Upstairs, ceramics and carving from Nishapur, bas-reliefs from Rey and Veramin where we still hoped to go on the next day, lustre from Mashhad, wonderfully carved mimbars, carpets and books. Unfortunately, no catalogue appears to have been published, nor were there postcards. No museum officials appeared, but our guide asked us to phone the National Commission on Saturday morning to arrange the appointment with the Director.

Hassan phoned as promised and put his brother Cyrus on. Cyrus explained that he and his family were taking Hassan away for the Sabbath, the next day. I said that we could make our own way to Rey and Veramin, feeling a sense of relief that we would be without our minder. Someone had told us, moreover, that traffic entering the capital was restricted on Fridays. Cyrus wished us well and said they would phone Saturday morning about 9.00 a.m. He gave us his surname and phone number, a thoughtful act which proved to have been unnecessary.

Even before breakfast the next morning, Friday, June 5th, I phoned the Consulate. The duty officer said that five Iranians had been expelled by London on Thursday. They were now awaiting the list of expulsions from Tehrān to be phoned through by the Ministry of Foreign Affairs. They feared demonstrations outside the Embassy, which never materialised, and again urged that we keep off the streets until we could leave Tehrān and the country. When I had repeated all this to my colleagues, we agreed then and there to make Friday a rest day, to forego the ancient centres at Rey and Veramin and to leave as early as possible on Saturday taking the shortest route to the Soviet border. That meant abandoning the road to Samnan, Nishapur and Mashhad, but we took seriously the warnings to keep a low profile, not an easy thing to do in our vehicle. Mashhad contains one of the holiest shrines in Shia Islam. Would that we had been able to stick by our resolution to avoid the city. As to leaving the country quickly, just when would depend on the Soviet Consul.

Did I panic? It did not feel that way at the time. We feared an unpredictable event, only the probability of which had increased. Yet superficially there was no sign of crisis, and in Tehrān, little sign of war. In the small towns and villages, we saw displays of photographs of war dead in specially-constructed glass cases lining principal streets, but Tehrān looked busy, noisy and prosperous. In our hotel, we saw few fellow guests; they included couples and at least one family — grandmother, mother and father, possibly an aunt and three children. The hotel dining room was usually empty, and not even Tom, the most relaxed amongst us, had a casual conversation there. Our responses reflected first, the Consular advice, then the black market, Hassan, the woman at UNESCO who could have been an agent provocateur and a similar approach by a man that Don experienced on the street, the "full" hotels and the brooding omnipresence of the Ayatollah's gimlet-eyed image combined to make serious exploration and relaxed photography very hard.

I read a lot of *Lucy Barton* by Mrs Gaskell, the Penguin edition, mercifully abridged. We all caught up on our sleep. Our laundry had been taken by the hotel, but not without incident. Pants and some handkerchiefs had been returned with the stern admonition that such things were not washed in the Islamic Republic of Iran. Another chore for a rest day. It may have been during that quiet Friday that one of us was idly leafing through the passports and came up with the unexpected information that there was a discrepancy: my Iranian visa was good for two weeks from June 1st, the other three were valid for one month.

When we met at noon on Saturday, the Soviet Consul explained most apologetically that without permission from the Department of Foreign Affairs in Moscow, he could not alter our visas. He was eager that we should not interpret his refusal as bureaucratic obstruction. We could enter the Soviet Union any time after June 10th within the life of the visa, but not at an earlier date. Nevertheless, we had decided that morning to leave Tehrān in the afternoon. By heading for the Caspian, we could comfortably reach Bājgirān on the 9th. The worst that could happen, we naïvely believed, was that the Soviets would keep us waiting until midnight, and there was a good chance that our Soviet hosts would be already awaiting us at the border and could arrange our immediate crossing a day early.

Hassan was delighted. He would get home a day early. He and Cyrus would meet us at the hotel at three that Saturday afternoon.

Meanwhile, Mr Pourjavadi expected us at 11.00 a.m. and sent a car for us. His secretary was veiled, but she acted as his receptionist in the Western manner. He was an urbane and handsome man who spoke softly but enthusiastically in pleasantly-accented English. He had been commended to us by the British Vice-Consul as well as by our Iranian friends at UNESCO.

I asked what he made of the diplomatic crisis. He began by talking about Western failure to appreciate the sensitivities of all Muslims, not just the Iranians. But because of uncritical Western support for the Shah, Iranians felt this insensitivity even more. It was exacerbated now, of course, because the Western countries, and the Soviet Union, refused to denounce Iraq as the cause of the war. Thus, any European accusation that an Iranian national had behaved improperly or illegally was interpreted as an attack on the Iranian revolution. Such accusations were never made against the agents of the Shah abroad. The government could enroll public opinion in the form of demonstrations if it believed that by doing so Britain, in this case, might be embarrassed. Should this happen, we understood without being told, we would be best out of the country. The interview did not last much longer. When Mr Pourjavadi learned that we were going to Dushanbe where Don would inspect the new paper conservation facilities in the Tadzhik national library and museum, he asked if Don would deliver a book of poetry recently published by the Iran University Press to a friend there. Of course, Don agreed. Though neither he nor we reached Dushanbe, the book was posted from London and an acknowledgment duly received.

# Chapter 4

# THE BORDER

مرز

Hassan and Cyrus arrived forty minutes late, but the latter guided us in his car on to the ring road before saying goodbye. The busy four-lane motorway began a steady climb into the Elburz Mountains in the draining heat which threatened constantly to boil the radiator. To our left we could see Mount Damavand, at 5,600 metres the highest mountain in Iran, a snow-capped volcano but otherwise as brown and dry as the surrounding landscape, excepting for a sprinkling of green that must reflect the spring.

Cyrus had warned us that for about fifty kilometres the road was very rough. He and his family had taken Hassan to the Caspian the day before. There had not been time to repair winter damage, he said. After the first pass, four lanes became two. It is a mountain road, following the contours of natural passes cut by various rivers. In many places the road has been blasted into the sheer cliffs and then covered by metal sheeting as protection against the falling rock. Approaching them, these tunnels look like worm casts. The potholes in their surfaces made the roads outside seem like Brands Hatch. It was probably the diversion of money to the war effort that explained the only bad road surface we encountered in Iran.

The surface changed for the better after we had passed Damavand and begun to descend. The climate of the northern mountain slopes is dominated by the Caspian Sea. Forests begin quite high up, and beside the rushing stream in the valley below, cultivation also begins again. The descent lasts far longer than the climb because Tehrān is already at almost 1,200 metres.

It was getting dark as we entered the narrow fertile plain between the mountains and the sea, but we could make out the rice paddies clearly enough. Hassan knew the Hotel Ohra just west of the little resort town of Bābol Sar. It was cheaper, he said, because it is about a kilometre from the sea, but new, clean and brazenly ugly. A very good dinner with fresh sea fish cost me £90 and two rooms with four beds, £65 – at the legal rate of exchange, of course.

The next day, Sunday, June 7th, was to be a day off at the seaside. Outside Tehrān, we felt less pressure. First, however, Tom wanted to change travellers' cheques. There was a Bank of Iran in Bābol, a nondescript market town fifteen kilometres south of Bābol Sar. We noticed a number of abandoned and uncompleted new buildings, mostly shops but some houses, as we drove through the straggling suburbs. With Hassan, Tom approached the bank manager. He agreed at once to exchange the dollar cheques, quoting the black market rate quite openly, Tom reported, making no attempt to hide the transaction from his interested staff. When Tom refused because of our UNESCO connection, there was a surprised silence. Then the manager said he could only send the travellers' cheques to Tehrān and await the cash because only in Tehrān was it possible to exchange them. Tom did not get his riyals.

We returned to the beach at Bābol Sar. After paying a small admission fee, about a pound each in our money, we walked on the soft brown sand beside the gentle rollers. It was hot, and the sea looked inviting though it seemed very salty. We looked for shells, took some photographs, especially of Hassan, and observed the decaying shops and wooden pavilions in need of paint. One stand offered bottled soft drinks which were cool at least. The wide beach was all but deserted although Hassan assured us it had been very busy two days before, a Friday.

About one, we drove back to the hotel on the way to finding a place for lunch. No sooner had we appeared in the forecourt than the bearded young manager flew out of the office and began to upbraid Hassan. It seemed that the police had come to look for us and demanded that we go at once to the police station. The manager insisted on coming with us. For almost two hours, we four sat in the vehicle while Hassan and the hotel manager dealt with our papers and passports. To this day, I have no idea what it was all about. Had the bank manager reported that we were trying to trade on the black market? Were the police simply annoyed that we had been out when they called? Was it to do with our being British? It was around this time that Hassan began to assure us regularly that we were foolish to go to the Soviet Union where people were poor while in Iran everyone ate well and was free to do as he pleased.

Early the next morning, we left Bābol Sar and headed east across the fertile alluvial plain. Fields of cotton were being weeded by women. Near the town of Gorgān, wheat cultivation began, interspersed with fields of potatoes, salads and other market garden products. We stopped in Gorgān to buy bread for breakfast, but there were queues at the bakeries and none to be had. Instead, Hassan loaded us up with sweetened toast and sweet bread rolls. A few kilometres further on, a subsidiary track beside the highway gave us a place to make some coffee. A row of trees and a flooded irrigation channel separated us from a wheat field. A woman with half a dozen small children was resting a hundred metres further on. One tiny girl was washing an infant in the irrigation water. When we had finished our bread and butter, Hassan washed his plates in the same way. I think they were later rewashed with ours in soap and water containing a little Savlon.

Despite our sense of flight, I could not resist the proximity of the fifty-five-metre-high Tomb Tower at Gonbad-e Kāvūs. Built during the first decade of the eleventh century, it can be seen for a great distance across the plain. Entirely of plain tan brick, its eight vertical flanges add massiveness to the tower. At the top, below the conical dome and around the door, bas-relief inscriptions in the same colour brick are the only decorations. The tomb of the local ruler has never been found, and the story goes that the body was suspended in glass by chains from the dome.

In Gonbad and Gorgān, both men and women wore brighter clothes than we had seen elsewhere in Iran. The men's white turbans left an end hanging behind. The women wore red, yellow or green blouses and scarves under their cloaks and veils. A man riding a motorbike carried his wife pillion wearing a red shawl and green trousers. These people are Turkmen from what is now the Soviet side of the mountains to the north and are Sunni Muslims.

In Gonbad, we saw carts for the first time in Iran, but very few horses. Donkeys, bullocks and water buffalo did the work in what seemed a very prosperous region. The plain soon became a valley with fields spread stamp-like up the hills to the south-east. Just beyond a small town called Minudasht, a woman wearing a grey cloak and carrying a child sat on a donkey led by her husband.

As the road continued to rise, cultivation gave way to flocks of long-haired sheep and goats. At last the hills closed in on both sides and we entered a forest called the Gulestan National Park. Hassan said tigers and wolves roamed there, and we did see a dead wild boar by the side of the road. There were prepared campsites along the highway and lush scenery until at the top of the mountain pass, geographical conditions changed completely again. The land was dry and covered by scrub. This was the Abshar National Park. Abshar means waterfall, according to Hassan. Beyond, where the villages began, cereal crops and sheep looked like the principal products. High in this rolling treeless land, we stopped to photograph a mud village. A man in the fields between us and the village also stopped his work and photographed us. He had been ploughing, evidently with a camera near to hand. The most likely explanation for this unusual event would seem to be that he too was a camera buff.

When we reached Qūchān and left the main Mashhad road to turn north towards the border, the sun had set. A rock quarry, probably used for road building, provided some shelter against the evening wind. Again, despite a bit of shelter in a shallow cave, it was hard to keep the cooker flame steady. Hassan had a long wait for his tea, and we made do with cold coffee. It was not just the wind this time, but also the hour. Hassan was intent on an early arrival at the border next morning followed by his early departure for home and insisted we keep moving. Don hated a late stop because it made cooking that much harder, though that night Tom did the rice. Hassan had to have his rice!

We woke very early on the day intended to be our last in Iran, made tea and coffee in the quiet dawn and set off on the non-metalled road which became more spectacular as the kilometres slowly passed. With 180-degree hairpin curves, it ascended a good 1,000 metres, and in the same manner, descended into the valley beyond. The ranges seemed without end. There was plenty of water and in most places spiky vegetation, but no snow. Occasionally, green veins of what may have been malachite shot through the black rock. On one stretch of relatively level road, we passed a party dressed like gypsies, about ten dark-faced men and women with roughly an equal number of children and heavily-laden donkeys beside which they walked. Concrete bridges crossed the streams, but they were slabs without such luxuries as railings. In one astonishing spot, roughly 500 metres in length, the valley narrowed to the width of the road, about two metres, partly natural and partly hewn from the towering rocks. It is sixty-three kilometres from where we camped to the sprawling hillside village of Bājgirān, very little of it level and none of it boring.

On the far side of the village stands the neat frontier post. Straight ahead, the road continued through a locked guarded gate up a gentle hill amongst trees to disappear at the top. Beside the gate was the entrance to a white cluster of buildings that housed barracks and probably a mess and kitchen. The white single-storey guard post containing several large rooms stood to the left of the road before the gate, and on the right were various lock-up warehouses. We were directed to the guard post. The Customs officer in charge asked us to come in to his office. We were given tea while he examined our passports and had a word with Hassan. It was about 9.30 a.m.

After consulting with his colleagues, the officer said through an interpreter that the border was closed. We could not cross and had no business being there. No one used the crossing. I explained, only for the first time that long day, the purposes of the expedition, the jobs each of us did, our work for UNESCO, how the Iranian National Commission for UNESCO had arranged our visas specially so that we could cross at Bājgirān to meet our Soviet hosts who were awaiting us two kilometres away at Chowdan. He said he would be able to ask the Soviet Customs police if they knew anything about us because they had telephone communication at about noon when either side had something to put to the other. He also said he would have to communicate with his superiors.

The latter phone calls took roughly an hour during which we were allowed to wander more or less freely within the building and to the car parked in front. Some time later, a volunteer Indian doctor assigned by the government to work in Bājgirān for two years came in to chat with us. He had been visiting patients in the barracks. His practice consisted largely of treating farm accidents and children's diseases. His role in childbirth was extremely restricted by the segregation of women who depended largely on midwives. Although our research into oesophageal cancer was to begin in the Soviet Union, we were naturally mindful of it. There was not much disease, the doctor said, some gastro-intestinal disorders due to improperly stored or cooked foods. But he had seen three cases of oesophageal cancer, two men and a woman in their thirties, one of the men and the woman from the same family, an unusually high incidence although this was north-eastern Iran where the disease was common. One of the men was still alive. The doctor hoped to stay on in Iran for another two years before returning to India, but perhaps not in Bājgirān.

The Customs officer reappeared and said that we would be spending the night in the large recreation room outside his office. Hassan was evidently to stay elsewhere . We were to take whatever we needed out of the car. He did not know how long we would be there or whether we would be going on the next morning. He himself would not be around to find out, furthermore, because today was his last in this post. No, he had not yet spoken to the Soviet guard post. He directed me to drive the car into one of the warehouses. I locked the car, and a Customs policeman bolted and sealed the door. Hassan, the policeman and I had started back to the Customs post when the officer in charge appeared, admonished the policeman and ordered that the car be moved to another shed directly across from the post. The door was unsealed and unbolted, the car unlocked and driven fifty metres up the hill again into the new warehouse, after which the original procedure was repeated.

By this time, lunch was ready. With Hassan, we were shown where we could wash and taken into a small side room with clean mats spread on the floor. An enormous meal of soup, kebabs, pigeons, rice, yoghurt, salads, bread and tea awaited us, all of it replenished, principally for Hassan's benefit, by the people looking after us. Clearly, we were honoured guests.

We were all relaxing after lunch, reading, writing letters or dozing, when the officer in charge appeared with Hassan who said instructively: "Go to Mashhad."

"We are supposed to stay here."

"No. Go to Mashhad. Customs headquarters."

"But we cannot possibly go to Mashhad and enter the Soviet Union tomorrow when we are expected. Our Soviet hosts are waiting for us." They were, too. They had arrived a day early just in case we should cross very early the next morning. Apparently, the officer in charge had been told not to communicate with the Soviet border post.

"You must go. Orders. Go at once. Maybe you will come back today."

It is 220 kilometres to Mashhad, sixty of them over the unmetalled road. Again the car was released. The others began to reload.

"I would like to telephone to the National Commission for UNESCO," I said, forgetting that the office closed at 1.00 p.m.

"Impossible."

"It will be your responsibility that we cannot complete our work for UNESCO."

"Go now. Maybe come back soon, but go."

Hassan was angry. After all, his colleagues were mucking up his plans too. Two guards with automatic rifles appeared from the barracks. A four-door Toyota van pulled up driven by a third guard with a fourth beside him. Both had automatic rifles.

"You must go at once. Him," he gestured at Don, "in our car, you three in the other."

I had not foreseen that we might be divided, and the thought that one of us should travel alone with our guards, like a hostage, filled me with dread.

"Why should he go alone? I will go with him, the other two in the expedition van."

After a word with Hassan, they agreed. One of the armed guards rode in our van, the other three made room for Don and me in the back seat of the Toyota. They laid all three automatic rifles against the crankshaft casing between the front seats. Two seemed to point directly at me sitting beside the left-hand rear door. We set off, Tom driving our van behind.

As we drove through the peaceful village of Bājgirān, I half believed we might be back by tomorrow, June 10th, the date on our Soviet visas. Hassan's farewell to his mates at the border post had been tinged with conspiratorial annoyance. You could interpret their manner to mean that the officers were just making work as usual for privates like themselves. They would confirm the acknowledged stupidity of all bosses when Hassan got back tomorrow.

We stopped in one of the tiny settlements by the road about ten kilometres past Bājgirān. Evidently, the guard beside us in the back seat lived there. He climbed out and reappeared three minutes later carrying a jug of yoghurt, accompanied by his family. Each of us was offered yoghurt before the guards and Hassan had a drink. Even now, we were some indeterminate kind of prisoners.

Friendly grocers, Tabriz, Iran.

The museum director at Kokand, USSR.

Portrait of a craftsman, Andizhan.

Portrait of a herb-seller, Samarkand.

It was dark when we reached Mashhad. We were confined to our hotel, if not technically under house arrest, until we left the next day. I saw a large, low city with wide avenues lined by many trees and no trace of a mosque, let alone a shrine.

None of our guards seemed to know the location of their headquarters, actually the headquarters for Customs, the police and other functions of the Ministry of the Interior for the province of Khorāsan, comprising north-eastern Iran. After many enquiries, we parked beside an office block, perhaps three storeys high, and were ushered past guards to a large, ground-floor reception room with three or four overstuffed armchairs at one end and two desks at the other. I reminded Hassan that our baggage was unprotected on top of the car, now parked on what seemed to be a public street, but we were assured it would be watched.

After a delay, a dapper young man appeared who spoke excellent English. Mr Sultanija works normally in the office of the provincial Governor General. He explained to us that the Ministry of Foreign Affairs had not informed the Ministry of the Interior that we wished to enter the Soviet Union through a border crossing that was normally closed. It had been closed, Mr Sultanija said, for ten years. In London, I had been told that border was closed in 1985. The next morning, according to the Customs officials who came to execute our sentence, it had been closed for eleven years, "by law". Mr Sultanija added that the Soviets had not informed the Ministry of Foreign Affairs as they should have done, he said, that they intended to meet us at Chowdan on their side of the border. Finally, Mr Sultanija said that the Ministry of Foreign Affairs had heard of us and acknowledged that they had issued visas to us, but denied all knowledge of where we wished to leave Iran. Apart from the fact that his last point seemed to nullify his first point, Mr Sultanija was unaware that visa application forms ask where the applicant intends to leave Iran and whether the applicant has permission to enter the country on the other side of that crossing point. Though they were politely put, these objections seemed not to interest Mr Sultanija. In addition to our passports, however, he did take letters from UNESCO asking the expedition to act as scouts for its proposed Silk Road studies and from the Institute of Geography of the Soviet Academy of Sciences stating that they wished us to enter the Soviet Union from Iran near Ashkhabad; i.e., at Chowdan. Copies were telefaxed to Customs headquarters in Tehrān along with copies of our passports and visas, all of which were eventually returned.

We had been given tea, but had eaten nothing since the large lunch provided by Customs at Bājgirān. After the tensions of the day, we were also tired.

Mr Sultanija said, "You will have to wait in Mashhad until tomorrow morning."

"We certainly have no objection," I said, "but we also have no Iranian money. We had expected to leave the country today. We have only travellers' cheques, and we have been told that they can only be exchanged in Tehrān."

"Although your government hates us, we do not hate you. You cannot sleep on the street. We have arranged for you to stay in a good hotel. Do not worry about payment. The important thing is to get some rest."

Naturally, we thanked Mr Sultanija sincerely.

"Please wait in your hotel rooms for our call. We expect an early decision," he added. "Good night. Rest well."

Hassan was our guard as usual. The five of us in our van followed a Customs vehicle to a first-class, new hotel with a lock-up parking area. Tom, Geoff and Hassan had dinner. Don and I felt too exhausted and passed up that late-evening meal.

I telephoned Mr Afkhani of the National Commission for UNESCO at nine o'clock next morning. He promised to get in touch with the appropriate section of the Ministry of Foreign Affairs immediately. I also mentioned the added irritation of the date discrepancy between my visa and the others'. He suggested that I ask the Customs officials to arrange a visa extension for me with the police, normally a routine matter, and promised to phone back as soon as there was something to report.

Three men from Customs appeared about eleven. All had been present during the conversation with Sultanija the night before, but none spoke English. The hotel manager acted as interpreter. We were required to leave Mashhad at once. We could cross the border into the Soviet Union at Āstārā on the western Caspian coast. I explained that our Soviet visas would not allow this. Then, said the Customs spokesman, we must return to Turkey. We must go at once because my visa expired in three days' time. No, it could not be extended. I phone Mr Afkhani so that he could speak to the Customs spokesman who repeated what he had told us.

Furthermore, there was the matter of our hotel bill. I pointed out that Mr Sultanija had kindly said that Customs would see to our accommodation. No, we had to pay the bill. At the legal rate of exchange, it amounted to £474! They would not accept travellers' cheques, but they would accept Eurocheques! Now, as far as we knew, Eurocheques are unusable in Iran, the Soviet Union, China and all other countries whose banking systems are not integrated with those of Western Europe and Japan. Nevertheless, the hotel manager accepted two Eurocheques from Don adding up to the necessary amount in pounds sterling, and both were eventually cashed.

I was able to phone the British Consulate who thanked me for the information and wished us good luck. I said that if we did have to return, which now seemed probable, we would avoid Tehrān.

The Customs officials left. At 12.45 p.m., Mr Afkhani phoned me. The matter had been sorted out. We must not leave Mashhad because the Governor General of Khorāsan himself was going to stamp our visas. I thanked him, but said that because my visa expired in three days, I could not delay our departure past three o'clock. What is more, Customs had ordered us to leave Mashhad immediately. We would have lunch in the hotel and hope to hear from the Governor General, but we must leave at three. Mr Afkhani promised to pass on the message.

As the minutes passed, my hopes plummeted. The others claimed that they had never been hopeful. At three, we drove out of the hotel car-park. It was a hot, cloudless day. Almost at once, Hassan's inability to read signs got us on to the wrong road. We added about five kilometres and lost perhaps fifteen minutes before regaining the main highway from Mashhad to Qūchān, but in so doing, we missed any chance at the remains of Tus, the ancient capital of

Khorāsan, that might have been seen to the right of the road as we sped by. The heat, dust and wasted opportunity deepened my already considerable depression to the dimensions of a Turkish meteor crater, the walls rank with vegetation, the floor littered with non-biodegradable rubbish. Back the way we had come stretched the four-lane highway through a fertile valley that spelled defeat. I drove very fast.

The first police check, now more irritating than ever, came as we entered Qūchān where the road to Bājgirān turned north. The second followed about twenty kilometres to the west as we approached another village. There was a message for Hassan, proof that communication between the checkpoints was possible. He was to phone the Customs post at the border. Suddenly, there was hope again. Like most villages, this one had a public telephone centre. I accompanied Hassan into a concrete room with the operator in his own enclosure on one side and two dark phone cabinets on the other. The call went through quickly, and Hassan chatted cheerfully for a minute or two. When he hung up, I asked what had happened. "Am I coming back today? I say no," he answered. I lagged behind him as we returned to the car.

We camped that night in an official campsite for the first time, and by midday, June 11th, we had returned to Bābol Sar. From there, the road ran close to the seashore, sometimes beside it, at others separated only by villas, many of them recently built but few showing signs of use. As in other parts of the north, unfinished buildings, both public and domestic, frequently stood out. To our left rose the heavily-wooded foothills of the Elburz Mountains. Mist gave the landscape the soft edges of traditional Chinese painting. Between the towns where there were no villas, semi-tropical crops abounded. In addition to rice, cultivated often by women bending from the waist, we saw tea, pulses, citrus fruits and cereals, always in small fields. Near Rasht, there were palm trees.

The road was excellent but very busy with local traffic. We entered Rasht in deep twilight and turned south away from the sea, camping beside the highway, treeless and noisy. That marked the nadir of the entire journey. The occupant of a house just beyond a hedge to our right appeared as we were pitching the tents, but he was extremely friendly, merely curious. That night's dinner came for the first time from our stock of Raven dehydrated iron rations, a delicious shepherd's pie, to which Don added rice.

The Rasht-Qazvīn highway climbs back again through the mountains to the central Iranian plateau, but it is gentler and even more beautiful than the road past Damavand. That evening, the twelfth, we drove into the Customs compound at Bāzargān at about half past seven. Hassan greeted his mates, and directed us immediately up the hill to passport control and the final police check. Tired as we were, the chance for a beer that night in Turkey appealed even to relative non-drinkers like Tom and me. But the border was closed. Down the hill again we drove. After pointing out the cafeteria in the office block nearby, Hassan left us to unroll our mattresses and bedrolls literally on the steps of the Customs hall. "Morning. Eight a.m.," he said, and went happily home.

The cafeteria offered enough food but no choice. It was tense. We did not imagine the angry looks from several other diners and ate quickly.

After driving 1,200 kilometres in two and a half days and a disturbed night, we slept soundly. Awakened by the morning light, we were soon joined beneath the canopy in front of Customs by a crowded car carrying a Pakistani family from Kuwait, where they had been working, back to their home in Karachi. They had a radio that worked. Although it was the morning of June 13th, we had escaped so far without news of the general election. The opening bulletin on the BBC Overseas news broadcast announced a Tory majority of 102. We had left England almost two weeks before the election had been called but had regretfully agreed that Mrs Thatcher would win. I suggested a kind of pools: each of us would select a number for the size of her majority and the one who was closest would win drinks from the other three as soon as we left Iran. Geoff had said 102.

Hassan did not appear until nine o'clock. I confess to a very bad hour although the others seemed to remain calm. I imagined every possible reason for the delay: Hassan had been our contact with the black market and needed to protect himself; the authorities wanted us held, at least until my visa expired. I even realised that he might have found it hard to get out of the connubial bed after two weeks away. In any event, when at last he did arrive, cheerful and smiling, the Customs check was cursory. No one asked for the currency declarations we had completed on entering the country. Hassan was genuinely warm in his farewells, either because he had grown to like us, as two of my colleagues maintain, or because he was glad to see the back of us. I was overjoyed to see the back of him, and his countrymen. Not even the young Turkish Customs policeman who told us how great the Ayatollah would be for Turkey could diminish my relief.

We had escaped from Iran. The adventure actually cost £1500, three times what I had budgeted. But what were the real costs? Would the Soviets allow us to enter from Turkey? How long would new visas take? We had to live in Turkey too. Should we abandon the expedition, try to sell what we could, return home failures? In that case, how imminent was personal bankruptcy? Our return to safety left us afloat on a sea of daunting questions.

# Chapter 5

# ERZURUM AND ANKARA

First priority: revised Soviet visas allowing us to enter the Soviet Union at Leninakan from Kars in Turkey. But whatever I might do, the authorisation for new visas had to originate with our Soviet hosts who we presumed were still in Ashkhabad and must be very worried about us.

In Doğubayazit we knew where to find the Post Office, and Tom had long since discovered the secrets of Turkish international telephone calls. Secret 1: only tokens can be used in the machines. They must be purchased from the operator on duty in the Post Office. Secret 2: the prefix numbers for London are 99 44 1. The language barrier had made this discovery difficult. To repeat the triumph by obtaining the prefix for Moscow, or Ashkhabad, proved impossible in Doğubayazit. Secret 3: patience. The number of lines to London (or any other destination, domestic or foreign) is restricted, the system is ancient and the completion of a call, the merest chance. Secret 4: the instrument must be primed with tokens continuously because a) the cut off signal is followed immediately by a dead line, and b) the value of the token (about 20p) does not go far towards a call to London. Even so, the call might well be terminated for no apparent reason. In that case, the instrument generously returned all the tokens you had put in and, sometimes, a bonus paid in by the previous caller.

My best chance to tell our Soviet friends what had happened was by talking to Paul Crook who was still in London. Earlier in the summer, he had been in touch with the USSR Academy of Sciences, and they could reach the people in the field. Eventually, he was able to speak to them directly from London. Even I had two frustrating conversations over terrible lines with Dr Badenkov, the Deputy Director of the Institute of Geography, in Bukhara and Samarkand, but by then I was in Ankara.

It was Nigel Morley, the British Consul in Ankara, who sensibly pointed out that our applications for new visas had to begin at the Soviet Consulate in Ankara. On Tuesday, June 16th, therefore, we drove to Erzurum, the nearest commercial airport, and I flew to the capital while the others camped six kilometres west of the city for the next thirteen days. To them, the delay seemed particularly endless.

Nigel Morley, and the Vice-Consul, Engin Bey, made arrangements for me to see the Soviet Consul, and because the Consul spoke Turkish but no English, Engin Bey enquired informally several times about our visas, very much above and beyond the call of duty. The Soviet Consulate at first expected approval of the revision before the end of the week. Our Soviet colleagues in Ashkhabad, who had moved on to Bukhara and Samarkand in accordance with our agreed schedule, repeatedly made the case for urgency with the

Foreign Affairs Department of the USSR Academy of Sciences. The British Consulate also checked with the Turkish Customs authorities and police that we would be able to leave Turkey at Kars in order to enter the Soviet Union. Towards the end of the ordeal, the people in the Foreign Affairs Department were giving me details of the messages sent by the Ministry of Foreign Affairs to the Ankara Consulate, including the number of the cable approving our revised visas. I also managed to have one phone conversation with Dmitri Oreshkin, my Institute of Geography contact, who had come to Jerevan to meet us. He told me that he understood we would have to put the car on a train either to leave Turkey or to enter the Soviet Union, he was not sure which. This information was also checked by the British Consulate who told me on the same afternoon our visas finally came through that we could drive out of Turkey but that our car would be put on a train from Leninakan to Jerevan. I had already learned from Moscow that the car would be driven from Jerevan to Ashkhabad by Soviet drivers while we flew to Ashkhabad, and that we would continue our journey by road as planned from Ashkhabad. So the report from the British Consulate made sense.

My Ankara hotel, the Haneçioglu, had been recommended by Engin Bey. It was cheap, very clean and comfortable and marvellously located in a wholesale section of the Ulus district. Several Iranians were staying there awaiting visas. One family from Tehrān with two small children had been promised entry into Canada. A second couple with one young daughter had expected to go to the United States because the wife had a place to study physics at the University of Kansas. When their application was refused, they decided to apply for a British visa because she had also been offered a place by the University of London. Two single businessmen were hoping to work in the United States. None of these people, with the possible exception of the emigrants to Canada, talked about a permanent exile. All of them explained why they would be returning to Tehrān or Isfahan. None of them openly criticised the regime. That made sense when one of the businessmen decided to await his US visa in Isfahan because it would be less expensive.

Meanwhile, Paul flew from London to Samarkand as planned. Arriving on June 22nd, he was met by Dmitri Oreshkin's chief, Dr Yuri Badenkov, and the Soviet contingent. The rest of the team at Erzurum kept in touch by phone, often twice a day, their frustration growing because they had even less control over events than I did. When June 26th passed with Moscow saying that revised visas had been approved and Ankara saying they still had no instructions from Moscow, Don decided he had to leave. The plan had been for him to travel with us to Dushanbe to visit the new conservation facilities in the library of the Tadzhik Republic and to return to London on June 27th. With sadness that we all felt, he came to Ankara and flew home early Monday morning, June 29th. Monday afternoon at three o'clock, the Soviet Consulate told me they had the revised visas!

The next day, Tom met me at the Erzurum airport. We picked up Geoff in the town and retraced our steps as far as Horasan. Entering the town, I triggered a speed trap of the sort that used to bedevil the American middle west. The posted limit, which we had not noticed, is fifty kilometres per hour. Evidently, I had been travelling at sixty-three kph. Unlike the American middle west, the two policemen understood a little English and kept us only long enough to check our passports and warn us about speeding.

Between Erzurum and Horasan, we had stopped briefly beside a river at Çobandede to photograph an Ottoman bridge attributed to the great Sinan. It is a graceful structure 220 metres long with six arches and still in use, albeit for a side road. We had noted the bridge with some excitement during the drive to Erzurum and would have stopped then for pictures but for the presence of a military convoy by the side of the road and an encampment nearby. In such circumstances, photography seemed unwise, but by June 30th they had all disappeared, signalling the end of some manoeuvres.

The road north to Kars passed through a green, well-watered valley climbing on to the rolling north Turkish plain. North-east of Kars as we approached the border, road markings became rare and erratic. Indeed, of the three maps we carried that covered the region, only one spelled the name of the Turkish border town, Akyaka, correctly. Nevertheless, we reached this village beside the railway at about 6.00 p.m., prepared to cross into the Soviet Union immediately if possible. The road being unmarked, we stopped at the gate of an army barracks as we entered the town to ask directions. Imagine our sense of *déjà vu* when we were finally informed by an officer in charge that we had no business being there and could go no further. We had to return to Kars and the Customs headquarters there. When we protested, we were accompanied by two soldiers to the local police station. A haughty and extremely rude police sergeant repeated much the same story, through a German-speaking interpreter, and ordered us back to Kars.

By this time, it was not only dark but we had had nothing to eat since midday. The police sergeant gave us permission to camp outside the village and on the way back to their barracks through the main street, our military escort knocked up the one local restaurateur and arranged for us to have a meal.

The next morning, Monday, June 30th, we held a council of war. Near the border, the road from Kars had become an unmetalled four-lane highway, as though someone sold the idea that, with a good road, heavy traffic might use this crossing point, and then lost his job when construction had begun. It actually bypasses Akyaka, running along the edge of the grass-covered, treeless hills a hundred metres higher than the railway in the valley. We thought it might be worth a try to follow the road towards the border, nine kilometres away. We just might be able to talk our way through the final Turkish checkpoint and our brand-new visas would get us into the USSR. There was a chance that soldiers or police in the town would see us and give chase, but we figured we could stop and turn around before anyone started shooting.

We reached the border post without incident. The road continued through a gate past a Turkish barracks, and, as far as we could see across the relatively flat terrain, to the border itself. We stopped by the gate. Shortly, a man in pyjamas appeared from the barracks. He was unarmed, but he was also the army lieutenant in charge of the border post. He was very friendly and spoke excellent English, having worked in England and been educated at Portsmouth Polytechnic, but he was also astonished to see us.

"How did you get here?" he asked.

"We just followed the road."

"But you cannot cross the border. There is no road." An accurate statement because at the border itself, as we later discovered from the train, the road has been destroyed.

"We understand from the British Consul in Ankara that we may leave Turkey by road."

"Impossible. Have you reported to the army post in Akyaka?"

"Yes."

"What did they say?"

"What you say, but there must be some mistake. See, we have valid Soviet visas."

The cheerful lieutenant offered to phone his superior officer in Akyaka. Within five minutes, he returned: "You must certainly go back to Akyaka. I can do nothing else. Have you a piece of paper?" I handed him a notebook. "Here is the name of the officer you should speak to in Akyaka. But please, destroy this page," he said, pointing at the notebook. "It is bad security for me to give you his name."

At the barracks in Akyaka, we were sternly told we must return to Kars. Then in the care of the officer in question, we were again taken to the police station. This time the sergeant failed even to look up. "Where have you been?" he demanded.

"As you know, we drove to the border."

"You had no right to do that. If you do it again, you will be arrested."

"What for?"

"For disobeying my orders."

"Your orders are unjustified. I will report your threat to the British Consul in Ankara immediately."

Both of us were by now filled with righteous indignation as he dismissed me. For despite the repetitive aspect of events in Akyaka, there was a profound difference between the Turkish and Iranian threats.

From the local Post Office, I phoned the Consulate. Mr Morley promised to speak to the sergeant himself and to check further on the matter of transport out of Turkey. I rang back at eleven. The sergeant, he said, was pacified. Morley had also spoken to his police superior in Kars. As to the train, the Akyaka authorities spoke the truth. I fear Mr Morley believed that I misunderstood what Engin Bey had told me in Ankara. If the Consulate has a taped recording of our phone conversation which proves otherwise, I would like to know about it. Meanwhile, as old ladies in central Ohio used to say: "I heared what I heared."

The high spot of this return journey to Kars was a hilltop field of wild flowers of a brightness and superfluity hard to describe. Poppies, varieties of daisy, grape hyacinths, relatives of the daffodil and iris and a dozen species beyond my power to identify waved gently in the breeze. They shone in the sun, a Turkish carpet made by a demented weaver.

With the help of a young man from the Kars Tourist Office splendidly named Cengiz Alp who appeared opportunely, attracted by the peculiarities of our vehicle parked outside the Customs office, we made preliminary arrangements for the car and us to be transported across the border. Trains run on Tuesday and Friday at 10.00 a.m. It was now Tuesday afternoon. Cengiz recommended the Hotel Asie. The rooms were extremely dirty and noisy, but had a private shower of sorts and were cheap. Our guide then took us to the Tourist Office, because we had decided to make the best of a frustrating situation and visit Ani, for several centuries the capital and principal trading centre of the more or less independent kingdom of Armenia. More or less, because first the Arabs then the Selcuks and then the Mongols conquered the kingdom, but in those days of slow communication and cumbersome, expensive defence, many regions with established regimes continued to be governed by the native rulers under threat of death and destruction should they fail to pay their taxes regularly. Armenian kings usually enjoyed this vassal status until they became too feeble to maintain their authority. Under the Ottoman Empire, the destruction of Armenia extended to the people themselves. They were Christians within the major Islamic power, of course, and no doubt in regions like Erzurum and Van, they also controlled valuable resources like land. As to Ani, it was destroyed by an earthquake in 1319, an event which confirmed the decline in the city's fortunes brought on by the Mongol conquest and the shift in trade routes to the east. It was not rebuilt.

You need a police permit to visit Ani, forty-one kilometres east of Kars, because it is sensitively situated today on the Soviet border. All visitors must stop at an army barracks twelve kilometres before the monuments to check in their cameras. A camera found after that halt is subject to confiscation.

Just before the massive medieval walls stands a modern village so that you get the best view four or five kilometres away. Entrance is through a Lion Gate, so called because of a bas-relief animal carved inside the wall, high above the road. Ani filled an extensive triangular plateau. From the gate, you can see the land on either side of the deep canyons defining the area, the Soviet Union to the left. Ahead at the apex stands the citadel, now a fortress used as a barracks and defensive point and closed to tourists. In the middle distance stand manmade piles of reddish stone, half a dozen of them scattered across the waist of the plateau. They are the remains of great churches that served what must have been different quarters of the city. One was built as a mosque and has a minaret beside it. Another is the apse of the cathedral, its northern wall riven by a great crack from roof line to foundation. Western authorities identify ruins with a great central crossing still standing as the Church of the Holy Apostles, but on the plateau the small directional signs in English call it a caravanserai. Well down on a rocky headland in the canyon separating Turkey from the Soviet Union stands the latest of three churches dedicated to St Gregory the Illuminator. It was built about 1215 and retains its high drum and part of the conical roof characteristic of Armenian churches. Its frescoes, the usual gospel scenes in pink and blue, are now unique at Ani. At the base of the cliff below this church, the River Arpa is crossed by a ruin called the Marco Polo Bridge. He may well have reached this immensely important trading centre.

Ani had been a bonus on our journey, as the forthcoming weekend in Jerevan was going to be if we got across the border at our third attempt. Kars has an interesting small museum, its exhibits divided in the usual way between

A tranquil hillside north of Kars, Turkey.

A Turkish mountain village between Tatvan and Akhtamar. ►

Tillya Kari Madrasa, the Registan at Samarkand.

the ground and first floor, a citadel, parts of which are in use as municipal offices, and an Armenian church which became a mosque after the Ottoman conquest. Near the market, each block along the main street is given over to a trade: wood-working, carpets, auto repair and metals. Though the busy animal and vegetable market is relatively small, the sight of sheep being driven along a main street in a modern city still catches the eye.

During the afternoon before our scheduled departure, we delivered the car to the freight yard for loading. The grossly fat man in charge greeted us in his office eating melon seeds from plastic packets. Our friend Cengiz Alp acted as interpreter that long difficult afternoon. There were two problems. The simplest to overcome was money: the station master had told me two days before that the charge for the car would be about £12. After much searching through books of charges, the freight boss proved to my satisfaction we should pay about £50, a far more reasonable amount even in Turkey where goods and services are incredibly cheap. An emergency trip to a local bank provided the missing cash.

The second problem halted operations throughout the freight yard for almost three hours. Still munching melon seeds, the freight boss first directed the measurement of the car. It had to be shipped inside a closed freight car because of vandals who might try to break into it or throw rocks at the windows. Against all the commonsense visual evidence, he satisfied himself that it could be got into the closed car providing we removed the roof rack. Like all Land Rover roof racks, this one covered the entire vehicle and was attached to it by at least a dozen nuts and bolts. Nevertheless, off it came. With at least three people shouting directions at any one time, I then manoeuvred the vehicle back and forth at every conceivable angle for about three-quarters of an hour. Between four and six strong backs even tried to lift us in, but you cannot bend a four-wheel-drive vehicle around a corner. At that point, the freight boss could have given up and just sent us away. After all, he had insisted on the closed car for our protection. We were relieved and grateful that despite his initial pigheadedness, he now ordered a flat car, a floor and two-foot high sides on hinges, on to the siding where we were labouring. Loading on to the flat car took five minutes. Our vehicle was then tied in place with steel wire, and we agreed that one of us would sleep beside it. Even this concession to the boss's ego was unnecessary because the yard is guarded at all times. His insistence that one of us must ride in the car all the way to the border, furthermore, was frustrated next morning by the railway staff who ordered that passengers ride in the coaches.

Crowded with people and livestock travelling to the villages along the way, the train left Kars at about 10.30 a.m., half an hour late. At Akyaka, we shunted backward and forward far more often than seemed really necessary and my palms began to sweat again. But we reached the border about 3.00 p.m. Our friendly lieutenant, now in uniform, was in charge of the border police and smoothed our way with Customs. Indeed, the only problem arose because we were ordered yet again to empty the roof rack, though not to remove it. "Soviet Customs insist that everything be locked inside the car, and the car must be sealed," the lieutenant explained.

The Soviet Customs officer who released the car to me at the border looked surprised by the sand tyres and folding chairs piled up inside. When I explained, he cast his eyes toward heaven and said in English, "Nonsense."

With this officer as a guide, I left Tom and Geoff on the train and walked fifty metres to the siding where Soviet freight workers had already released the cables holding the car. Accompanied by the Customs officer and one soldier who had business in town, I drove the four kilometres from the border post to the Customs office in the Leninakan railway station. Conflicting advice to the contrary notwithstanding, there were no more train rides on the Silk Road.

# Chapter 6

# JEREVAN AND ASHKHABAD
Ереван    Ашхабад

The border train carrying my colleagues arrived at the Leninakan railway station soon after we did. The Customs officer directed me to drive up a concrete ramp on to the platform where Customs inspection would be carried out behind a hastily-erected barrier to separate us from the public part of the platform.

"Someone from Moscow is waiting for you in the station," he said.

I knew from our phone conversation that Dmitri Oreshkin had been in Jerevan and hurried into a waiting room out of which a long dimly-lit corridor extended to the left. Indeed, it was Dmitri approaching. We both quickened our steps and embraced. It was a reunion against all the odds in the wrong place and certainly at the wrong time. We both wept a little.

Dmitri was the principal liaison between the Institute of Geography of the USSR Academy of Sciences, of which he is a candidate member, the Marco Polo Expedition and the hotels, local political and party officials and republic Academies of Sciences who saw to the minutiae of our journey along the Silk Road within the Soviet Union. About thirty-five, of average height with hair and beard of tan, greenish eyes, an impish smile and the flexibility of attitude and response that go not just with brilliance but with genius, Oreshkin's fresh openness set the tone of Gorbachov's USSR for me. He is an accomplished publicist in a land that supposedly knows nothing of such dubious refinements: two excellent articles in *Pravda* before and after our Soviet transit and the participation of a film cameraman from Central Television, Moscow, throughout our stay in central Asia are proof enough. From Jerevan, he had managed to make contact with me when no one else had during the blackest hours of the expedition by cleverly using the telex belonging to the Armenian Academy of Sciences to get a message to the British Embassy in Ankara. I was very glad indeed to see him again.

Today, July 3rd, not only were we a month late, but we were 1,500 kilometres west of Ashkhabad. Although we didn't yet know it, there were eleven Soviet members of the Marco Polo Expedition, scientists, administrators, interpreters, drivers and photographers. They had followed our route and schedule as far as Leninabad, ancient Hodjent 2,500 kilometres to the east in Tadzhikstan, where they awaited us with Paul Crook. They all had schedules of their own which in theory meant that their stays in central Asia were to end about July 7th, four days from now, when we had been scheduled to cross the border into China. There were other complicating circumstances, especially our Chinese visas which expired on July 22nd and could only be renewed in China. Rescheduling was to dominate our truncated stay in the Soviet Union.

Not for the moment, however, because the relief that came when we crossed the border had left us a little disoriented. In accordance with Soviet time, our clocks had gone forward two hours, moreover, and we had not eaten since breakfast in Kars. But first, we had to be cleared by Customs. This lengthy task required among other operations the inspection of every item of printed matter we carried, including the Cambridge local newspapers in the flower press Geoff had brought along. Dusk was gathering when Tom at last drove the 100 kilometres to Jerevan.

One enters Jerevan over the top of a hill quite high above the city lights in the valley below. In the dark, it looked larger than it is. The Hotel Ani, on a main street, was built to a common Intourist pattern within the last ten years. The restaurants always have dance bands during the evening meal, and people dance. Menus are identical, but the dishes that are "off", the large majority, vary from place to place. All Intourist hotels in central Asia charge foreigners 40 rubles (£40) for a single room and 50 rubles for a double, both with bath. The rooms are small, modern and comfortable, often with balconies, and they were always available, despite the uncertainty of our schedule.

Dmitri had used his week of waiting in Jerevan to arrange for specialist historians and archaeologists from the Armenian Academy of Sciences to guide us through the sites nearby. This was the pattern the Institute of Geography had established with the Academies of Sciences of each republic through which we were travelling. It was this fabric that the Iranians had effectively unravelled.

We were greeted on behalf of the Academy by Academician B. H. Arakelian, an archaeologist of Armenian antiquities. He was in his seventies, short and square with a mane of grey hair, and spoke some English. Our interpreter, Gayaneh Makhmourian, was an historian of Armenian communities abroad. Dr Henry Grigorian specialised in the history of Arab relationships with Armenia. Iranian and Persian influences were the province of Dr Vahan Papazian. Dr Hratch Bartikian was a Byzantine specialist. We all sat round a large table in a board room drinking tea and eating local grapes and peaches.

Academician Arakelian asked if we had seen any Armenian buildings in Turkey. I said that just three days ago, we had visited Ani. He was very excited. Although he had travelled in Europe and America and taught Armenian archaeology in London, he had never been allowed to visit Ani or any other Turkish site. The Turkish authorities do not welcome nationals of the Armenian SSR, especially not scholars. It was his heartfelt wish to visit the former capital of the Armenian kingdom, but he knew it was impossible. He could only dream. He recounted the history of the city and was interested that the Church of St Gregory was identified as a caravanserai. Academician Arakelian was an intellectual exile from the Armenian heartland in Turkey despite being at home in his own land. He set the tone of nationalistic warmth and nostalgia within a framework of academic crispness that characterised our stay in Jerevan.

As I had expected, our days of haphazard self-reliance had come to an end.

For better or worse, our creature comforts were arranged precisely as we had asked with modifications imposed only by our exigent schedule. We were being looked after now, being shown what we had specified and similar monuments and artefacts that were entirely new to us, by the people who could write the guidebooks. For the next eighteen days we enjoyed the benefits of careful joint planning.

Later that first morning, we were taken to visit the Matenadaran Archive, the Armenian National Library and a museum of books and manuscripts. Housed in an impressive new building incorporating conservation workshops and facilities for scholars, the display of illuminated manuscripts and bindings is full of wonders. Like the carvings on the church walls, the books overflow with brilliantly-coloured plants and animals, as well as miniature scenes from the bible and Armenian history. Our guide told us that to assure supplies of cochineal from which reds were made before the nineteenth-century aniline dyes, they are now farming the small insect whose carapace gives the colour.

Though there has been a town at Jerevan for 2,000 years, almost nothing of the past remains in the modern city. Except that the snow-capped northern slopes of Ararat seem to dominate the rural as well as the urban landscape, the surrounding regions offer a different perspective. Perhaps most impressive among the ancient buildings we saw was the mountain-side monastery of Gegard, begun in the eleventh century. The principal buildings including the church are partially or wholly carved out of the rock. The typical barrel vault and conical dome of the church are decorated with carvings of plants and animals in the red stone, though less profusely than at Akhtamar. Inside, the major supporting columns and arches are carved rather than constructed. Our academic guides had arranged for us to meet the Abbot who offered us tea at the end of our visit. He was a handsome bearded man of middle age in orthodox clerical dress who seemed quite sophisticated enough to cope with the local intelligentsia as well as us foreign visitors. Not only is the monastery a tourist attraction and a shrine for worship, but it still houses a small permanent religious community.

Next day, Sunday, we drove to Echmiadzin, the cathedral city south-west of Jerevan, and stopped first to see an eighth-century church at Hibsima. It has the familiar drum and conical dome but none of the external carving that characterises Armenian churches of a somewhat later date. A service was in progress with an impressive choir singing what sounded like nineteenth-century hymns. The congregation consisted primarily of foreign tourists.

The cathedral itself was built in the fourth century, but has been much rebuilt and restored. It was jammed with tourists and worshippers, the former probably outnumbering the latter. Tourists appeared to represent all the nations of Europe and of course Japan. It was too crowded to move about, but flash photography went on without interruption. Gold is the prevailing tone of the vestments and trappings of the mass; incense and a choir trapped the other senses, but they also added to the heat and noise of the crowd. We were standing to one side in a position to watch the ballet of genuflections behind the great gold curtain that was drawn across to separate the laity from the priests and acolytes around the altar. The Metropolitan's Palace, a nineteenth-century pile, stands in front of the cathedral but that personage was absent from the mass that day.

At Zvartnots nearby, the ground plan of a seventh-century church has been excavated, revealing a unique circular structure. The remains of a palace indicated that, at one time, Zvartnots and not Echmiadzin was intended to be the religious centre of Armenia. We were also taken to see a reconstruction of a fifth-century Greek temple at Garni associated with the scattered ruins of a fortress built about the same time.

More impressive than either, I thought, was the new ethnographic museum at Sardarapat, the site of a military victory over the Turks in 1918. The two-storey red brick structure is windowless and fortress-like. The collection is relatively recent, summarising the immediate past. For example, the large and beautiful carpet exhibition contains nothing earlier than the last century. Above the large central hall housing the carpets rises a remarkable dome consisting of concrete bars laid tangentially to the angles of the rows above and below and decreasing in length towards the apex. My colleagues had observed a dome of the same construction but with the bars made of wood in a mosque in Erzurum.

The museum sits at one end of an irrigated tableland about three kilometres from the Turkish border, Ararat shaping the southern horizon. In a large new restaurant nearby, we were guests of the Academy of Sciences at a stupendous lunch of salads, kebabs and Armenian wine.

That night, or rather very early the next morning, we flew to Ashkhabad. Dmitri and Valery, one of the drivers from the Soviet party, had left on Saturday afternoon to drive our car there. Why the Soviet authorities insisted on this arrangement, I cannot say. Perhaps there was just not time to arrange with the local police or the military for us to drive through a region, part of which is not open to tourism. Henry Grigorian arranged our Aeroflot tickets, not an easy procedure, and at midnight took us to the airport, a final act of Armenian hospitality.


We landed at Ashkhabad at about 4.00 a.m. local time, an hour later than Jerevan and four hours ahead of London. There, awaiting us with few signs that the hour was inhuman, were the head of the Foreign Affairs Department of the Turkmen Academy of Sciences, Valentina Maslukova, the archaeologist Academician T. Hodjanejazov, fortunately a generation younger than Dr Arakelian, and a young, rather nervous interpreter, Nadya. She was very blond and managed somehow to look newly-showered each time we met despite temperatures that rose to 44°C.

Ashkhabad, the capital of the Turkmen SSR, is an oasis much enlarged by irrigation. Despite wide avenues and many trees, the town is flat, low and unprepossessing. The Iranian border is fifty kilometres away, but the mountains to the south, hazy in the heat, are much closer. We would have liked to have driven there to complete the circuit, as it were, but for another twenty-four hours our transportation was laid on by the Academy who had already planned a programme in accordance with our requests.

Before it began, there was a phone call from Yuri Badenkov in Leninabad,

750 kilometres to the east. Dr Y. P. Badenkov, Deputy Director of the Institute of Geography in charge of administration, was a tall, enthusiastic, smiling man who enjoyed food, drink, good company and the challenges of field life, though not necessarily in that order. His commitment to what became our joint project in the Soviet Union was as great as mine. At our first meeting in Moscow, I had questioned the route of departure prescribed for us by the Soviet authorities. It was much longer than the route I had suggested and seemed less interesting historically. Badenkov agreed. "I think the army have made a mistake," he said. In the event, the route remained more or less unchanged, but Yuri Badenkov's experience organising and leading research groups in the field was invaluable.

Both of us were delighted to talk at last on Soviet soil, but the dominant theme was not a happy one: Yuri insisted we must make all speed to reach the Soviet party by July 12th, five days hence. Dmitri could not reach Ashkhabad before July 8th. After 1,200 kilometres in the Turkmen Desert, the car would need servicing, to say nothing of Dmitri and Valery. If we left for Merv on the 9th, we could stay one night at Repetek in the desert, one night in Bukhara and one in Samarkand. Yuri insisted that we had to give Leninabad and the communities in the Fergana Valley, Kokand, Andizhan and Osh, a day each, not only because they contained places of interest to us, but also because they were closed cities opened for us, and local officials had planned receptions to mark the occasions. I replied with what I hope passed for respect that the mosques, madrasas and tombs of Bukhara and Samarkand were ultimately more important than a reception in Osh. Thereupon, Yuri won the argument: "Dick," he shouted down the terrible line, "you have to compromise and do exactly what I say." More phone calls followed after Dmitri arrived the next day. In the end of course, there was no alternative to compromise. We gained one more day but agreed to reach Leninabad on July 13th.

In the late morning, we searched out the General Post Office in the searing heat but there was no poste restante to cheer us. I sat briefly under the trees in a park and then examined an outdoor display of Turkmen carpets for sale. The price on one particularly fine room-sized rug was 1,200 rubles, about £1,200. By the time the cost of shipping it home had been included, it could not have been much of a bargain.

In the early afternoon we attended a formal meeting in an air-conditioned board room chaired by the President of the Turkmen Academy of Sciences, Academician Oraz Oriezgeldiev, himself a biologist, and to aid the digestion of our new concentrated schedule we were served with plates of magnificent grapes and plums, along with apple juice and mineral water. Travellers from the days of Marco Polo onward have written about the institution of dastar khan, a variable meal depending not on the time of day but on local produce and the status of the visitor. It might be served by the side of the road entering the oasis, in the caravanserai or the reception room of the local potentate. The custom continues throughout Soviet central Asia and Xinjiang, as far east as Xi'an. In a hospital practising traditional Uigher medicine at Kumul, we were served three types of melon. Peaches and apricots enhanced meetings in the Fergana Valley. Tea was invariably offered in China, but in the Soviet Union, soft drinks as well as green tea. Western tourists in China have been heard to complain about the delay entailed, and, perhaps partly for that reason, some places have either abridged or abandoned the custom. We could not always do justice to what we were offered, but happily did our best.

First objective on our Ashkhabad schedule was the major excavation nearby which has revealed the remains of Nissa, capital of Parthia, an Iranian Empire dating from the last centuries before Christ. We were taken to see the ark or citadel, the central most defensible feature of these ancient mudbrick cities. The ark was usually surrounded by a walled town inhabited by military leaders, court officials and probably the most important local merchants. Often these central zones were built around a natural spring, long since dried up. Outside the walls straggled the houses and shops of the supporting population, including tillers of the nearby fields. At Nissa, a village still occupies part of this ancient outer precinct. It was while we were there that Tom thought he heard the muezzin call, the only occasion during our stay in the Islamic lands of Soviet Asia.

Some mudbrick remains are more evocative than others, depending on how much is identifiable as walls, altars or religious sculpture to the amateur eye, and how much one knows about the history. At Nissa, the unvarying, hard-packed tan clay and the heat did nothing to stimulate my interest. Other sites, like Jiaohe near Turfan in Xinjiang, produced much more of an effect.

I liked it better when we drove to the other side of Ashkhabad to see the Karakoram Canal. About fifty metres across, it is a ribbon of water running 1,500 kilometres from the Caspian Sea into the desert near Merv. Nothing grows beside its concrete banks except where the precious liquid is allowed to run off into side channels. We observed the results time and again as we drove east through the Turkmen Desert, through one huge collective or co-operative farm after another. When we got back to the hotel about six thirty that evening, the temperature had fallen to 40°C.

Dmitri and Valery arrived with the car during a meeting with the Deputy Director of the Ministry of Public Health and four clinicians the next morning, July 7th, so I missed much of the first of our discussions with local doctors about oesophageal cancer and the relevant epidemiology. Meetings of this kind were arranged, often at very short notice, at almost every stop we made in the Soviet Union and China.

Immediately after this meeting, we were taken to the Museum of History and Archaeology, normally closed on a Tuesday. There were several beautiful small artefacts, some from the era of Marco Polo, some much earlier. In particular, I was struck by a shell amulet with a deer pricked into the mother-of-pearl surface. The polychrome opalescence gave depth to the simple outline. Tom decided that here certainly were objects worthy of holography. The Deputy Director of the museum responded enthusiastically, offering a room that could be darkened and running water. It was four o'clock before the necessary permission came through from the Ministry of Culture. With one of the two twelve-volt car batteries for power, Tom used the portable holographic camera for the first time and with stunning effect. Copies of five holograms were presented to the museum.

While Tom worked with Geoff's assistance, I went with Dmitri and Valery to buy food and service the car. It was about three o'clock. At an under-patronised supermarket on the edge of town Dmitri sought out the manager, a small but formidable woman of forty or so, because he wanted to buy tinned meat, a kind of spam, and for that it was necessary to demonstrate that he had a priority: specifically, us. In the shopping area itself, the light level was low to the point of dimness, but it avoided the terrible jangle that characterises Western supermarkets, as though the more excited you become, the more you will buy. This danger was further reduced by the absence of variety. We wanted bottled water. There was carbonated water. We wanted jam. Rows of one-kilogramme jars filled a section, all plum jam. On the other hand, there was none of the careful standardisation of EEC eggs: the local product came in a variety of shapes and sizes, like eggs do. Prices were consistently lower than at Sainsbury's. On the evidence before me, I believe no one in Ashkhabad goes hungry, but there are few gourmets.

The car was serviced at the Academy of Sciences garage by experienced mechanics who welcomed the diagrams in our manual. Dmitri and Valery had also discovered its propensity to overheat. For the first of many times, the radiator was drained, flushed through and refilled from a special stock of water reserved for radiators. It contained a lower mineral content than the local supply and came from the mountains! Each time we drained the radiator, overheating became less of a problem, for a while. I sheltered from the heat and the work in the ramshackle but air-conditioned office of the manager, a friendly Muscovite who ended by presenting me with a bottle of Turkmen brandy. Despite its tendency to blow the top of your head off, it was very popular, while it lasted, at celebrations, for example, when we finally connected with our Soviet colleagues at Leninabad. Like much else in our Soviet experience, there was no charge for the car service.

The garage sold neither oil nor petrol, but it was decided that the oil was still in good condition, and that the local product was likely to do more damage than any impurities already present. On the way back to town we located a petrol station. When they are available, there are three grades of petrol, the highest being ninety-three octane. This station was fully supplied. The procedure was the same along our route. At a kiosk located more or less centrally, you announced how many litres and the grade you wanted and paid. You then went to one of the overhead delivery hoses. Often there was only one working, and you waited your turn. When you reached the pump, you showed your receipt to the office, or, on rare occasions, to an attendant. The start-and-stop mechanism tended not to work, making our job quintuply hard because we had four supplementary tanks to fill as well as the main one.

The same system operates in most of China, except that Chinese stations almost always exclude anyone other than the driver from the precincts, making you wait in the road. Inasmuch as smoking amongst the male population occurs with the same frequency in both countries, the Chinese seem more cautious, in this respect at least. New Chinese petrol stations, however, use Western-style pumps, permit payment after delivery and allow passengers to remain in or near the car.

The road east from Ashkhabad follows one of the oldest routes in history. To the right are mountains. Almost empty of scrub, the flat desert extends from the mountains as far to the north as the eye can see. Apart from the road itself only the canal, occasionally visible from the road, and rare mudbrick villages in the distance towards the mountains indicate that social life exists. About 120 kilometres past Ashkhabad, we stopped to look at more mudbrick ruins. The seventh-century city of Abjeverd stretched some five kilometres between the road and the mountain. In the outer precinct a tomb, still visited as a shrine, stands alone. The outer precinct is said to have been inhabited in the last century. There is still a hamlet there with a mosque, and the inhabitants shepherd flocks in the nearby hills.

These stops always seemed to go on too long, but I had to learn to suppress my childish impatience to get there, wherever there might be. Tom's pictures should not be rushed. What is more, the first law of observation, whether archaeological research or sightseeing, is, "Take your time". Tom later generously asserted that, at such stops as these, he also sensed impatience in our Soviet and Chinese colleagues as well as Don, Geoff and even the patient Paul. Nevertheless, at Abjeverd, the mounting heat and the featureless piles of eroded red mudbrick added strength to the elastic pull of "there".

Due east the black road ran, splitting the desert floor until it reached a flourishing agricultural area and turned slightly north at a level-crossing in a nondescript village. As far as the road signs indicate, the ancient town of Dushak has disappeared, absorbed into the mammoth Moscow Kolkhoz. A branch of the road still turns south-east towards Sarakhs, once a capital of Khorāsan, when this highway linked the trading route followed by Marco Polo through Herat and Balkh to the more northerly route through Merv. Without a pause, we sped along the well-paved northern road.

We reached the scattered ruins of old Merv, dry and windworn by the sand, about three o'clock with the temperature at 45°C. From the tenth to the sixteenth centuries, this too was a thriving capital city, a trading centre blessed by water that has disappeared. The modern Soviet city, Mary, is twenty-two kilometres south-west and we skirted it on a ring road. Beside the ruins in the prosperous village of Bajram-Ali, a small but colourful market provided tomatoes and cucumber for our dinner, and a white "Young Pioneer" cap for me. My disreputable headcovering seemed to have blown overboard, and I had been reduced to wearing a handkerchief against the sun like a character from *Monty Python*. Entering the market, we passed a stall where caps and hats were on offer. I lingered behind the others. The stallholder noticed that the white cap had taken my eye and offered it to be tried for size. It fitted, but when I began to count out the price, less than a ruble, he insisted that I have it as a gift. After first refusing and then accepting, I was still sufficiently unsure, language being the barrier it is, to ask Dmitri to confirm I had understood and acted properly. I was very proud of that useful cap. Sadly, it went the way of its predecessor some time later, having become pretty grubby meanwhile from dusty hands and sweaty forehead.

At old Merv the sixteenth-century tomb of Sultan Sanjar is being restored. New blue tile is being applied to the outer dome. The inner dome reveals yet another architectural solution to the problem of mounting a round structure on a square building. There is no drum, but squinches compress the square walls into supports for the round dome. The dome is constructed using curved courses of brick that stand out like beams and touch tangentially so as to support each other. The space between the beams appears to be filled with mudbrick. Any of this detail that might have been visible from the outside is of course hidden by the ceramic tiles. The tomb cover has also been restored to its proper place on a concrete plinth. Other parts of the original structure, such as an entrance porch or side chambers, can be guessed at because of bits of masonry or beams sticking out of the central chamber. But now, only the square central tomb chamber remains, as at Soltānīyeh in Iran.

Nearby stands the ruin known as Chiz Kala, the Maiden's Tower, although I cannot explain why. The ground floor appears to have been completely buried beneath debris, probably that of the first floor and the collapsed roof. But the remarkable features of this tower are on the outside. The south and west walls are fifteen metres high and flanged vertically in great triangular columns of brick. Were the flanges purely decorative, did they provide more surface for cooling the interior or were they merely buttresses?

The extensive site of the ancient city contains many less well-defined ruins. The walls of the ark still stand grimly against the bright sky, softened by a flock of sheep straggling through a break, feeding on thin patches of vegetation, a bonus derived from irrigated fields nearby.

From Merv, the desert becomes more pronounced with stretches of drifting sand ribbed by the wind. Irrigation cannot penetrate this far from the Karakoram Canal, but the land is occupied. Camels wandered towards us. To our right, the railway, in the distance, high-tension lines, and an occasional tyre slung on to a sand dune are not quite the only signs of man. Occasional side roads, not usually signposted, lead to watch towers and other structures obscured by the rolling terrain, possibly the military establishments.

One such nondescript side turning to the right was signposted to the village of Repetek and, just beyond it, the desert research station belonging to the Institute of Geography where we spent the night. The permanent staff at this eighty-one-year-old station live in attractive, white-painted wooden houses with wide verandas and space for a garden if time and water are available. Desert trees and shrubs domesticate the dominant sand. We stayed in an air-conditioned bungalow. The evening was long and very warm. Dmitri prepared dinner on the same principle that had applied to Don: he could not drive. We had two tins of spam and salad carefully washed in the boiled water provided in a large enamelled bucket. Two additional sources of water were available for each bungalow: a tap supplying non-potable water for boiling and dishwashing, and a special tap opened by a plunger that fell back shutting off the supply as soon as you removed your hand. That water could be used for brushing your teeth and rinsing your hands and face. It tended to be hot, probably because the pipes lay just beneath the sandy surface. Just to complete the survey of available water at this desert station, there was a shower block near the bungalow with a supply of hot water.

Soon after leaving Repetek, we passed a serious road accident, a motor cycle on its side, oil, petrol and the contents of panniers scattered across the road. The driver lay unmoving. Two police cars had arrived. This was the first of a depressing series of accidents we saw, though the only one in the Soviet Union.

The morning began clear and bright, but haze became yellow smog as we entered the industrial ring surrounding Chardzhou. At a police checkpoint where we were stopped I was invited to accompany Dmitri into the office. There was a brief exchange between Dmitri and the officer in charge, and the atmosphere, never especially menacing, changed to one of embarrassed welcome. The officer said they had been told a foreign car on some sort of expedition would pass through in June. Dmitri explained. While the officer phoned his office in the city to clear our way on to the ferry across the Amudar'ya, we were served green tea.

Old Chardzhou near the river is smog-free and tree-lined. For centuries, it has been the busiest crossing point on the Amudar'ya which rises in the Afghan province of Wakhan in the Pamirs and empties into the Aral Sea. Dar'ya is the Turkic word for river and Amu means swift. Two weeks later on the banks of the Syrdar'ya, we learned Syr means clean. Now there is a railway bridge at Chardzhou, but the ferry still carries all other wheeled and foot traffic.

The ferry was a large flat barge, capable of carring upwards of twenty fully-laden lorries and an assortment of vans and official cars. Its draught could not be more than perhaps fifteen centimetres, a depth dictated by the shifting sand banks near the shores. While we were waiting to board, a small tug trying to pull a dredge into position just beyond the ferry slip got itself stuck on one. Tugs provide the motive power for the barge. A larger tug attaches itself by a cable to the offshore forward side of the barge, gradually pulling it round and into the stream. It travelled downstream near the shore and was then joined by a second tug, in this case the one that had been stuck half an hour before, which took the lead, adding its power to the first by a cable connecting the two. The crossing takes about half an hour. In mid-stream, the current seemed very swift judging by the eddies around the supporting piers of the railway bridge just upstream. The position of another barge being towed upstream suggested that the main channel was on the north-east side of the river towards our point of disembarkation. As we approached the far shore, the small leading tug was released, and the remaining tug manoeuvred the barge for disembarking. Huge arched steel gangways on each side towards the bow formed high barriers – the only barriers except for a railing of rusting iron pipe – during the crossing and reached far enough on to the sandy spit to make it safe for lorries to roll on and off. Seldom have I seen experience and patience win so signal a victory over low tech.

We would have liked to photograph both the river and the boats. In Jerevan and again in Ashkhabad, I had asked Dmitri if we could take pictures of something, the Karakoram Canal in the latter town. On that occasion, he had replied with asperity: "Photograph anything you like. There is no need to ask. If anyone objects, send them to me." It was yet another welcome expression of glasnost. So while we waited at the ferry slip to cross the Amudar'ya, Tom prepared to take some pictures of the open-sided shed with a galvanised roof that provided some shelter for pedestrians. Dmitri said: "I will just say a word to the military guard before you start so they know who we are." He returned with chagrin writ large across his face and annoyance in his voice: "We must not. I am sorry. He forbids it, and his chief is not here. He can cause trouble, delay our crossing. I am afraid we must not." It was the sole occasion when we were told not to take pictures in the Soviet Union, and I am reasonably sure the incident was reported to higher authority.

# Chapter 7

# BUKHARA AND SAMARKAND

Букара  Самарканд

For centuries, the Amudar'ya has formed a natural border between contending forces. Though scarcely in contention today, the Turkmen and Uzbek Republics, the former to the south and the latter north of the wide river, are divided by it. To us, the major difference was the deterioration of the highway in Uzbekistan. Although there is no large town north of the river, a belt of lush, irrigated agricultural land containing several villages extends at least ten kilometres beyond its shores. A canal runs northward toward Bukhara, but excepting for tamarisk in full flower and scent, the desert reasserts itself until the traveller enters the Bukharan oasis.

Like all central Asian cities, the suburbs gradually engulf the road with haphazard ribbon development in brick or mudbrick, often with corrugated metal roofing. But there was less industry along route M37 entering Bukhara from the south than, for example, in the environs of Chardzhou, and more historical sites to be seen at the outskirts. To the left at Chorbakir, about six kilometres from the centre, three fifteenth-century tombs built by three brothers are in process of restoration.

Bukhara and Khiva to the north near the Aral Sea continued to be governed by their own puppet rulers until 1921, the last two cities in central Asia to be absorbed completely into what had become Soviet Russia. Bukhara had a reputation as a centre of Islamic learning, qualified by evidence of arbitrariness and cruelty unusual even by the standards of other medieval autocracies. Slavery and trade in humans, mostly landless Turkmens from the mountainous Iranian border region, persisted at Bukhara into the 1870s. Appropriately, its conflicting reputations are symbolised by the juxtaposition of Bukhara's most familiar buildings, beautifully restored in the centre of the city. The Kalyan Minaret, dating from the twelfth century, is a miracle of Qarakhanid brickwork with horizontal bands of varying widths containing non-repeating geometric designs. At the top, its wide balcony provided a platform for the muezzin to call the faithful to prayer and a favourite style of execution for the Khan who ordered offenders to be thrown over the arched and decorated parapet. The Kalyan Mosque, from about the same time, and the spectacular Mir-Arab Madrasa, built 500 years later, face each other on either side of a broad public square in front of the minaret. The Mir-Arab Madrasa is the only one in Uzbekistan where Islamic scholars are still being trained. The great minaret and the institutions of learning form a polychrome tile landscape of culture and barbarity.

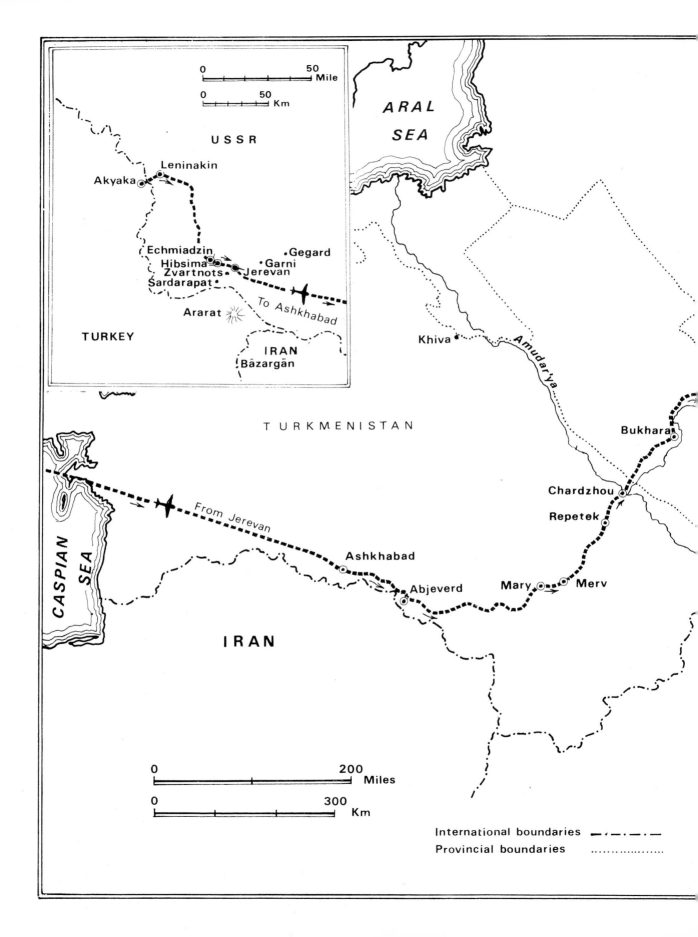

ARAL
SEA

USSR

0 ———— 50 Mile
0 ———— 50 Km

Leninakin

Akyaka

Echmiadzin
Hibsima
Zvartnots
Sardarapat

Gegard
Garni
Jerevan

To Ashkhabad

Ararat

TURKEY

IRAN
Bāzargān

Khiva

Amudarya

Bukhara

TURKMENISTAN

Chardzhou

Repetek

CASPIAN SEA

From Jerevan

Ashkhabad

Abjeverd

Mary

Merv

IRAN

0 ———— 200 Miles
0 ———— 300 Km

International boundaries ——·——·——
Provincial boundaries ··············

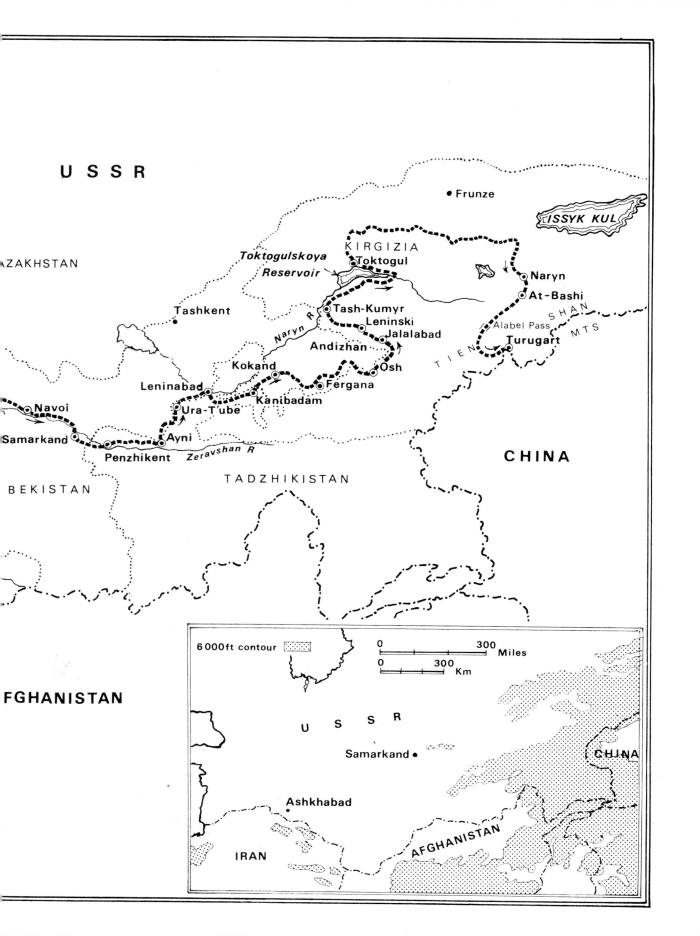

U S S R

KAZAKHSTAN

• Frunze

*ISSYK KUL*

K I R G I Z I A

*Toktogulskoya*
*Reservoir* • Toktogul

• Naryn
• At-Bashi

*Naryn R*

• Tashkent

Tash-Kumyr
Leninski
Jalalabad

Alabel Pass

T I E N   S H A N   M T S

Turugart

Andizhan
Kokand
Osh

Leninabad
Fergana
Kanibadam
Ura-T'ube

• Navoi
Ayni

Samarkand
Penzhikent   *Zeravshan R*

BEKISTAN

TADZHIKISTAN

CHINA

FGHANISTAN

6 000ft contour

0                    300  Miles
0          300  Km

U    S    S    R

Samarkand •

CHINA

Ashkhabad •

AFGHANISTAN

IRAN

In 1875, Eugene Schuyler was an American Consular official stationed in St Petersburg. He was able to obtain permission from the Russian government to travel alone in Turkistan which then included Bukhara, Samarkand and the Fergana Valley, as well as Khiva and Tashkent, the modern capital of Uzbekistan. He began his report of Bukhara where we also began our tour, at the ark or citadel. Its massive walls have been restored, but its vast arched entry has not changed at least since Schuyler's visit. A carriageway paved with blocks of stone like those used to build the wall rises about ten metres to the elevated floor of the fortress itself. Perhaps the most striking building is the Friday Mosque with its wooden porch supported by intricately carved and painted wooden pillars. Built originally in the seventeenth century, it has been rebuilt several times, most recently at the beginning of this century.

The throne "room" of the Khan is about ten metres wide and roughly twenty-five metres from entrance to throne. It is unroofed except for a raised arcade on three sides which has a wooden roof supported by carved wooden pillars, not as recently restored as those of the mosque. Between the entrance and the room proper stands a baffle which screened the court from the eyes of its approaching suppliant until the last minute. The seventeenth-century marble throne decorated with ceramic tiles still sits at the centre of the arcade opposite, a little the worse for wear.

We went to see the Director of the Ark Historical Museum, a young administrator who was enthusiastic about holography despite a disappointing experience he had had with it a few months before. The museum had acquired three unique but unidentified silver coins from an excavation nearby and wanted the prestige of publishing them. It occurred to the Director to use holography for the purpose because it gives so much more information than photographs. Scholars could study the holograms as though they were the real thing. What he did not want was to send the coins to a major museum like the Hermitage in Leningrad which would almost certainly not return them. So, he invited holographic specialists from Leningrad to bring their equipment to Bukhara, but they failed to obtain usable images. The museum Director offered to let Tom holograph anything we selected providing he would also try again with the coins. To our delight as well as the Director's, Tom succeeded with two different holographic pictures. Ironically, the man who had invented the mechanical technique incorporated in our portable Holofax camera was a Russian scientist teaching in Leningrad.

As we left his office, the Director motioned us to the parapet above the huge parking lot stretching across the entire front of the citadel. That was all part of the registan, the public place, originally the principal Bukharan bazaar, he explained. Registan is an Uzbek word meaning place of sand, and the sand was used to spread across an open area after heavy rain to cover over standing water that had no place to drain and would not soak into the hard-packed earth. The American diplomat, Schuyler, wrote about this one:

> . . . the Righistan or public place . . . is immediately in front of the *ark* or citadel, and is surrounded by fine large mosques and *medressés*. On the west side of it which is raised above the rest . . . there is a large pond surrounded by trees, about which are placed barber's shops, tea houses and refreshment

The restful inner courtyard of the Ulugh Beg Madrasa, oldest of the three beautiful colleges forming the central square of the Registan.

In the grounds of the Ulugh Beg Observatory.

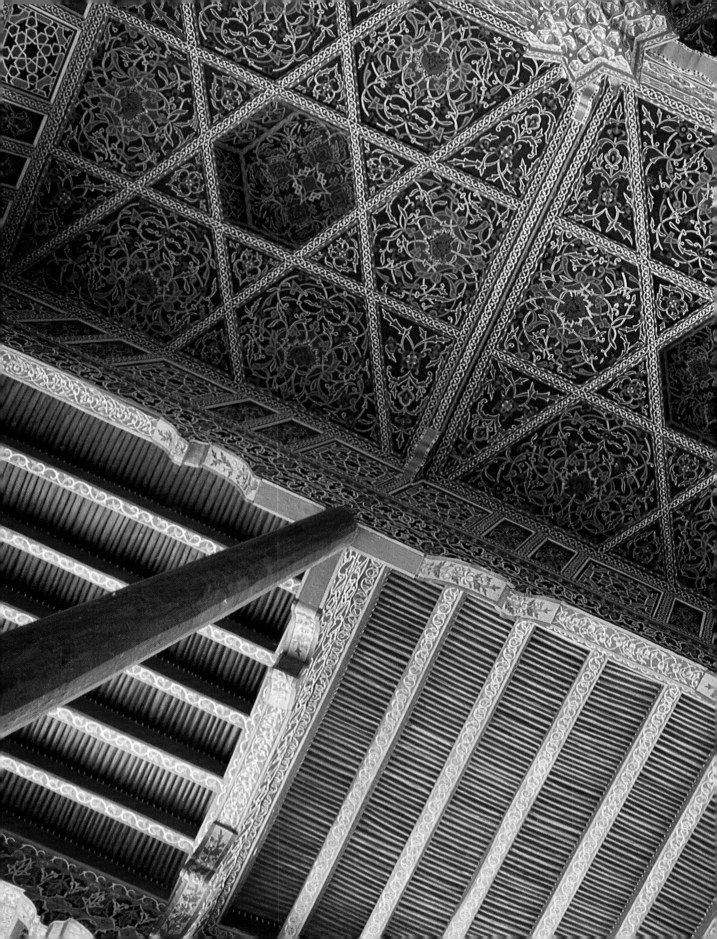

The entrance iwan of the Ulugh Beg Madrasa, Samarkand.

◄ A restored ceiling at the Mir Hajab Dawla Madrasa at Kanibadam, Uzbekistan.

booths of various kinds. The rest of the square seems to be a general market for bakers and butchers, dealers in skins, and small wares of various kinds. It is the real centre of the city . . .

Perhaps it was in this market that Niccolo and Maffeo Polo traded when they sought refuge in the city for several months from just the kind of internecine political strife which caught us in Iran. The pond and the trees are still there, enclosed by a one-way traffic system, but the shops, the booths and the market have moved on. In the sixteenth century, a great new central market was built towards the great madrasas and the Kalyan Minaret. It consisted of three brick market crosses, each devoted to a single trade, but excluding the perishables and "skins, and small wares" sold near the registan. One, Tak-Zargaran, is still surrounded by the cupolas of other trading areas, and all three provided intersections for the covered ways that formed a large bazaar. The crosses, about 100 metres apart, have been restored, but are now separated by other buildings. They demonstrate the marked changes in street levels that have taken place over the years. Opposite one of the entrances to the market cross used by the hatters stands an older mosque with the restored entrance iwan two metres below the sixteenth-century street level.

Even when Schuyler was there a century ago, Bukhara still used this central bazaar, for the slave trade among other specialities. Today, there seems to be no permanent market. Perhaps even more surprising, the city whose name is famous in the West because of its carpets has no carpet museum nor even a carpet trade.

However, there is a central square consisting of a garden, an artificial lake large enough for a few boats, and in the trees between them, tea houses and refreshment booths with both Western-style tables and the wooden divans preferred by the men of the town. Schuyler observed censoriously that this was "the resort of the idlers and loungers of Bukhara", and so it was in July 1987. But there is another aspect to this square which impressed us twentieth-century loafers. To the north, east and west it is fronted by madrasas. They sit above the level of the lake, approached by flights of steps on the north and west. All three are sixteenth-century buildings of limited architectural interest, but they are certainly being maintained if not restored. The fourth side of the central square consists of shops in a nondescript row of whitewashed buildings, a late addition to the prevailing restfulness. In this recreational space, the Muslim ideal of a garden amongst buildings, like the Topkapi, was enhanced by the institutions of learning.

Nearby, in a square filled with raised beds of geraniums and other perennials, there were two sixteenth-century caravanserais. Only the façades have been restored, but the arcaded, two-storey interiors are also in process of reconstruction. We were told that they were for transient traders and their goods. Animals were kept in special compounds at the edge of the city.

Between the central bazaar and the Kalyan Minaret, two madrasas have also been rebuilt. The earliest is the Ulug Beg Madrasa, named for the grandson of Timur who was one of the world's great astronomers. His glory shines even more brightly in Samarkand, but Bukhara was part of the realm he inherited. Across the road stands the sixteenth-century Khan Abdul Aziz

Madrasa. Its large decorative courtyard, formed by the two-storey arcades on to which the rooms of the students open, was filled with wooden beds of the sort used by coffee and tea drinkers in the central square. It looked like the city fathers had found a place to store their unwanted beds for auction. We were told that the anomalous furniture was there because both madrasas were now used occasionally for conferences.

Conferences strengthened Bukhara's ancient reputation for learning but now it is also a major tourist centre, as the numerous restored buildings demonstrated. More than any other great city, Bukhara itself seems to be an artefact, a restoration, as though the Soviet tourist authorities wanted an Islamic version of Disneyland. Thanks to the pressure to move on, we spent two nights and not quite two days in Bukhara, barely enough to acquire a sense of direction in the town. The Intourist Bukhara Hotel was the best we used. Its architectural and culinary ingredients were much of a muchness, but the staff seemed more interested in running a hotel. On the first afternoon, we located the local bookshop near the citadel so that I could buy a town plan. Although it was only 5.30 p.m. the doors were locked. On the steps stood two women chatting. Dmitri asked whether they were connected with the shop. With only the smallest protest, one of them unlocked the shop for us, and provided a suitable map in Russian. No other languages there.

Perhaps because of all the restoration, the most beautiful and evocative monuments we found were not in the centre at all, but in a park on the western edge of the city. One was the ninth-century tomb of a Samanid ruler, a small, square building of great beauty. The complex brickwork of the walls, the four entrances and the arched arcade at the top from which the dome rose directly was symmetrical and timeless. It is said not to have been restored, but the maintenance has been excellent. About 250 metres north of the Samanid tomb stands the mausoleum of Chashma-Ayub built in 1380. Only the squat brick minaret, topped by a conical dome, is from the original construction, the rest of the low, three-domed building being largely rebuilt.

At five o'clock on the day of our departure, we picked up Tom and the heavy holographic equipment from the ramp in front of the ark. The museum Director would have liked to entertain us with a cool drink in his office, but there was to be a visitation from some Moscow official. His special car was expected momentarily, and our baggage was scattered across the ceremonial entrance. The local police urged us on but hesitated to lend a hand with the packing. Nevertheless, there was time for Tom and the museum publicity person to take a few photographs of the museum Director and members of his staff in various combinations with us and the equipment. We got away as the bigwig's car drove on to the former registan.

Samarkand is 268 kilometres from Bukhara. My notes say, "Now on the road to Samarkand. Sounds like a Hope-Crosby movie." They also say that the road surface was appalling, like Emmenthal cheese without the smooth bits, which is perhaps why I never managed to think of this stretch in terms as elevated as *Hassan*: "Golden road to Samarkand" it was not.

Near Bukhara, farming is intensive, mostly market garden produce. This is part of the fertile valley of the Zeravshan River, another of those central Asian rivers which never reaches the distant ocean. This one rises in the mountains north-east of Samarkand and peters out in the desert near the Bukharan oasis, a relatively short river by comparison with the Amudar'ya, but it has nourished civilisations that have been fought over throughout history.

Amidst the green about thirty kilometres past the city, we saw what looked like a lone sand dune. It was a partially excavated mound or tell, the piled-up remains of a town site built upon and rebuilt upon after destruction by war, earthquake or the natural decay to which mudbrick is subject. Tells such as this one dotted the landscape outside of Ashkhabad, in the vicinity of Merv and north of the Amudar'ya. We had seen them in Turkey and Iran, too, though less frequently. There, as in the Soviet Union and China, they can be positively identified from the road by a characteristic stick-like tower, a kind of ancient monuments sign which means a site of archaeological interest.

After the cultivated area, a semi-arid region stretched away to mountains on the north and south. The dreadful road was lined with artemesia, a smell that puts me in mind of Elysium. Clouds near the northern mountains looked like rain, something almost unheard of at this time of year in Uzbekistan. Dmitri called it Zeravshan weather: i.e., unpredictable.

Nearing a town called Navoi, Dmitri stopped for us to see the astonishing remains of a caravanserai, probably sixteenth-century, but the brickwork decoration could be much earlier. To the right of the present road stood a water reservoir consisting of a pool about three metres deep covered by a brick dome, five metres across. The dome, its top now broken away, had been built by insetting the courses of brick at widths of one metre.

Across the road from the reservoir stood the decorative brick entrance arch of the caravanserai, about twenty-five metres high and twenty wide. Around it were courses of cross-over brick raised above the surface, and the same motif was repeated around the entire outside rectangle of the structure. Mongol knots, interspersed with six-pointed stars, covered the surface above the arch, and towards the top, wonderfully angular Kufic lettering completed the decoration.

Though it was still light as we drove into Navoi, we estimated our arrival in Samarkand would be about 11.00 p.m. A roadside café with tables outside under the trees was serving dinner. These state-run village restaurants were consistently dirty in the Soviet Union, but the kebabs with salads and plof, the Uzbek and Kirgiz equivalent of pilaf, were well cooked and decently served. Before we had finished, drops of rain could be heard on the dusty leaves above us. The storm did not develop then, but darkness enclosed the last 100 kilometres of the Zeravshan Valley. Valery drove. He had experience with the local night-driving technique: you turn on your headlights when you think another vehicle might be approaching and keep them lighted until you have passed. Late as we were, the hotel had rooms for us, the last positive comment I can make about Intourist in Samarkand.

Appropriately, as it would be in any central Asian town, our first visit next morning took us to the bazaar. I felt only a little inhibited by the company of two city officials, the Deputy Director of the Uzbek Institute of Geography and an interpreter named Ludmilla, but the Soviet tendency to keep everyone

The expedition parked by a water-hole serving the caravanserai near Navoi, USSR.

together in groups impaired Tom's essential freedom of action. Ludmilla, a tall, well-groomed woman of thirty-eight, married late and just returning to work after the birth of her second child, feared that she had forgotten her English vocabulary. Her English was impeccable. If she had forgotten anything, it was how to listen, as events were to prove.

Nothing could diminish the pleasure of this large new market occupying an area that had fulfilled the same function for at least 600 years, since Timur made Samarkand his capital. Vegetables, cereals, fruits, spices, meat and a whole department store of non-food merchandise each occupied their own areas. Huge open-sided sheds looked like patchwork quilts and smelled like a chef's paradise. We were offered samples of almost everything to taste or touch. The bazaar was crowded and chaotic when you could not understand the language and knew little of the customs, but it flourished. Probably a majority of the enterprises were private. Choice did not seem to be restricted though I had some trouble locating a shop that stocked handkerchiefs. It was explained that Uzbek weddings are huge affairs with dozens if not hundreds of guests each of whom must receive a present from the bride's parents. What better than a handkerchief? And there had been several weddings in Samarkand within the last few days.

To the left of the Samarkand bazaar, forming its eastern wall, towers the great Mosque of Bibi-Khanum, a favourite wife of Timur. After an hour of melons and metal craftsmen, I sought out its quiet courtyard. The walls and glazed-brick decoration of the entire structure were being restored, scaffold obscuring the façade of the mosque itself. The exuberant, blue geometric designs were interspersed with courses of Kufic lettering. False windows outlined in blue tiles against the underlying tan brick, the frames filled with regularly-placed blue rosettes, rose one above the other on the corners of the truncated minarets. What really distinguishes this building, however, is its scale. In the middle of the courtyard stood a stone sculpture in the shape of a reading lectern which was required to support an enormous Qurân whose pages could only have been turned by the co-ordinated efforts of two or three people. The lectern measured roughly two metres by four metres and stood on six huge stone legs, each a metre high. Said to have been moved outside the mosque after an earthquake, it is attributed to Timur's grandson, the astronomer Ulug Beg.

After lunch, our two-car cavalcade drove to the Ulug Beg Observatory, built by the ruler himself to make possible the completion of his remarkable star charts. The restored building has a small, lifeless museum in its basement and was jammed with tourists of every European and Soviet nationality. At the brow of the hill on which it sits are the carefully-preserved remains of the last half of Ulug Beg's large stone quadrant which gives some sense of reality to the site.

Our return drive took us past the new museum built to house the wonderful murals of Afrasiab. Samarkand occupies a site at the confluence of the Zeravshan and two tributaries that has been inhabited for upwards of 40,000 years. Perhaps the first urban settlement developed from the fifth century BC as the capital of the Soghdian kingdom, a conquest of Alexander the Great that was said to have been sealed by his marriage to a Soghdian princess. This city, called Afrasiab after a legendary king of the region, covered a defensible hillside juxtaposed to the present city. The murals decorated a principal room in a palace built in the seventh century AD, only seventy-five years before the conquest and destruction of the city by Arab invaders. The background colour is an earth red against which the artist has painted court and battle scenes full of action and, one suspects, realism. Within the mudbrick ruins themselves, we were shown the palace cheek by jowl with tenth-century roads, so presumably the city survived in some form while at the same time Samarkand, Maracanda as it was called by Alexander's contemporaries, grew up in the lush valley next door.

Our caravanette returned to the wide piazza raised to the level of the present-day streets in front of the registan to be greeted by photographers from the local press and a burst of heavy rain. Both the photocall and our tour of the registan were washed out by the unseasonable downpour. Instead, we decided to explore the nearby Museum of the History of Culture and Art of the People of Uzbekistan, a vast, two-storey, purpose-built monstrosity in the glass-and-steel soulless-modern style of Brunel University. Its collection is no less disappointing. Not only was the administration uninterested by our portable holographic equipment, but more to the point, there was almost nothing small enough and of sufficient merit to warrant holography. To my eyes, the display of modern carpets alone deserved closer attention.

The museum was a disappointment, as was the much older and more attractive Art Museum which we visited the next day. But for our first day, the best was yet to come. Tom and I were able to walk from our hotel with Dmitri and Abdul Malik, our helpful troubleshooter from the Samarkand city government, to the Gur Emir, Grave of the Ruler. This is the tomb of Timur the Lame (or Tamerlane) and, therefore, launches its emotional impact from a higher pad. Small enough to absorb, it is the perfect example of the Timurid architecture that makes Samarkand so exciting. Inside and out, it has been carefully and elaborately restored. Rising street levels require you to descend a flight of steps to the entrance iwan in the surrounding wall. Through the decorative arch with its blue and yellow ceramic tiles you enter a pretty courtyard, a small bed of flowers surrounding a young mulberry tree in the centre. The tile work on the two minarets at the front corners of the façade has been restored, but the lost tops have not been rebuilt. The attention is drawn to the blue-tiled dome with its sixty-four gadroons, lifted on a drum.

Perhaps to protect the interior of the building, the main entrance iwan is walled off. An ordinary door to the left leads into a gallery from which you enter the main chamber. The tile work, onyx and gold leaf are breathtaking. The entire inside of the dome and the four half-domes is dominated by gold leaf. Yet the dimensions of the chamber are modest, perhaps eight metres square and proportionate in height. Inside, the drum is not evident, and the dome seems to be supported by the four half-domes and squinches.

In the centre just below floor level lies the green onyx tomb cover of Timur's grave, split in two, according to legend, when it was dropped by grave robbers. Somehow, I did not expect to see the seven or eight additional tombs. The monument was ordered to be built for Timur's grandson, Muhammed Sultan, in 1404. Timur himself was interred there the next year. There also lie two sons, Shahrukh and Miranshah, his better known grandson, Ulug Beg, his tutor and a brother. In one of the side chapels formed by the half-domes is the tomb of a mullah evidently important to Timur. The tombs themselves are two metres below their respective decorative tomb covers in a kind of undercroft entered through beautiful fifteenth-century carved wooden doors, their flat gravestone slabs covered with elaborate inscriptions and carvings.

In the courtyard again, we were offered green tea by the keeper. It was served as we reclined on the wooden platform within the former entrance iwan. Abdul Malik, a small, wiry man in his thirties, talked with the keeper in Uzbek and Russian. Like all the local people with whom we exchanged more than a nod and a thank you, the keeper, who knew about tourists in coaches, was a little unsure about us. Were we scientists and, if so, what were we studying? He veiled his curiosity behind a lifted eyebrow and a slightly condescending smile.

In the morning, we again parked our car in front of the Mosque of Bibi-Khanum at the entrance to the bazaar where it attracted larger crowds more continuously than any market stall. The weather had returned to normal so that the sun already made the skin prickle as we walked the short distance to the registan past the unusual hexagonal domed structure built 200 years ago and now used for market stalls. Having approached the registan from the front on the first occasion when rain made us look indoors for amusement, we now entered the great square between the Tillya-Kari Madrasa opposite the main approach and the Sherdor Madrasa on the east. No one who has seen pictures of Samarkand can have forgotten this remarkable public area with three elaborately-decorated educational institutions facing the central square like the buildings of a modern university campus. The Tillya-Kari is the newest, finished in 1660, and the largest. Its courtyard is still formed by the cubicles of the scholars except that the west end is a mosque, now a museum, with a giant blue dome. The restorers were having difficulty making the ceramic tiles stay in place, a problem we had also been told about in Iran at Soltānīyeh.

Dmitri and Abdul Malik had laid on the chief of works for the restoration of the registan to give us the facts, but I'm afraid it was too hot. I sloped off to the madrasa built for Ulug Beg on the west side of the square, the earliest of the three. Here the colours are much more subdued, perhaps because the tiles are older. The deep entrance iwan leads into a beautiful garden courtyard where the prevailing tile colour is blue with designs in green, orange, darker blue and white. For fifteen minutes, I rested against the entrance wall in deep shade enjoying the birds, which I could not identify, and the passing tourists who were less mysterious.

The Sherdor Madrasa is sometimes called the Lion because of the two bright orange and blue beasts that decorate its iwan. From its courtyard, the construction of the inner façade of the entrance iwan can be observed. It consists of eight arches across the top, the two at the ends being wider than the six in the middle. Below them is a roof-like structure that extends backward towards the courtyard. This courtyard had been set up for a concert or lecture with rows of chairs facing a wooden stage in the small iwan on the south side.

The Registan is understandably the centre and symbol of Samarkand, the Florence of medieval Islam. But we were also eager to visit the Shaki-Zinda, a necropolis, which provides a link between Samarkand and Afrasiab. It rises up the south-east slope in the hill that was surmounted by the ancient settlement. The entrance iwan, decorated with ceramic tiles in geometric patterns, is one of the latest structures, having been built in 1434. A carriageway leads uphill between a series of tombs dating from the thirteenth to the sixteenth centuries, although construction in the complex continued into the last century and restoration has begun more recently. Shaki-Zinda offers a rich variety of detail if only because construction took place on the orders of different patrons over so many years. Most of the tombs are domed, usually resplendent with the prevailing blue ceramic tiles. Domes are supported by drums, some of which are lettered in Kufic script, some covered with geometric designs and others undecorated. There are carved wooden doors, inscriptions and tomb covers often of great beauty. Both Tom and I preferred to see these variations in our own way despite Ludmilla's eagerness to fill in dates and numbers. She had come to accept his lone meanderings because of his cameras, but she expected more of me, the expedition leader, and she had her job to do. Nevertheless, I left her talking to Geoff and crossed the narrow carriageway to the mausoleum of Shah Li Mulik Akka, 1372.

"Where are you going?" she asked.

"To look at this tomb."

"It is not interesting."

"How do I know if I don't look?"

"I can tell you because I have been here."

I tried to explain that her experience could not be matched to my curiosity, but she was both unconvinced and hurt by my apparent rudeness.

"I'm sorry," I said, "but sadly we have so little time."

"Exactly. I will tell you what you ought to see."

It was a cultural stand-off. I was annoyed because she interfered with my freedom of action; she because, as a professional guide, it was her job to save me time. Not all Soviet and Chinese guide-interpreters fall into this trap, but those like Ludmilla assume they are hired because they know what is good for you and take the view of the apocryphal Lufthansa airline captain who called over the loudspeakers as the flight began: "You vill haf a good flight if you do as you are told." In the Soviet Union, however, the problem never arose again because the scholars from the Academies of Science, not being professional guides, understood our needs.

Intourist hotels all display signs saying that you may use certain credit cards to obtain cash providing you give a day's notice. In the morning of our first day in Samarkand, a Saturday, I went to the Intourist desk. "May I please use my Visa card to obtain 400 rubles?"

"We close at noon today. It will have to be Monday."

"Yes, that will be fine. Monday morning."

On Monday morning, the Intourist desk opened at nine thirty instead of nine o'clock, the hour posted, and the clerk was a different person. She found no record of my request and said there was nothing she could do. When Abdul Malik intervened, she said the cash was not available. He suggested she take it temporarily from the hotel safe. It seemed that the person with the keys was not coming in that day. Abdul Malik then insisted that she arrange to obtain the cash from the bank immediately. The Intourist manager for the city was called, and Abdul Malik offered to drive him to the bank, an arrangement which the manager finally accepted.

When we left Samarkand at eleven instead of nine o'clock, Abdul Malik, Ludmilla, the Deputy Director of the Uzbek Institute of Geography and two reporters from the local paper shook hands and wished us well. They washed away the Intourist flavour, and Tom generously kissed Ludmilla goodbye.

# Chapter 8

# FERGANA

*Фергана*

My compromise with Yuri Badenkov, arrived at by bellowing into the phone at Ashkhabad, required that we meet up at last with the Soviet members of the Marco Polo Expedition and Paul on July 13th at Leninabad in the Tadzhik SSR. Thus we left Samarkand in anticipation of joining forces by the end of the day.

From Samarkand to the Chinese border as the crow flies is about 600 kilometres, but the route we had been authorised to travel more than doubled the distance. All of this country is closed to foreigners so we were not surprised to learn that we could not use the shortest route to Leninabad along the main road to Tashkent. Not even Dmitri had an explanation. Instead, our route ran due east.

At 12.30 p.m., just before reaching the historic town of Penzhikent, we crossed the Uzbek-Tadzhik border. We were awaited by a police check with a difference: a police escort. It accompanied us, blue lights flashing, through the town without stopping for red lights, pedestrians or other traffic. Dmitri said it was a mark of respect. We found it mildly embarrassing.

The road now descended into a rich valley with the Zeravshan on the left and beyond it the Turkestan mountain range. To the right, the mountains are also called Zeravshan. Orange groves and grapes indicated a long growing season, and the weather was sunny and very warm. But not for long. The road climbed as the valley narrowed. The river narrowed too and became a rapid. The road crossed it several times on suspension bridges. High above a curve of the river, we stopped for a photo session. These unscheduled stops occurred whenever Tom or anyone else wanted to take a picture or for any other reason, like when Geoff collected samples of cereal. Dmitri identified three ravens flying low over a field of grass beside us. Falcons swooped in the river valley below. At this point, our police escort changed from an ordinary police car to a jeep which had been awaiting us by the roadside. The reason was soon apparent. A poor road surface now deteriorated further, especially where it had been damaged by landslides. We had learned in Jerevan that we could not drive to Dushanbe because landslides had closed the road entirely. Evidence that it had very nearly happened here lay all about us. As if to underline the threat, clouds were gathering as we entered Ayni, a Tadzhik mountain town.

At the municipal building, we were met by the local party leader who led us to a restaurant where she helped to serve an enormous lunch. It consisted of all the usual ingredients, salads, kebabs, rice, but the meal ended with bowls of the most delicious white apricots, products of the valley. This hospitality at midday seemed sadly misplaced, not just because most people find it that much harder to drive after a heavy meal, but because on this occasion we were feeling the excitement of the meeting in Leninabad, 120 kilometres further on.

Yet we had been warned. Foreigners in a forbidden land, we were indeed honoured guests. The hospitality of these isolated people has been reported by travellers for hundreds of years. Though hospitality was traditional, it might be less than wholehearted if the local potentate was unfriendly for some reason. We benefited not only from tradition but also because of a friendly government embarked on the new policy of glasnost. Whatever the Ayni partyleader might have thought of us, she was the perfect hostess, warm and welcoming. She even travelled in the police car until it turned around at the base of the pass to the north. In the misting rain, everyone got out and made little speeches of thanks including our mutual hopes for a peaceful world. In our small way, we had become involved in the difficult business of improving international relations. That was what Badenkov had meant when he said that the small town ceremonial visits were an imperative part of our journey. Had we crossed the border as scheduled, the visits and the hospitality would have happened all the way from Ashkhabad.

It was raining and cold when we said goodbye to the Ayni group and began the climb on a narrow, unmetalled road through the most difficult pass we had traversed so far. The scenery would have been magnificent, I have no doubt, but it was obscured by the clouds through which we were driving. Only occasionally could you see forests and a strip of road far below the hairpin curve. We had been told when we parted that the summit lay thirty-two kilometres ahead of us. At about twenty-five kilometres, the rain turned to snow. At thirty kilometres, the snow had begun to lie. The summit offered a winter landscape restricted to twenty metres in all directions. Of course the snow continued for some time, but the descent was more gradual. There was rain again, followed by a fairly rapid lifting of the clouds. We could see trees rising up the sides of a narrow valley, apparently higher than the tree line on the southern face, with a stream. The valley broadened and was very green, though uncultivated like a pristine land. Species roses lined the river. The hills seemed much lower, and there at last grazed a flock of sheep. Very soon, the landscape became a gently rolling plain across which the road ran in a very straight line towards Leninabad.

At Ura-T'ube, Dmitri was expected to report at the party headquarters so that news of our progress could be passed to our waiting colleagues. The need for this became apparent later. The local people told him that it had already rained for two days, the first rain in July for twenty years. We seemed to spawn new records.

Dusk was adding to the grey as we came down a long hill towards an intersection where there seemed to have been an accident. A crowd surrounded several vehicles including two police cars. Suddenly people in the crowd looked familiar. Before Valery had actually stopped in the intersection, I found myself on the road and then sharing a Russian hug with Yuri Badenkov. Paul stood beside him. There was Olga followed by general introductions, handshakes, hugs and a tear or two. Yuri passed out badges they had designed showing our logo combined with the Institute of Geography logo. "At last." "When did you leave?" ". . . wonderful to be here." And so on, in Russian and English which everyone understood. There were eleven of the Soviet members of the Marco Polo Expedition, including the historian from the Tadzhik Academy of Sciences and five of us, so the police had to pacify several drivers delayed by our obstruction of these busy roads. The rain fell steadily.

At last we redistributed ourselves in three vehicles, a Russian jeep, an official car and our own. A police car led the cavalcade for not more than a kilometre. The road in front of shops and a school seemed to fill with people and lights. Two men were blowing the enormously long Tadzhik horns, the curve beneath the bell resting on the ground. We all got out. Yuri and I approached a group of people in local dress. Children handed us bunches of gladioli, and two women presented me with bread and salt. About fifty people had gathered, drawn by the commotion despite the rain, but on this occasion there was no speech of welcome. After everyone shook hands with everyone, it seemed, we set off again.

The next stop was a chaikhana, a tea house or in fact a restaurant. Here we were greeted by two more horn players on the steps in front of the entrance, and between them, our hostess, the deputy leader of the Leninabad City Soviet and two or three more local government and party officials. We entered a large, high-ceilinged room brightly lit by a crystal chandelier. One long table stretched across the middle of the room covered by a white table-cloth and set with bowls of fruit and bread, platters of tomatoes, cucumbers and onions, white table napkins, cutlery and glasses. We were hungry, and no sight could have been more welcome. First, however, we were taken on to a covered terrace at the back of the building. Had it been warmer, we might have eaten outside because the terrace overlooked the Syrdar'ya itself.

Except for the sweet, white local peaches, the meal was not remarkable. Nor were the speeches of welcome and of thanks by the city official, a party leader, Yuri Badenkov and myself, in part because soft drinks only are served at such functions in the Soviet Union these days. It must have been near to midnight when we shook hands and were driven off to the campsite occupied for the last two weeks by Paul and our Soviet colleagues. "Campsite" fails to sum up the attributes of this shaded garden complete with swimming pool lapped by the waters of the Syrdar'ya. It belongs to the local electricity workers' union. At the side of the pool away from the river stood a large dacha, a summer house consisting of two large rooms separated by a roofed sleeping porch open front and back. Bunks, complete with mosquito nets, had been set up ready for our sleeping bags.

In all of this comfortable, not to say luxurious, accommodation, I found only one drawback, perhaps because I needed it more than the others. The toilets consisted of a privy. That would have been perfectly acceptable had it not been one of the dirtiest privies it has ever been my misfortune to experience. In fact, in Moscow, Leningrad, Irkutsk and Soviet central Asia generally public toilets, whether privies or plumbed, are a disgrace, far more filthy than those in any other country I know.

There was time before bed for a cup of coffee or a measure of vodka. We all sat around an oil-cloth-covered table in the partly-roofed kitchen area near the river. For the first time, we had a chance to look at each other. Olga Omelchenko was the third member of the group which had arranged the

Soviet part of the expedition with me at the Institute of Geography in Moscow. She is a translator and interpreter with tact, accuracy and wit. A translator is someone who works through a manuscript with time if not leisure to find the exact word or phrase; an interpreter works simultaneously with at best an interval of a few seconds while the words are spoken. As interpreter, Olga conveyed confidence that the meaning was precisely what the speaker had intended. Her expressiveness went beyond words, of course, to her small hands, blue eyes and the set of her small mouth. On the second morning of my Moscow visit, at a meeting arranged for me to meet the then head of the Foreign Affairs Department of the Academy of Sciences, Olga was sitting just behind this official of the old school. Whatever the directive that had come down about us, he was full of doubt that our proposed journey across the Silk Road could be useful let alone practically possible. His feet were dragging so heavily that I was beginning to feel the strain when I looked up to see Olga watching me; with equal weight, she lifted her eyebrows and cast her eyes prayerfully towards heaven. The struggle not to laugh restored my balance.

The kitchen seemed to be in the charge of Olga and her less experienced fellow interpreter, Natasha, who was pert and petite with long reddish-brown hair. When I questioned this MCP arrangement, Natasha assured me she preferred to know what her food contained. I know the answer to this one, but it was far too late to display my feminist erudition. Tolya, their stills photographer, was a saturnine forty-year-old willing to help with anything. Boris, short, square and crewcut, was the film cameraman from Central TV, Moscow, assigned to make a documentary about us. Yuri Badenkov's son, Artiom, teaches literature at Moscow University and was a dogsbody with us, improving his English. Gena was the second driver, responsible for their lorry. In theory at least, their vehicles could be driven only by Valery and Gena. Unlike our Soviet hosts, we had had a long drive topped by the excitement of our meeting and the two receptions. And we had to attend a reception in our honour in the offices of the Director of the city government, the Mayor, at nine next morning. We went to bed.

The Mayor's office is on the top floor of a new eight-storey block overlooking the river with mountains at some distance, apparently on all sides. As Hodjent, the settlement has existed for centuries, though very little of the old city remains today. It is on a main road connecting the fertile Fergana Valley to the north-west along the river. The Mayor wanted us to know about the modern town, of course, and made a long speech of welcome as we enjoyed fruit, cakes and green tea. To this speech, again, I was expected to reply. The content of these responses became somewhat standardised as time passed and need not be preserved for posterity. For the past two weeks, Paul had been delivering them on our behalf but was relieved, he said, to be relieved.

Paul had become the old stager, of course, having even picked up a few Russian words. It was very good to see him again. Like everyone else, he had doubted whether we would ever enter the Soviet Union, but his cheerful good sense had helped to lighten the gloom. One of his Russian words was a Muscovite gem, *triocha* (*tri*=three; *ocha*=a quantity of money of unspecified minuteness). Thus, "it is worth *triocha*" became the Russian expedition's estimate of our chances.

Leninabad has two museums, a new Archaeological Museum in a disused mosque near the centre of the old town, and a much larger Historical Museum also in a former mosque and a madrasa. Neither collection is especially exciting, but in the latter there is a Qurân dated to the eighth century in an astonishing state of repair. The wooden coffered ceiling of the Historical Museum has been brightly but insensitively restored. The Historical Museum forms part of a complex of buildings, however, that includes a large Friday Mosque in regular use. It was built in the last century and recently very well restored. The courtyard, covered with arbours of grapevines loaded with grapes, has very attractive wooden pillars and wood and plaster decorations set off by modern tiles. There are two large rooms inside, a plain wooden ceiling supported by wooden columns with elaborately-carved capitals. The simple, undecorated mihrab has blue-tiled Kufic lettering above it. Behind these buildings, a twelfth-century mausoleum is being restored, so far with only basic undecorated brickwork. It is intended as part of the museum.

On the other side of a large public square stands the Leninabad bazaar, a huge arched hall built in 1960 to replace an old market. We were there at a little after noon, and though the bazaar was busy, there was room to move about and inspect a mezzanine lined with shops for clothing and manufactured goods, and the ground floor filled by row upon row of food stands selling, in the height of summer, an immense variety of locally-grown fruits and vegetables. Various cereals and flour, spices and dried vegetables were sold from stands in the hall, but bread seemed to be available from sellers outside the main entrances.

About 1.00 p.m., the rest of the team in the Russian vehicles found us in front of the Historical Museum, and we set off for Kokand in a convoy of five cars: first, a police car clearing our path, followed by a car carrying the local party and civic officials whom we had first met the night before. Third was the jeep, painted British racing green or Soviet equivalent, driven now by Yuri Petrovich despite his complaints that we had detained his second driver, Valery, for far too long. The jeep was in full expedition mode: i.e., it pulled a trailer containing most of the kitchen equipment and food. We had by that time contributed what food we had, the white enamel plates and cups and our Dutch cutlery to the general good. After the jeep, our white van, with the BRG Russian lorry as tail-end-Charlie.

Our first stop was to be given another enormous lunch by a small town called Kanibadam. This agricultural community is near the eastern end of the Kairakkum reservoir, one of many we were to pass on the Syrdar'ya.

After the meal, we were taken to see the disused Madrasa Mir Hajab Dawla at the edge of the town, which was in process of restoration. It had a beautiful garden courtyard and the carved wooden doors on the former scholars' cells were very well made, while the large entrance iwan had a decorated coffer ceiling similar to that in the Leninabad Historical Museum.

Soon after lunch, our caravan re-entered the Uzbek SSR. Having said thanks and farewell to our Tadzhik hosts and hostess, we greeted and were welcomed by the Uzbekis yet again, complete with a new police escort and official car, of course. These republic borders in the Soviet Union seem to be like state borders in the United States: officialdom changes personnel. The eastern tail of

Uzbekistan we were now entering was the remarkably fertile and prosperous Fergana Valley, so named for a small tributary of the Syrdar'ya which waters part of the region. Cotton is the most important crop, and we also saw fields of cereals, but the orchards of peaches, almonds and apricots and the melons could hardly be overlooked during mid-summer. Fergana has been a major trade route for centuries, properly a part of the ancient Silk Road from China to the Mediterranean.

A century ago, Kokand was the principal city of the region, capital of a Khanate. Today, its population has declined to less than 200,000. The American diplomat-traveller Eugene Schuyler described Kokand in 1875:

> Kokand is a modern town, not more than a 100 years old, and therefore has wider streets, and is more spacious than most Asiatic towns. From the roof of the caravanserai we may see the whole city set out before us, and not only the city but the Khanate as well. Immediately around us are the broad flat clay roofs of the bazaar, most of the streets even being covered, so as to allow an easy promenade from one end to the other. Near by, to the left is a group of mosques and medresses built of reddish grey brick, with high melon-shaped domes, the cornices covered with blue and white tiles, forming texts from the Koran . . . To the left is the beautiful facade of the Khan's palace, glittering in all the brightness of its fresh tiles, blue, yellow, and green, half hidden in luxuriant verdure, and surrounding all the brilliant green of the gardens and orchards.

Schuyler's caravanserai was specially pointed out. Now a motor-repair garage occupies the site, not inappropriately, I felt. At first, we were told the caravanserai had been built in the eleventh century, but Dr Ashraf Akhmetof, the historian from the Uzbek Academy of Sciences, said quietly that no one knew when it was founded.

The Khan's palace is the Museum of History and Art. The collection is less interesting than the nineteenth-century building with its decorative tiles and ceramic quotations still intact. The Director, Mme Mansurova Mansura, has the enthusiasm and charm which may transform the collection. Behind the museum, the former Friday Mosque built in 1820 was being restored, and the Kydoyar Khan Mosque, also restored, continues in use.

For me, the most significant moment in Kokand, however, had a contemporary meaning. In the midst of our tour of the town, the whole caravan stopped in front of a monument with a flame burning beneath it, the local memorial to the dead of the Second World War.

The Mayor spoke to me. Olga translated: "Kokand lost 40,000 men in the War of Liberation. The city and district sent 52,000 to the front. Would you be willing to honour our dead?"

"Certainly. The honour will be ours."

"We ask our guests to place a rose at the eternal flame."

We were each handed a fragrant, long-stemmed red rose and walked with the Mayor, Yuri, Dmitri and Olga fifty metres along a wide pavement lined by trees to the memorial. After standing in silence, I placed my rose and the others followed. I said to the Mayor, who was aged perhaps forty-five, that I too was a veteran of that war. He nodded.

At Kokand, all our meals were provided by the municipality. Dinner the evening before and breakfast were cooked and beautifully served at the guest house just outside the town where we spent the night. On the far side of the building was a small swimming pool used before breakfast only by Paul and Natasha.

Unexpectedly, the 125-kilometre drive to Andizhan returned us again to desert conditions. Boris, the television documentary-maker, saw an opportunity at last to film our vehicle in the sand. We turned off the main road toward a nature reserve entered by a sand track through scrubby dunes. He took some background shots but nothing very dramatic. The track ended in front of a steep dune. Happily, Boris suggested I drive up. Nothing would have been easier except that the dune had a double tilt: the route to the top rose to the right but the slope fell off to the left. With our roof racks filled by sand tyres, full twenty-five-litre water bottles, tools, parts and personal baggage, the topography looked like a recipe for disaster. Boris took it in good part and made do.

"Andizhan, the chief place of the Khanate after Kokand, and one of the oldest," Schuyler wrote, "made a very pleasant impression on me." He was able to buy eggs and fresh fish. Though lacking these products, our meals were again supplied. This time, our campsite was a semicircular pavilion on top of a wooded hill. Beside it grew nectarines and plums in full fruit. At the centre of the circle, a modernistic fountain played in a rather deep pool. A kitchen at a little distance enabled local people to give us dinner at a long table in the pavilion. Later, the pavilion provided a marvellous roofed shelter for the cots and sleeping bags, open otherwise to the night.

The only missing amenity was a bath. Our hosts, led by the Mayor, made up for this lack by driving those who wanted a shower to a local hotel. I stayed behind, preferring a rest to cleanliness. In an access of goodwill, the Mayor had then offered to make phone calls to London for Tom and Paul entirely without charge. I had chosen to do without a shower but not a free phone call, and felt some envy at least, but the next afternoon the Mayor made good by placing a call for me from his own office.

In a large nineteenth-century madrasa, the city has opened an Historical Museum devoted primarily to displays of the works of local writers. Only the more recent are original manuscripts or publications. From the Islamic middle ages, however, Andizhan can boast two famous and important native sons. Al-Khwarizmi (1381–1446) became an astronomer and mathematician. He did his work primarily in Bukhara and Samarkand. The other Andizhani about whom one is told was Babur, the first Moghul Emperor of India. A descendant of Timur, his father had inherited a sheikhdom centred on Andizhan where Babur was born in 1483.

Another madrasa just behind the bazaar was being restored to become a museum of art and culture. The bazaar itself was more crowded than at Kokand but seemed less colourful. Behind it in a semicircle runs the Street of the Handicrafts, consisting of workers in wood and metal whose products were often combined in large highly-polished wooden chests with showy brass hinges, handles and decorations. The colours varied from maroon and red gloss to the tones of natural pine, but the general effect was old-fashioned and slightly barbaric. We saw vans and cars throughout Fergana carrying chests such as these lashed to their tops, probably being carried off to become a central furnishing in a new home. Handicrafts for sale in the street included ceramics, kitchen utensils and knives, many of them clearly mass-produced in Omsk or Leningrad. Nevertheless, the Street of the Handicrafts seemed to Boris a suitable setting for filming us. We walked through parts of it more than once, pausing at designated shops until he was satisfied.

As at Kokand, there had been a caravanserai adjacent to the market and the madrasa now being restored. This site, too, is occupied by a car repair garage.

Lunch that day was served at an open-air restaurant beside a lake in a city park. Again, the table was beautifully, even magnificently, set with bowls of fruit, platters of salad, white linen and sparkling cutlery. A feast to the eye, but whereas the fruit was a great treat, the kebabs and plof had been repeated too often. Paul said he would eat no more lamb for a year. Pork is not served where the population is chiefly Muslim, and beef is not produced locally. My own complaint was much less subtle: I was having too much trouble at the other end to find any food interesting, except the fruit, and that was about to be banned.

After completing various phone calls from the Mayor's office and the requirements of protocol, the cavalcade departed on the short drive to Osh. The border between the Uzbek and Kirgiz Republics runs a few kilometres before Osh, and again we said goodbye to those who had looked after us before turning round to greet our new hosts. They had agreed to keep the civic reception to a minimum, but we were taken on a tour of this nondescript town, barren but for an accident of nature. Schuyler travelled east as far as Osh:

> . . . I was given a comfortable house, with a large clean court, near the "throne of Solomon". This celebrated rock, *Takht-i-Suleiman*, is a bare high ridge of rugged stone, standing out of the midst of the plain, on the edge of the town . . . An old tradition represents it to be the place where the great Solomon once established his throne, to look over that part of the world; though probably, this Solomon was some local saint or hero who has been confounded with the Jewish king.

In fact, there is a spectacular new almuminum-and-glass-fronted archae-ological museum built into the side of the Takht-i-Suleiman with very little being exhibited yet, I was told. My regimen of rest and blandness had already begun the next morning when the rest of the expedition inspected it.

We were comfortably accommodated in a large guest house built in the 1950s, possibly with the expectation that it might become a rest home in competition with the Crimea. At the urging of Yuri Badenkov, I agreed to see a doctor who would call at the guest house. Four doctors, two nurses and four hours later, it was agreed that I had some form of dysentery, should rest in the hotel for the next twenty-four hours while the others went off to visit the ruins

A free-enterprise stall in the Samarkand bazaar.

A restored tile screen in Bukhara.

Approaching the Toktogulskoya reservoir, Kirgizia. ►

Sardarapat Ethnographic Museum, Jerevan, Armenia. This central dome uses concrete in a manner reminiscent of a wooden mosque dome in Erzurum, Turkey.

at Uzgen and would restrict my diet to bland food and liquids for five days while taking a course of antibiotics. The Russians decided that my rest could only be secured if the language barrier did not exist, and Natasha sweetly agreed to stay behind too for the day. She did an immense amount of laundry for Olga and herself. So central did this illness become, for me at least, that I shall ask your indulgence and skip ahead to the end of the expedition and beyond in order to summarise its course.

The Russian cure worked for a few days but in Kashgar, the trouble was as bad as ever. I was taken to a traditional doctor in a large hospital. He examined me cursorily and prescribed three different pills. Again, relief followed but not for long. I tried to control the trouble with careful diet, avoiding spices and most of the other attributes that make Chinese cooking varied and worthwhile. In Luoyang, the symptoms became much worse. The local hospital is run by doctors who practise Western diagnostics and for the first time a test was done. I did not have amoebic dysentery, though they could not say what was the cause. They prescribed three more drugs including a new Chinese antibiotic, piperic acid, which added indigestion to my other complaints until I stopped taking it on the advice of another doctor. For the third time, temporary relief. Incidentally, all of these visits and treatments were free in the Soviet Union, and very nearly so in China. As far as my kind of dysentery is concerned, furthermore, I have demonstrated that Soviet medicine, Chinese traditional medicine and Chinese scientific medicine have in common their failure.

It took three months and a degree of serendipity before NHS medicine improved on this record. No causative organism was ever discovered, but a drug used to cure a bug found worldwide but most commonly in China did the trick.

I felt much brighter for a day of sleeping and lying about, and we left Osh on Saturday, July 18th, for a long detour to the Chinese border. Our Chinese visas, only renewable in China, expired on July 22nd, so we had to be sure to enter the day before. The original itinerary called for us to cross the border at Irkeshtam, a village about 150 kilometres south-east of Osh and due west of Kashgar. The Soviet authorities rejected this proposal, and we later learned that the Chinese too had closed their border at this point. The alternative, the Turugart Pass, is about 200 kilometres due east of Osh as the crow flies, but the road certainly does not, due to the mountainous terrain. The route agreed through Jalalabad to Naryn and Turugart is roughly three times as long. But even this road could not be used by the time we reached the region. Unseasonable rain had caused landslides which closed it too. We were forced to drive much further north and had to cover more than 1,000 kilometres in the remaining three days. Only in Idaho and Colorado have I seen such consistently wild and spectacular mountain scenery, and we had not yet reached the much higher Tian Shan range that forms this part of the Soviet–Chinese border.

The drive began quietly enough through rich farmland irrigated by water from mountain streams. Tobacco, corn and cotton dominated, with orchards of peaches, apricots and apples at frequent intervals. Soon after starting, a vast diversion through a cutting for a new bridge approach gave Boris another

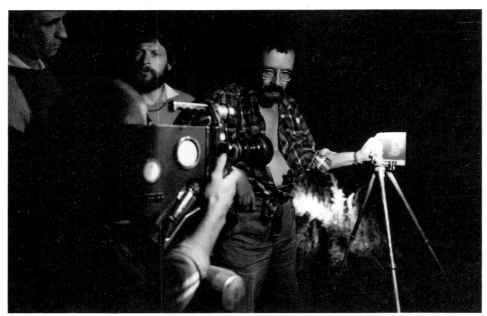

Filming a hologram by truck search-light for Soviet Central TV, near Toktogul, USSR.

chance to film us descending a road through sand. Lunch was early at the sensible request of the Osh authorities who knew we had had only a scratch breakfast. It was served to us in a village called Leninski by the village soviet, the Mayor attending. Leninski is also the home village of the historian, Sulaimanof Ertabyildyi, sent to accompany us by the Kirgiz Academy of Sciences. Here and in towns further along the route, we had to detour across temporary bridges because spring floods had destroyed the road bridges. As the road rose, the mountains we had seen in the distance moved closer. Cotton and corn were still the principal crops in the narrowing valley which looked as though it was closed off completely by the ranges ahead of us. Just to the left of the road, the first of many extraordinary rock formations like the carvings of a vanished race of giants. This one consisted of lighter grey rocks in a pattern of ninety-degree angles, apexes at the top, against the basic tan of the mountain.

At a village named Tash-kumyr, the road crossed the Naryn River and ran beside a new reservoir in process of filling. The water was so dark green that it must contain dissolved minerals. Soon after entering another fertile valley, we caught a glimpse of the great Toktogulskoya reservoir completed in 1974 beside which we were to travel the rest of the day. As the valley narrowed, a settlement of yurts sheltered shepherd families whose sheep had come to summer pastures. Snow could be seen on the mountains for the first time. Dr Ertabyildyi said we were at about 3,000 metres, and the mountain peaks must reach another 3,000.

When the road returned to the south shore of Toktogulskoya, we could see a blue oval like a postage stamp surrounded by blue-green vegetation beneath an immense blue sky, all of creation in emeralds and sapphires. The eastern end of the lake is swampy where the Naryn enters, but hills run down to the north shore almost until the town of Toktogul where we intended to spend the night. The Russian jeep which had been leading needed petrol, as would the lorry when it caught up. Because only low-octane was available, we decided to use our spare capacity with the expectation of finding better further on. Slowly, we began the ascent along the valley of the narrow, swift Chichkan River which runs into Toktogulskoya from the north. We found a perfect campsite between the quiet road and the stream about twenty kilometres from Toktogul and stopped to await the others. Half an hour passed. Though it was quite light at seven thirty, dusk was approaching. We drove back to the petrol station to find the lorry had broken down. Gena and Valery had been able to make basic repairs, but until they could buy a new battery, it was necessary to lend them one of ours. We camped in a field nearby, adequate though far less beautiful than the spot we had selected.

Dmitri had already located the local government and party headquarters and had arranged to obtain a battery from a local garage the next morning, Sunday. At nine o'clock, I went along with Dmitri, Yuri and Olga because I could drive our car legally and the battery was to replace the one we had supplied to the lorry. The three-storey municipal building set amongst trees was open, and the party official eventually appeared. He summoned the garage operator by phone, but this personage did not have a suitable battery. I went with Olga to sit in the sun so I am not sure how the police became involved, but I was asked to drive everyone to a police barracks nearby. There, the necessary twelve-volt item was cannibalised from a police car. At no cost other than time, we could move.

We led the way on that morning's drive, fifty kilometres up the Chichkan Valley to the Alabel Pass at 3,100 metres, surely the most beautiful drive of the entire journey. Until it left us, a tiny rivulet above the tree line, the Chichkan River flowed down on our right. The narrow wooded valley of the previous evening continued twenty kilometres past the place we had turned around. The trees were conifers mixed with oak and beech, plane and maple. There may have been walnut trees amongst them. Above the tree line, the valley widened considerably. A grassy floor made it green as far as the rocks of the mountains themselves. Now, we could see snow on the peaks. Across a large meadow to our right on the river bank were two yurts, grey with high walls and sharply-peaked roofs. They were separated by perhaps fifty metres, possibly housing two related families. We could see the people, their sheep and their horses. We were nearing the summit now. Where the narrow new Chichkan flowed down from its source, scree covered the slopes, but green vegetation persisted.

A few kilometres past the summit, there was a roadside café on the right and a petrol station just down the hill on the left. We ordered lunch and some of us had walked down to the sparkling mountain lake behind the shabby buildings to wash our hands when one of the girls called out in alarm. Geoff had misjudged a leap between two boulders, fallen and broken a tooth, but it was the bleeding abrasions on his forehead, left arm and leg that attracted attention. Fortunately, they were superficial, and the tooth had had the nerve removed. That was our only casualty in the whole expedition.

Lunch left much to be desired, but the petrol station had ninety-three-octane petrol for sale to unofficial vehicles. The rest of the day was very long because we had set off so late. The final 150 kilometres took us through a well-watered valley with many villages, each with its Muslim graveyard, a few small mudbrick mausoleums and many rounded gravestones with a triangle looking as though it had been stuck on top like an early exercise in sculpture for beginners. These cemeteries were all quite new. So too were the villages in most cases, the old mudbrick buildings have been left to decay next door. It was almost eight o'clock when we finally camped beside a river called Karakudzhur. Cattle had used the area before us and caution was necessary.

For the first time since we entered the Soviet Union, we awoke to discover an overcast sky. The road seemed to be rising consistently again, and the population was notably more dense. About midday, we reported in at the municipal buildings of Naryn, our last Soviet town of any size. At the outskirts, a police checkpoint halted us briefly. Then, we began to climb through the buff-coloured hills of the Kuzel Bel Pass. From the top and the road beyond, across a flat, grass-covered plain, we faced a great wall of jagged grey mountains topped with snow, the Tian Shan.

To the left was the village of At-Bashi, one of those straggling places that occupied an ancient site. Great mudbrick walls just north-east of the settlement dominate it. With the jeep, we drove off the main road and, after once being thwarted by the banks of a narrow stream that looked a little too challenging, finally reached the walls by another road. Dr Ertabyildyi explained that this was the Ark of a town than had been built at the time of Timor, perhaps as a defence against him. The massive walls enclosed an area about 100 metres square which was absolutely empty except for wild flowers and grasses. The walls too were featureless though there was evidence of former watch towers, at least at the corners. Although they have been breached in several places, as if to admit farm machinery, and display the kind of erosion that might be expected, I wondered whether these walls could have stood through almost 600 years of heat and cold unless they had been rebuilt more recently.

Our objective for the last night in the Soviet Union was a caravanserai called Tash Rabat and reputed to be in a remarkable state of repair. It would provide not only a comfortable campsite but sheltered facilities for the farewell party planned by our Russian hosts. They would remain there for two nights because only a small group would accompany us to the border in the jeep the next morning. About ninety kilometres before the border, therefore, we turned off the main road on to a dirt track made soft and yielding by the persistent rain that had begun an hour before. The land was rolling and green but featureless until we descended to the banks of a wide stream that looked as though it had been raining longer than we knew. Having forded this obstacle, we carried on beside broad pastures, crossing a smaller stream on a wooden bridge near a shepherd's house, the only habitation we saw. The gravelled track entered a narrow valley beside the stream we had crossed most recently. Just as the rain stopped, the caravan halted. Ahead lay a mudslide covering the road and all but blocking the stream at a point where it ran cheek-by-jowl against the rocks of the hills forming the valley to our left. It was a fresh slide, thick, black and at least ten metres across. Tash Rabat was still four to five kilometres away. No one knew of an alternative road and although we might have walked, the cookers and other equipment were not intended to be portable. Then the sun came out.

Boris alone benefited from this defeat. Not only did he film while the lorry was turned within its own length because the valley was so narrow, but his camera saw its left rear tyre go flat and watched at least part of the process of pumping it up again with the compressor they carried for such emergencies.

We returned past the house and the bridge to the wide pastureland beside the second stream. Except the hills, there was no shelter anywhere, but at least it was green and reasonably warm in the sun. The grass was a heavy stemmed plant mixed with others like an odourless artemesia. An irrigation channel overflowing with muddy water ran through the meadow nearby, useful for rinsing and boiling. We set up our tents near the road, using rocks to hold down the flaps because the ground was almost too hard for pegs despite the rain.

The cold of the evening and a wind that could have been worse were tempered by conviviality laced with an astonishing cellar of wine, champagne and vodka which the Russians had managed to assemble. Considering the alcoholic drought which had prevailed so far, both the quantity and variety indicated the perseverance of our Soviet friends. Dinner I can barely remember, except that it consisted of plof and many wonderful tins of fishy Soviet delicacies. The speeches were almost equally unmemorable but none the less heartfelt for that. We had all become remarkably close in the eight days since we had met at Leninabad. The chemistry was right, helped by the relaxed, not to say laid-back, manner of Yuri Badenkov. Experience combined with natural talent had taught him to direct a large group apparently by keeping still, and Dmitri Oreshkin was an ideal lieutenant, inventive and witty. The two interpreters smoothed our lives together and took the edge off the dominant maleness. Not only was there an absence of strain or competition, but we all realised that, despite the Iranians, excellent planning had made our Soviet journey fruitful. The party broke up about ten o'clock, but it is still going on.

Before we left the next morning, two minor chores had to be completed. We assumed that our cookery equipment would still be needed in China, incorrectly, and the girls, with some help from Artiom, had sorted out the cutlery, plates and cups. They also insisted we must have supplies to replace those we had contributed. Fortunately, I was able to hold their generous overcompensation to a minimum.

The second chore was to obtain from Dmitri an account of money we owed them. In some cases, he had paid for our petrol, hotel accommodation and food, and I had been singularly unsuccessful in keeping the books balanced. Furthermore, Paul had been their guest for two weeks. Finally, I had no idea what expenses the Institute of Geography had incurred to mount the entire expedition. Nor have I ever learned. Reluctantly, Dmitri listed specific payments he had made for us adding up to roughly 225 rubles. And then, using what remained of the 400 rubles obtained with such difficulty in Samarkand, plus all the Soviet currency possessed by my colleagues, we were unable to meet the entire sum! The shortage was small, perhaps 10 rubles, but embarrassing in the circumstances. I suggested a travellers' cheque, but Dmitri would not hear of it. We are left to repay the balance owing along with our debt of gratitude when they come to England.

Yuri drove our car, and Dmitri, Tolya, Boris and Dr Ertabyildyi followed in the jeep with Valery driving. We waved goodbye to the others at 9.00 a.m. Asian time: i.e. 10.00 a.m. Once we had to turn around because Yuri had forgotten his passport. After climbing through a 3,200-metres pass, the road climbed gently across a green plain towards the towering mountains. The only prominent vegetation was large cactus-like plants with pretty pink-white flowers. To the left, a lake around which the road turned along its southern shore gave no indication of our elevation of 3,700 metres. At about noon, we reached the border post at Turugart.

Yuri induced the Customs officials to permit the jeep to drive the two kilometres between the border post and the Russian-built arch of brick and stone marking the actual border. We all shook hands and exchanged hugs. Then we drove through the arch to the stone hut manned by two teenaged Chinese soldiers in overlarge uniforms. As they inspected us and our passports with some curiosity, we waved again to our Russian friends standing beside that monstrous arch.

# Chapter 9

# KASHGAR TO HOTAN

قەشقەردىن خوتەنگە

We descended quickly from the summit on the same kind of un-metalled road through the same gentle mountains, the high peaks seldom visible from the floor of the pass. Although we had now entered the Xinjiang Uigher Autonomous Region, the Customs post was manned by officials who represented China. The post was a village of one-storey whitewashed stone buildings on both sides of the road. The first of these on the right contained passport and Customs control. Now began Paul's long ordeal as interpreter.

The fact that Paul is bilingual led to perpetual double-takes by the people we met. He is over six feet tall and looks every inch an Englishman. Tom Ang is not only the shortest member of the team but has the yellowish complexion, the epicanthic folds and the straight black hair of the Oriental. He knew a few words of the language when we entered China and rapidly acquired more, being blessed with linguistic aptitudes, but contrary to the expectations of both Uighers and Chinese, and of the occasional European, he was relatively tongue-tied. Most thought he must be Japanese and simply refused to believe that he was ethnically akin to the Chinese amongst them.

While our passports were checked, we were told that the Kashgar road might be closed because of the unseasonable weather. We might have to spend a day or two with them. We had just returned to the car to prepare for Customs inspection, however, when a brown Toyota van came up the hill at speed. The six occupants were our Chinese hosts.

I had met Zheng Xilan, the youthful manager of the Mountain Scientific Expedition Advisory Service, in Beijing eighteen months before. Of average height, his face was dominated by the black-rimmed glasses that seem to be used universally by those who need them. Zheng greeted us with warm handshakes and at the top of his considerable lungs in a voice made even louder by his excitement.

With him was his deputy, Liu Guanjian, a tall slender whiplash of a man in his early thirties, best described as a Beijing yuppie. He too had a voice that would explode into the conversation like a cannon lit by verbal touchpaper. He could speak quietly but preferred not to. Someone supposed it was because he came from a large family, but he was an only child. He was to accompany us across China as our liaison with local authorities and proved himself to be hard-working, sensitive and intelligent.

Zheng Yupei, a charming and witty doctor from Urumchi, was to help us arrange medical contacts during our travels in Xinjiang. Zheng Yupei was a nutritionist who had done some work on the epidemiology of cancer in Xinjiang. He had a good English vocabulary which he used enthusiastically if

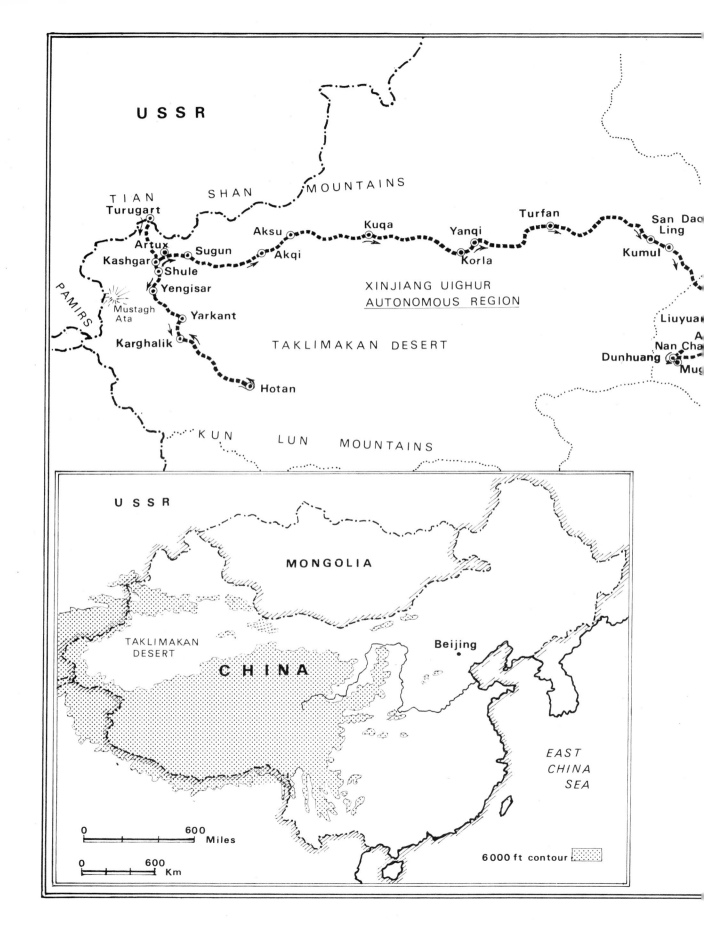

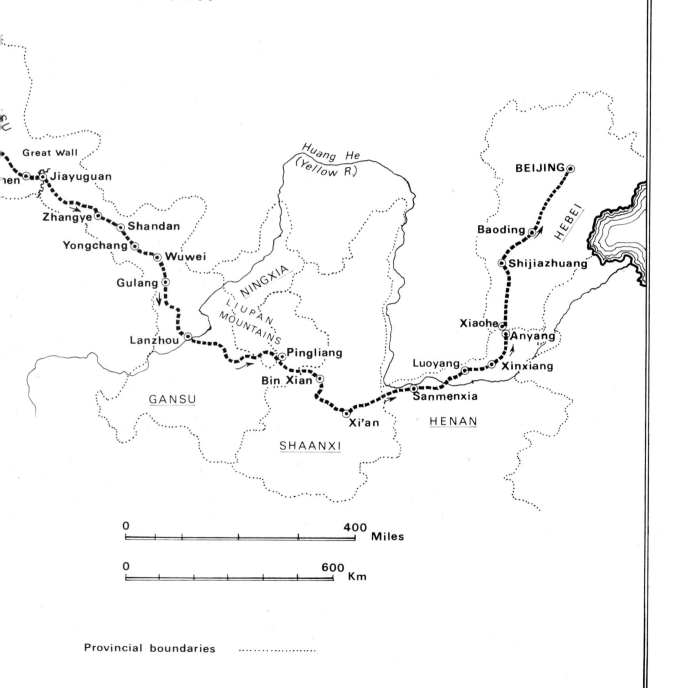

CHINA

Great Wall

Jiayuguan

hen

Zhangye

Shandan

Yongchang

Wuwei

Gulang

Lanzhou

NINGXIA

LIUPAN
MOUNTAINS

Pingliang

Bin Xian

GANSU

Xi'an

SHAANXI

Huang He
(Yellow R.)

BEIJING

Baoding

HEBEI

Shijiazhuang

Xiaohe

Anyang

Luoyang

Xinxiang

Sanmenxia

HENAN

0                          400 Miles

0                          600 Km

Provincial boundaries        ..................

inaccurately. He would "cough" instead of "sneeze", "come" when he meant to "go" and admitted his instructor in Urumchi complained, "I will practise not enough." His medical vocabulary filled in one of Paul's major lacunae, however.

Hu Youquan, a round-faced journalist from the *Guangming Daily* in Beijing, emerged from the Toyota snapping pictures. He embodied in his twenty-five-year-old person all that is most boring and least charming about the ideologue. He spoke no English, but Paul had to cope with him, and so did his Chinese companions! He occurred to the Advisory Service as a substitute for the TV coverage I had suggested. They paid his way.

The function of the youngest, Shen Peng from Beijing, was to drive our car. Shen was a quiet-spoken man with a huge smile, a wife and a very small baby. His mother was also part of the Advisory Service.

The sixth man was the driver of the Toyota, Liu Ziai, a cheerful family man from Urumchi. He was a serious man with a wicked sense of humour which he exploited at the expense of the Beijing journalist, capable of apparently endless driving and physically very strong. He was called Xiao Liu, Little Liu, to distinguish him from Deputy Liu. It is a diminutive and not applicable to a liaison officer.

The six of them had driven 1,500 kilometres from Urumchi to Kashgar in just two days. Their late arrival at Turugart proved that the road to Kashgar was open, barely.

Customs inspection turned out to be a non-event. An officer looked through the car windows, but waived even an examination of our luggage. We were the first people from the West ever to enter China through Turugart according to their records, the officer said. The light traffic consisted entirely of local people visiting friends or delivering goods on the other side and occasionally vice versa.

Here, as when we entered the Soviet Union, our clocks were set ahead two hours. Here it seemed less reasonable. Eastern Anatolia keeps the time of Ankara, 1,000 kilometres to the west, so that the sun rises and sets absurdly early. Soviet Armenia, due north of Mount Ararat, keeps sun time. Like all of China, Xinjiang keeps Beijing time. It grew dark about 11.00 p.m. and the sun rose around 8.00 a.m. Local life reacts accordingly. Shops open at 10.00 or 11.00 a.m. and close at 8.00 or 9.00 p.m. From our standpoint, we left the USSR at 1.00 p.m. and suddenly the clock said 3.00 p.m.

We were given our first Chinese meal at Turugart by the village authorities before beginning the long drive to Kashgar. A mere 160 kilometres, it took five hours. To say the road had been badly damaged by the recent rains is British understatement. Whole sections of it, amounting to 500 metres at a stretch, had been washed away and replaced by stream beds, haphazard piles of rocks ranging in size from pebbles to boulders. Not only was there a risk to the springs and suspension, but the tyres might so easily have been gashed by a knife-edged stone. Fortunately, these rocky rivers were dry.

At first the road – the phrase "such as it was" being understood for the next 100 kilometres – descended quickly through a jagged landscape lightly coated here and there with scrub. The stream on our right carried water from the high mountains. A little, two-wheeled cart pulled by a horse transported three soldiers up to the pass. We had been forbidden to take photographs until we reached Kashgar.

The first habitation was across the stream, totally nondescript but in brick and stone, probably a barracks. Very soon yurts appeared by the stream followed by small villages, three or four red mudbrick houses enclosed by red mudbrick walls. These buildings looked more like central Asia than like China. Every village had a small stand of willows either surrounding it or beside it. About half of the trees were newly planted or very young. We saw no sheep in this narrow valley. Perhaps these people managed as subsistence farmers.

The valley widened, and the mountains became hills with more and more fields amongst them. Now, flocks of sheep grazed further up the slopes. We crossed the river on a concrete bridge, and were stopped almost immediately at a police checkpoint which examined the Chinese passports but not ours.

The police were satisfied, but our hosts intervened. We must allow Shen to drive our car from now on. Chinese law required that all cars be driven by licensed drivers. Foreigners could not be licensed. Our International Driving Licences meant nothing. I had known this was coming. The irony that we had just completed the toughest drive of the whole trip was not even mentioned. One of the charges included in their account covered the salary and expenses of a driver. Hoping they would seek and find a special circumstance that could circumvent the law, I had refused to pay that charge when the banker's order covering all other costs had been remitted before we left London.

Zheng Xilan, whose voice could be heard in Kashgar over any traffic noise, insisted: "You cannot drive in China. You know that is our law." Paul conveyed the spirit if not the tone.

"I had hoped you would be able to accommodate us as the Soviets did. We were allowed to drive in the Soviet Union, although their laws are much the same." I am afraid this kind of comparison became all too frequent. Occasionally it had some effect, but not this time.

"You cannot drive. You cannot drive. Shen must drive. Let's go." Liu seemed almost beside himself. He was intimidating but even now, we could see it was manner, not substance.

"I think we had better do as they say," said Paul, sensibly.

Shortly, we were able to use the credit that came with acceptance. Every one of them smoked. We could and did insist that our car was off-limits for smoking, but we had no such authority over theirs. Instead, we simply said none of us would ride with them if they smoked while driving. These strictures they all accepted with good grace, and that nuisance died an early death.

I must add in fairness that both Shen and his colleague, Xiao Liu, Little Liu, were excellent drivers. Though the same can certainly not be said for all of their countrymen, we never had a moment's anxiety on their account. They drove up to eight hours in a day and then often took us several kilometres to see some monument after we had checked into our hotel. There was a secondary benefit, moreover. They had to register our car with local author-ities, and of course Shen was registered as its driver. That meant he was legally responsible for its maintenance. Not only did the duty to find suitable oil and keep the tanks full of petrol slip from my shoulders, but the inevitable failures and breakages also fell into Shen's capable and knowing hands. After consulting Liu Guanjian and us, he decided to do without the two rear shock absorbers rather than make the vain attempt to replace them. In the small city of Wubei, in Gansu province, Shen located a shop capable of replacing our shattered windscreen, albeit with ordinary glass, and had it done without disrupting our schedule. Both Shen and Xiao Liu were also interesting, educated men with a stamp of their own.

In any event, Shen moved into the driver's seat, to be displaced only once with noisy results. From an unmetalled, often non-existent track, the road now became a highway. At the junction with the road leading westward to Wuqia, the route we had asked to take originally, we entered a wide, fertile valley with frequent villages. The road crossed a barren ridge from which a great plain extended south and east as far as we could see in the gathering evening. It was our first glimpse of the Taklimakan Desert. And so we came to Kashgar.

Although I felt a distinct thrill at entering this ancient nexus on the Silk Road, it was subjective. Almost nothing of the past remains. Even the red mudbrick walls of the villages that line the road merging into the city itself were new. We drove down a long hill through an immense amount of traffic, wheeled, four- and two-footed, into a wide street lined by buildings that could have been anywhere except for the occasional tiled roof and gable-end curved up at the edges. On the right stood the new Friday Mosque. A more inappropriate and ill-conceived structure it is hard to imagine. The minaret was encircled by an outside staircase which led to a platform and blue mosaic-tiled dome supported by curved reinforced concrete girders with no infill. The hall itself was a box set on its small end. The same kind of civic mind that authorised construction of this monstrosity also approved the angular concrete high-rise town hall that blights the centre of Aylesbury half a world away in Buckinghamshire.

The Kashgar Guest House was less unlovely and, by design, more comfortable. The Marco Polo Expedition occupied five rooms along a ground-floor corridor. This was sensible and convenient, too convenient. Deputy Liu had a habit, slowly broken by the drip of our disapproval, of calling "Pau! Pau!" as he set out from the door of his own room to the one which Paul and I shared. Like any warning, it was effective, especially when it woke us after midnight. The first morning, however, it was the journalist, Hu, who appeared in the midst of our dreams, eager to have us read and approve his dispatch. So full of errors was it that I believe it was never sent. Indeed, as far as we know, the *Guangming Daily* never published a word about the expedition. Hu was a political hack and somebody's nephew. His Chinese colleagues thoroughly despised him.

A visit to the Foreign Affairs Department of the China International Travel Service, Kashgar branch, began as a duty but evolved into a pleasant surprise. We all drove into the outer compound of a white, single-storey building that had certainly seen better days though its age was unclear. Its windows and doors had simple, undecorated posts and lintels that looked European. The barn-like reception room contained the overstuffed leather furniture arranged in an open square familiar to all travellers to China, and we were given green tea while Liu and the Deputy Director discussed our route to Hotan. It was this man who told us that the border crossing west of Wuqia was closed. As the conversation became more general, I asked whether the Deputy Director happened to know the location of the former British Consulate in Kashgar.

"Yes, it was here," he replied. "It is our hostel for foreign students. You may look around outside the buildings if you wish."

Through the wide gate into the inner courtyard, I could see immediately Chini-Bagh, the much photographed residence built for George Macartney in 1898 when he was still merely the representative of the Indian government in Kashgar. Like the snowdrifts of childhood, the white, two-storey house with the pronounced classical lines looked smaller than it should. To the right, the orchard is much reduced in area, I think, and at the back beneath the great bay window and terrace, nothing at all remained of the garden although the view over the river valley is unimpaired by the nondescript warehouses that squeeze up to the elegant house. A Pakistani lad in a jalaba and an American girl in shorts asked if we wanted to see someone. I explained that until about 1948, this had been a British Consulate. They both smiled politely but were not impressed.

The other Great Power represented in Kashgar before the First World War was Russia. The former Russian Consulate, a larger structure, is now a lower-priced tourist hotel.

The chores that make travel possible filled the remainder of our first full day in China. Liu renewed our visas for one month and registered our car. Both vehicles needed petrol. Tom collected what mail there was in Poste Restante. Dr Zheng took Geoff and me to the First People's Hospital, a busy warren with a smell of carbolic on the ground floor. A dentist saw to his broken tooth, and I was prescribed something for my diarrhoea.

For about half an hour, the three of us sat in the shade of trees on a low wall separating the hospital forecourt from the street. It was the main road we had used to enter the city. In the dust and rising heat, the traffic was even heavier than the night before. Official cars account for roughly a fifth of the vehicles, bicycles and an occasional motor bike for about half and lorries belonging to manufacturing enterprises and farm villages perhaps a fifth. The remaining fraction is made up of two- and four-wheeled horse- or donkey-drawn flat bed carts that comprise the privately operated bus and taxi services in Kashgar and throughout rural China. These proportions remained roughly the same everywhere we went.

The main event of the first day, like the match for the heavyweight crown, began at 5.00 p.m. and ran on for almost four hours. It was the last of the great negotiating sessions that had characterised both my face-to-face dealings and my correspondence over eighteen months with the Mountain Scientific Expedition Advisory Service, a commercial body within the Institute of Geology of the Chinese Academy of Sciences, our Chinese sponsors. I had agreed charges amounting to £9,950 which had been paid, plus the gift of our car when we reached Beijing. Our food, accommodation, petrol and taxes had thus all been prepaid. Today's marathon dealt with four problems: the itinerary, charges for our driver (agreed at £1,050, but not yet paid), charges because of costs incurred by the Chinese as a result of the delays imposed by the Iranians and the costs of employing Dr Zheng.

In one corner, Zheng Xilan and Liu Guanjian. In the other, Paul and me with support from the others. Until Tom sensibly left to bring his notes up to date after the first two hours, we were two to one, but that advantage was more than compensated for by their strident and purportedly angry clamour, always regulated by politeness. They also had the advantage that they enjoyed the struggle. I believe that without it, they would have felt cheated. When it ended, the issues had been compromised, but the "we" and "they" had been established irretrievably. It emerged because the Service, interested only in money, failed completely to understand our objectives.

That the southern route around the Taklimakan Desert had been closed to us by the military at the very last minute, I had been advised just before leaving London. We were to be allowed to go to Hotan, still officially closed, but would then return to Kashgar and travel the northern route at the base of the Tian Shan range. At that time, their itinerary seemed wholly acceptable. Later changes, especially the addition of an overnight stay in Kuqa, were arranged with apparent ease by Liu who was beginning to understand.

The charge for Shen had been agreed, and I paid it as soon as I had an opportunity to obtain Chinese currency.

The costs they had incurred because of our delays were a matter of compromise. Without very clear evidence, they asked for £1,000. We agreed on £500 after reaching Beijing, largely because I was already very short of travellers' cheques. That the Soviets had made no such charges carried no weight.

They claimed another £500 to pay the costs for Dr Zheng. I had made it quite clear in our correspondence that any medical personnel accompanying us would do so at their expense. Zheng Xilan denied this, arguing that he had stepped into the breach after the Academy of Medical Sciences and the Ministry of Public Health had withdrawn as our sponsors. The latter was true. As to what I had written, we agreed to wait to see the letters in his file in Beijing. Suffice it to say, this charge was dropped. It was an embarrassing disagreement because, in the event, we appreciated the help of Dr Zheng and enjoyed his company. I never found out whether he knew about the argument.

Because it was cheaper, and the food was more varied and interesting than the hotel served, we had all meals in Kashgar, except the first breakfast, at a restaurant in the town centre. In CITS hotels, foreigners and Chinese are discouraged from dining together because the former are charged about five times more for the same meal, and the charges are levied per table!

After breakfast on July 23rd, the day after our marathon negotiations, we walked through the town to the bazaar. It spreads north and south of a public square filled with flowers and artificial ponds. Facing the square to the west stands the Id Kah Mosque, the former Friday Mosque still in use for worship and as a place of rest in the busy market. Under a line of trees to the south, a story teller had gathered a crowd of two dozen men and boys. He saw us join the group and lifted his voice very slightly. The clothing bazaar, housed in a large new enclosed shed, displayed goods from Pakistan and India as well as Canton and Hong Kong. There was more variety than in the Soviet markets though, on this Thursday, fewer shoppers.

The main iwan of the Id Kah Mosque is closed ordinarily, but entry into the garden is through a large gate in the south wall. Stone benches beneath the trees provide seats for people like me who want a rest. The dry earth is ungrassed, and I saw no open water. Two or three older men were sitting there with their sons and one grandson perhaps. One or two women wandered in and sat down to chat quietly. About one in twenty women still wear a headcovering on the street, usually an ugly brown wool shawl draped across the head and shoulders. We were told they were young and newly-married, obeying the injunctions of their husbands. The number of women covering their heads is said to be steadily declining.

The mosque itself is at the west end of the garden opposite the entrance iwan in the traditional layout. A large open porch is approached up a full-width flight of steps. Lightly-carved wooden pillars painted green support a flat white wooden roof. The ceiling is very plain except for occasional carved central panels. The entrance iwan to the inner hall is plaster painted in ochre, orange, red and blue. Much of the building has been built or restored fairly recently, but the plaster-work is similar to some entrances in the seventeenth-century tomb complex which I prefer to think of as the Tomb of the Fragrant Concubine.

This marvellous necropolis stands amongst trees behind a large artificial lake ten kilometres from the centre of Kashgar. In the guidebooks, the central tomb is called Abakh Hoja after a sage who was the grandson of an Islamic missionary named Muhatum Ajam. Chinese historical legends are never simple or straightforward, however. Some authorities maintain that the tomb is that of a descendant of the Hoja's family who became the concubine of a Qing Emperor about two centuries later. So lovely was she, and so great the love of her master, that the body did not begin to corrupt in the normal way, thus the Fragrant Concubine. Yet another school of thought attributes her fragrance to an "earth-date-like smell" she exuded.

Certainly, the perfectly-proportioned square tomb with its blue-and-gold tiled dome and four short minarets at each corner banded with vari-coloured square tiles warrants the poetic name. The entrance iwan decorated with three courses of tiles around the Islamic arch was no less magnificent. It led into a perfectly plain white chamber twenty-five metres square. A mezzanine formed by the squat drum was supported by four undecorated semi-domes, each of which added six metres to the floor space. The room contained several tombs covered with drapery and is still a shrine. In the right-hand wall, there was another entrance barred with a carved wooden grille. From the outside, people had tied small strips of cloth, a sign of prayer which we saw elsewhere in Xinjiang and also in western Gansu.

The Tomb of the Fragrant Concubine faced a paved open area with a square inset at a lower level that might have been a pool. Over the wall opposite the entrance to the open area extended a large graveyard. Before this entrance, several more tombs had been built, none of them as elaborate as the central tomb, each containing between twenty and thirty graves. The same family

Dr Zheng (far right) works during the interview at the Minorities Hospital, Hotan, Xinjiang.

continued to expand the necropolis for a century or more, and now it is being looked after by a grateful state.

We were given a tour of the Hospital for Traditional Medicine after a discussion with the doctors and the pharmacist the next morning. To our untrained eyes, the only remarkable difference between this hospital and the First People's Hospital where Geoff and I had been treated was the widespread use in the former of the acupuncture needle. Out-patients were being treated for colds with acupuncture, and in-patients for physical ailments ranging from diabetes to arthritic disorders of the hip and knee. One ward of eight beds was devoted to psychiatric patients. Not only needles but finely-tuned blue laser beams aimed at the base of the skull were being used to treat anxiety and depression. Because most Western-style hospitals also use traditional drugs, all pharmacies have a similar rich and comforting smell.

As our tour ended, we saw a television crew setting up their lights. It turned out they were also interested in us. Back at the Guest House, their producer explained that they had come from Xinjiang TV in Urumchi to make a documentary about various aspects of life in the region today. We seemed to fit their brief. A rather formal interview was set up in the hotel lobby with their two stars, actresses from Urumchi, and then of course they had to have the inevitable shots of the expedition members emerging from our vehicle.

Kashgar is still a city of red mudbrick like the suburban villages we saw as we drove in. New construction and repairs use baked bricks of the same colour. Xiao Liu dropped us at a main intersection from which a baked clay and dust street ran uphill. To the right of another broad intersection, partly dug into the hillside, stood an open chaikhana, the Turkish name used in Kashgar as in Leninabad. On a platform two musicians sat, one playing a drum, a flap of skin stretched over a round wooden frame, the other, an instrument consisting of a short bowl and neck with four strings. On two sides of the platform, within a low wall, men sat at tables drinking tea while, in the space left between the platform and the tables, a middle-aged man danced for an appreciative audience of children and adults, men and women, outside the wall.

Across the intersection stood a small mosque. The entrance gate, hardly an iwan, at the top of a short flight of steps was of carved wood and led into a cupola with a pink wash opening on to a porch where prayer mats lay. Beyond the porch was an enclosed room. The district was dotted with these tiny mosques. At the intersection of two lanes nearby, an even smaller structure had miniature painted-wood minarets about a metre high at the three street-side corners. Steps led to a first-floor porch with a wooden mimbar, but there was no enclosed space.

The men might all be relaxing at the chaikhana, the women kept out of the way, but the children were everywhere. In one narrow lane with windowless walls seven or eight seemed to hover in the air and settle in front of me. Aged from ten months to as many years, ragged and unwashed, they seemed happy and curious. An older girl carrying a baby walked up to me, snatched a biro out of my shirt pocket and disappeared into a doorway. A little boy carried a dead snake across a stick.

The upper storeys of houses made the lane into a tunnel in places, supported by heavy timbers. House entrances often sported well-kept decorative wooden doors with brass furniture. The houses looked like those in villages everywhere along the Silk Road, featureless mudbrick with nothing to set them apart as Chinese. Similarly, the people are not Han Chinese, but Uighers, a Turkic tribe, often with Mongolian eyes, but pale or brown skinned without a notably yellow cast. Intermarriage has been limited by religious differences and, perhaps even more, by Han racism. Dr Zheng and Xiao Liu, who lived in Urumchi, were Han Chinese, and neither of them understood Uigher, although Deputy Liu spoke enough for basic communication. Our Chinese friends frequently mentioned how dirty the Uighers are. Shen especially expressed relief when we found restaurants operated by Han Chinese. In Hotan, the Han Deputy Curator, Mr Li, deeply resented the Uigher Curator whom Li said was practically illiterate. Such attitudes are not supposed to exist in the People's Republic, but of course they do, just as in Britain. Yet Xinjiang is called a Uigher Autonomous Region, and perhaps, in time, it will be respected as such.

The magic of modern Kashgar is limited. While my colleagues went to look at a silk factory which turned out to be a sales showroom, I had my hair cut in the hotel for about 60p. The three-day stop had provided very necessary refreshment, comfortable beds, good food, beer with lunch and dinner for those who wanted it. We were all ready to move on. A quick glance at the map will explain the difference between the northern and southern route, north and south of the Taklimakan Desert, respectively. Both have sites of immense historical and archaeological interest, but Marco Polo had travelled the southern route which is less populous and much less well known. The early excavations undertaken by the great British archaeologist Sir Aurel Stein began at sites near Hotan and moved slowly east-north-east. But the southern route runs closer to the nuclear testing area in the vast depression of Lop Nor than the northern, and that could explain the decision by the military, if not its tardiness in pronouncing it. However we were to see no evidence that it was closed. The towns of Yarkant, Karghalik and Hotan were also theoretically closed though there were coachloads of European and Japanese tourists everywhere. Beyond Hotan, there were villages unlikely to boast hotels, and we had expected to camp occasionally in China as before. But our hosts had arranged hotel accommodation for every night. Often, it proved, camping would have been far more pleasant. Could these arrangements have conditioned the itinerary? Will we ever know?

The flooded Kashgar River, a rushing mass of brown water 100 metres across, showed that in the mountains it was still raining as we set off on our permitted excursion to Hotan. In the distance on the right as soon as we left the town, the massive snow-covered mountains of the Pamirs came in sight, dominated by the bulk of Mustagh Ata which Swedish archaeologist Sven Hedin, as well as English military explorers from Colonel Younghusband onwards, had tried to climb. The countryside was well cultivated, with corn and sunflowers most evident. A rooster strutted along a whitewashed wall in a mudbrick village.

At Shule, the town built by the Chinese as a garrison for Kashgar two centuries ago, there was a large mosque with the kind of courtyard that would indicate a madrasa, but no one seemed to know if there had once been one there.

At the next town, Yengisar, we stopped for lunch in an open-air café with dubious hygiene. The market, a series of roadside stalls in front of the café, specialised in knives, some of them probably made locally, with decorative handles and sheaths designed for tourists. Although I bought one, our Chinese colleagues each bought two, three, four or more. An extensive cemetery on the south-eastern boundary had old Uigher graves near the town. Newer graves had spread away from the town over perhaps a century. Part of the wall was new, built on a worn but massive mudbrick foundation. Beyond the cemetery stretched a shallow lake, a sign of the unusual weather. To the left a moon landscape of craters, rocks and sand dotted with scrub stretched off to the tree-lined river valley in the distance.

The road was generally well paved and raised from one to three metres above the level of the desert, a protection against flooding. Additional defences included long parallel mounds of rocks scraped up perpendicular to the road to deflect flood waters away from the raised road bed.

Yarkant, the first town in a rich oasis, was for centuries the terminus of the trails entering China from what is now Kashmir and Afghanistan. Undoubtedly, the artists who brought the Greek draperies of Gandhara to the towns along the base of the Kun Lun Mountains and even to such northern centres as modern Turfan, travelled via Yarkant. Today, it is a desert town looking like the stage-set for *High Noon*. Dusty trees and bushes have been planted along both sides of the main road. Behind the drab market on the right stood pieces of a city wall that could have been very old. There was a sewer pipe down the right side of the road ready to be installed. Paul discovered a little restaurant in the bazaar run by two boys and a girl, recent high school graduates, who had set up their own business with money supplied by the local authority. We drank tea and bought some bottled soft drinks. They had been open for a month; we wished them well. At the other end of this huge oasis, almost 100 kilometres across, lies the equally ancient town of Karghalik.

I had never expected oases to be so large. A few palm trees struggling for life around a drying well of bad water fitted my Beau Geste image better. We did pass through narrow strips of trees along a watercourse, but the oases scattered along both the northern and the southern routes around the Takli-makan, as far as we were allowed to travel, were large enough to hold several good-sized towns. Their trees were never palms, perhaps because it really is too cold for palms in these regions. They were willows and poplars with occasional hard-wood specimens like walnut. Usually, you crossed a clear line of vegetation at the entrance to an oasis. First there would be sand or gobi, sand mixed with rock, and then sand supporting trees and bushes, followed by crops of all kinds. Oases take many shapes, stretching out fingers along rivers or underground watercourses. The road may enter and leave the same oasis more than once. Even if this puzzles a traveller who cannot see where the fingers connect, the local people know it is a single cultivable region and cross the strips of desert between their fields and homes on carts or on foot.

Perhaps the most controversial issue is whether any given oasis is expanding or shrinking. The map indicates that the vast centre of the Taklimakan is without oases. Yet miles north of Hotan, for example, Aurel Stein found the remains of a city at least as large as Hotan that had flourished from roughly the time of Christ for almost 800 years, and many similar examples have been unearthed by Stein and others. Obviously, there must have been water there. Our guide told us that the Hotan oasis is expanding, an observation she supported by pointing to new lines of willows planted at some of its edges. Mr Li, Deputy Curator of the Hotan Museum, rejected this interpretation. He said that new trees replaced some of the hundreds of old ones that died without water. He believed that the amount of water flowing from the mountains, in this case the Kun Lun range, varies. So did Stein, but there is as yet no hard evidence.

The guest house in Karghalik consisted of a group of single-storey buildings with large verandas, most of them built originally as a Christian mission compound. The rooms were very large, dark because the customary desert sunlight was obscured by clouds during most of our stay, and crowded with double beds, overstuffed leather armchairs, the ubiquitous multiple-speed, multi-coloured standing electric fans, and buckets of water for the enamelled wash basins on their wooden stands, with a small shelf for soap but no hook to hold the towel. Paul and I had a room which had been occupied the year before by Hu Yaobang, then the General Secretary of the Chinese Communist Party. The toilets were a privy at some distance.

These clean, comfortable accommodations grew upon us because dinner was served soon after we arrived. Nowhere in China did we enjoy better food than at the Karghalik guest house. The sweet and sour spare ribs were prepared with a minimum of bright red sauce but a maximum of carefully nurtured flavour. Chunks of aubergine breaded and lightly fried suited my fractious digestion as well as my taste. Good local tomatoes were served everywhere but seldom as attractively sliced and presented with cucumber. Even the ubiquitous watermelon seemed better than in all the other places where it was served. We looked forward immensely to our stop at Karghalik for lunch on our return from Hotan a few days later.

In the quiet evening, I watched a woman leading two black and white sheep home from market. Beside a tree on the far side of a wide street, she half tethered the sheep, half held them herself. She squatted, her back against the tree and ate her supper, which looked like vermicelli noodles. People passed walking and on bicycles. No one took any notice.

The Post Office was a line of single-storey buildings looking temporary behind a new multi-storey concrete block in process of construction and surrounded by thick dust as long as it was dry. Paul wanted a telephone, which we were shown. The tree-lined road continued past low buildings to a large irrigation canal at the edge of town. Just over the canal bridge were the stalls selling dumplings and other edibles common in all these Xinjiang towns. It was getting dark as we returned to the guest house at about eleven thirty.

The market itself, like the Kashgar bazaar, occupied the land in front and to the side of the Friday Mosque. Indeed, at the opposite corner of the Karghalik bazaar stood a second small mosque, also in use on that Sunday. The large Friday Mosque, called the Jiang yi (Cami?) Mosque, was being rebuilt, and its 400-year-old entrance iwan and façade were being restored. The main structures are nineteenth-century, with octagonal wooden pillars painted with vertical stripes of red or crimson and green supporting a flat ceiling. These buildings each occupy the three sides of a square construction site that will probably become a garden again.

There is a local legend about the building of the Jiang yi Mosque which we were told by an historian who came round to the hotel that night by arrangement with the municipal Foreign Affairs Bureau. When construction began, the work completed each night was found in the morning to have been dismantled. Obviously, the builders were getting nowhere. They set watchers who observed at midnight a white camel that carefully removed the bricks laid in place during the day. No one knew where the white camel came from, but they decided to dig beneath the foundations of the new mosque. Sure enough, buried in the sand were iron images of the Buddha. They were melted down and recast as cauldrons whereupon the white camel disappeared and construction went ahead normally. Furthermore, iron left over from the casting of cauldrons was sold, and, with the proceeds, additional land was bought which became the bazaar and a source of income for the mosque until all land was nationalised after the Revolution in 1949.

At my request, the local historian also outlined points of archaeological or historical interest. With the exception of one site, all of them were some distance away, and, in his opinion, now contained too little of interest to warrant the drive. The exception was a ruined mud city in the desert nearby excavated by Chinese archaeologists but now closed to all visitors without special permission. We applied immediately to the local authority, but they could do nothing without approval from the regional capital, Urumchi.

Though we found this man helpful, his colleagues in other towns seldom were. In Korla, our request for some historical briefing was fulfilled by a party hack who recited by rote and knew nothing. In Hotan and Kuqa, the "historians" were local Foreign Affairs Bureau guides with inadequate English and even less knowledge. In the end we gave up asking for them, as not worth the price or the time.

The bazaar was busy. Indeed on a Sunday it is so crowded that motor traffic is banned from the town centre. Directly in front of the entrance iwan of the Jiang yi Mosque, two booksellers displayed volumes in Chinese and Uigher, as well as pictures that looked like they had been cut out of magazines. I was surprised to be told that most books had to do with Islam, though there were also Turkish textbooks and Turkish-Uigher dictionaries.

Just across the unpaved walking space between the rows of booths, a jeweller repaired trinkets and silver and copper household items brought to him. He used two charcoal braziers, a large one to heat the object and keep it hot, and a small one for close working. A sheepskin bellows usually held beneath his left arm on the bagpipe principle directed air to both braziers through two tubes. He could direct the larger one to a place in the larger brazier, but he used the smaller tube for precise delivery of air to the coals beneath the spot undergoing repair.

There was no lack of vegetables. One stall was selling onions, garlic, piles of ground yellow pepper, green peppers, tomatoes, small piles of potatoes, what looked like parsley, small aubergines, radishes, cabbages, cos lettuces, cherry tomatoes, small white onions, marrows, pale local carrots and chili peppers. At another there were three different kinds of rice and at a third, raisins, currants, walnuts, various spices in bags and sunflower seeds. Beside them were old ladies sitting on the ground selling tomatoes and boiled potatoes. In the section near the small mosque were sold horseshoes and taps for the heels of human shoes. Naturally, a whole building was devoted to clothing and fabrics, many of them, as at home, from Hong Kong and Pakistan. Along one side of the bazaar and along the street in front, stalls and restaurants offered hot food: bread in various forms, plof, kebabs – the food we had eaten throughout central Asia.

There was a wind blowing as we left Karghalik. Despite the vapour haze and the clumps of green vegetation scattered across the desert, the land was dry enough for sand devils to appear, small tornado funnels that whirl across the surface. They carry sand and debris and look as though they could be easily avoided, at least until they coalesce into a sand storm, an event which we happily missed.

The desert could be either very flat or lumpy and full of jagged rocks. For a few miles, the road was built at the same level as the desert. It was covered with mud in many places. Standing water appeared frequently. At one point, a river ran down from the south, passed beneath the road in a culvert and emerged only to disappear in the sand in clear view. Still, sand devils raced across the green-spotted brown hills. The Kun Lun Mountains to the south remained distant, featureless objects.

The Hotan oasis is about the same size as the Yarkant-Karghalik oasis, but the former has two parallel rivers entering it from the south and leaving it to the north. Long green arms extend along these waterways. Until about a thousand years ago, the rivers running away to the north supported the cities excavated by Stein. They are thought to have crossed the entire desert and to have flowed into the Tarim, a river followed by much of the northern Silk Road which gave its name to the great central basin of the desert. Like the Hotan River, the Tarim too is dry now. It seems odd that so little attempt has been made to understand the fluctuations in these river systems inasmuch as the patterns might be used to predict future changes in the desert.*

Just before a village near the entrance to the Hotan oasis, the road was covered by half-flattened bales of straw. Farmers stood by with the horse-drawn carts from which some were still unloading straw. This became a familiar sight throughout China. The passing lorries and cars are being used to crush the straw as a preliminary to squeezing out the oils. What we saw was probably rape. One or two of the clinicians we met on our route expressed horror at the thought of the carcinogens being collected in the straw from the tarred road surface.

Though probably older and certainly more important historically, modern Hotan has less of the settled appearance of Karghalik and more the dusty, Wild West look of Yarkant or even Kashgar. As recently as the beginning of the last century, Hotan was the capital of a vigorously independent princely state. Before the beginning of this century, it was the first sign of civilisation visited by many of the British military explorers concerned about the threat that Russian influence in Chinese Turkestan might hold for India from which they all came. Because of the military experience, Aurel Stein's first expeditions also approached China through the 5,000-metre passes that lead to Hotan.

Our guide, an attractive Han Chinese mother of two, was confused about the role Stein played in Hotan. This account depends more on Mr Li of the Hotan Museum whom we actually met after we had visited the sites. Our first objective was Mei Li Ke Wa Ti, some twenty-five kilometres from the centre. The track led out of the oasis, through the city airport and into the desert, but then re-entered the oasis near one branch of the southern river, emerged again and climbed into barren desert hills above and to the west of the river. Impressive but completely nondescript piles of ruined mudbrick constructions were scattered some distance apart across a wide landscape. In a few places, the remains of walls lining what may have been cellars could be seen. Everywhere across the gobi, mixed with the stones and sand, were shards of pottery. The site is large, about 1,500 metres north to south by 450 metres, but it is oddly situated being both high above the river and a considerable distance from it, with no sign that the river itself had shifted its course just there. Li and others say it is the remains of pottery kilns which may have exploited the local clay and flourished in the last century. Almost certainly, it was not explored by Aurel Stein, at least not in any systematic manner.

On the other hand, he is said to have worked at Yeturgan as early as 1901, though there is no reference to the site in his publications. Either he found it unproductive or decided against systematic excavation there too. One can see

* A Sino-French air-survey team began relevant mapping in the Hotan region soon after our visit. Their work is to be continued and extended in connection with the UNESCO Integral Studies of the Silk Road.

why. Yeturgan is in the northern part of the oasis in the midst of irrigation channels and cultivated fields. According to Mr Li, the site was revealed two centuries ago by a change in the course of one of the two main rivers. The artefacts picked up by local people included gold and silver items so that a sort of gold rush ensued. The precious metals and certain geographical features of the site suggest that it was the ancient capital of a region then known as Yütian, but no direct evidence such as city walls or written records has ever been unearthed. This could well be because so much has been destroyed by continuous occupation and irrigation farming. Today, the casual observer sees nothing at all except one straight barrow-like earthwork which could be either the remains of a wall or the overgrown clay from the dredging of an irrigation canal.

The small collection in the Hotan Museum contains nothing from the local sites, but there is a handful of exciting items from further afield. One small red clay head from Niya, Stein's first important dig 100 kilometres further east and therefore closed to us, would have been a candidate for holography. Deputy Director Li was in favour, but the policy of the museum would require payment of a substantial fee. In the event, the amount was never discussed because the Director refused permission anyway. It was the first disappointment to arise directly from the failure of our Chinese hosts to prepare the way for our visits with local authorities.

Between heavy, squally rain storms, mainly without thunder and lightning, the sun would glare forth with sudden heat. All the women in the street were wearing headscarves, probably as protection against the rain. Men wore the square embroidered felt Uigher hats with the low peak, possibly also against the weather. In addition, both men and women had a white muslin scarf pulled over whatever headcovering they were already wearing, and some of the women held the muslin in place with a small hat on the crown of their head decorated with bead designs in black or gold. This final touch looked incredibly elegant.

My notes for the next day, Wednesday, July 29th, begin characteristically for this part of the journey: "Again an overcast morning and a bit chilly. To come to the depths of the desert to have London weather is a bit surprising at least."

We spent most of the day inside, factories in the morning and hospitals in the afternoon. Having been assured that the Hotan silk factory was indeed a manufacturing plant and not just a sales room, I went along and was not disappointed. We were shown how the worms in their cocoons are treated, how the fine fibres are unwound and immediately twisted with others into thread of varying dimensions. Each step in the process has been mechanised. Hand work is still required in certain printing processes, and the factory seemed to be labour-intensive, but machinery at least assisted the bleaching, dyeing, weaving, and so on. The noise in the spinning mill was deafening, near the permitted limit of eighty decibels, we were told. No attempt is made to protect the staff except by providing mid-shift breaks. The plant had expanded recently, and the huge new workshop was much lighter than the old with its clerestory windows, but much hotter because ventilation was less effective. The silk works had no sales rooms at all, a sign that it was off the tourist track.

The carpet factory, on the other hand, consisted of a reception room where tea was served, a large sales room next door and, at some distance, a wooden barn with a ceiling supported by magnificently-worked beams and high enough to take the looms, of which there were about a dozen. Some were being worked by three or four men and women. We saw no more advanced machinery in use by the Hotan carpet factory and were told that much of the work was carried out as a cottage industry throughout the oasis. Some of the carpets for sale, however, certainly could have been machine-made. A majority of the designs are copies or at least adaptations of traditional Hotan carpets, a blend of styles drawn from all over central Asia. To my eye, they were often coarse and overbright, probably because aniline dyes used today lack the subtlety of natural dyes. But the go-ahead young Director had found designers to produce new products, many of them beautiful. I was particularly attracted by a pile of kelim-style carpets where the bright colours fit angular modern designs effectively. They cost about £40 for a four-foot by six-foot carpet. Despite the transportation difficulties, Paul bought one and struggled with it all the way to London.

Oesophageal cancer is not common in this part of the Taklimakan and therefore not high on the list of clinical problems. The conversations at both the People's Hospital and the Uigher Minorities Hospital dealt generally with the health of the area. At the Minorities Hospital, we were shown into the usual reception room and seated along the window wall. Opposite us sat the senior hospital staff, the Director and eleven of his colleagues. All were men, this being a Uigher and therefore a Muslim establishment. Excepting one who wore a moustache, all were bearded. Their ages ranged from about thirty to about seventy, but age predominated, an unusual occurrence in modern China. The older men wore traditional clothing, white muslin pyjamas in the Indian rather than the Arab manner. Everyone wore a headcovering, varying from the Director's Mao cap to skull caps or high square black hats. Several of the older doctors had been amongst the founders of the hospital twenty-five years before. Their principal spokesman was a small well-spoken man about sixty with a close-cropped white beard and a grey moustache, dressed in modified European clothing and wearing a Uigher hat and metal-framed glasses. Although he understood Chinese, as did the Director who had been educated in Western medicine in Beijing, the spokesman and the others spoke Uigher which had to be translated for Paul into Chinese *pu tong hua*, and then by him into English. It was a long session. The melon, peach and pear seeds from the beautiful bowls of fruit piled up on the shelf beneath the tables in front of us. One of the pyjama-clad founders sat cross-legged on his bench. One nodded off. We talked about some of the drugs commonly used by the population, but the real interest remained with our hosts, collective proof that an ancient culture thrives, especially amongst the sick.

That night, Deputy Director Li called on Paul and me to interview us, he said, for the local paper. We were surprised because such arrangements are usually made in advance with an agreed appointment. It is one of those matters about which the Chinese are punctilious. A man of average height, aged perhaps forty, Li is a Han Chinese with a quick mind and dissatisfied manner.

He did begin with questions about the expedition and wrote down our answers in a notebook. Inevitably, he asked what we thought about Hotan and this led to our discussion about the expansion and contraction of oases. We were sitting in the gathering twilight on the large flat roof of the ground floor to which French doors from the hallway opened just in front of our room. We had the roof to ourselves.

"What do you think of the museum?" Mr Li asked.

"You have a few very beautiful pieces, unusual in our experience for such a small museum."

"I am sorry you could not take the pictures you wanted. I have been here ten years and can go nowhere because the Director must be a Uigher. He is an uneducated man, as you saw, but I must take orders from him."

"Perhaps you will be able to change jobs to a larger museum."

"I cannot travel. There is no money. I am not allowed to receive foreign publications, just an occasional article or picture. I cannot apply for other work. There is no arrangement."

Mr Li had brought us two issues of an archaeological journal in which articles by him had appeared. "Surely, you will become known by your articles. Perhaps another museum management will ask for you."

"Impossible. I have no resources for research here, no library. There is nowhere I can obtain books. Even the works of Aurel Stein, a great man. He did so much to preserve important examples of our past. People say he was an imperialist who stole from us. It is not true. He saved what would otherwise have been lost. I have only read about him."

"Can you not order books from other places?"

"How? I do not know where they are. Why should other libraries send them to me? We do not have such arrangements. We do not allow people to grow and learn."

"Can you enroll in a university so that you can take courses in archaeology? You would also have a library available, of course."

"I need special permission from the municipal party. They do not like me because I complain. Also, I am getting too old to attend university. Here, university places are for young people. No, it is not possible. Our system makes no allowances for people who already have a position."

Mr Li enjoyed the opportunity of unburdening himself to Western foreigners, one of whom spoke Chinese as a mother tongue. We offered to send him the course catalogue for the School of Oriental and African Studies at the University of London and one or two other items. Otherwise, we could only give him a sympathetic ear. Paul knew something of Li's complaints, especially from the time of the Cultural Revolution. But there was obviously nothing we could do to help, and there was always the possibility, though it seems very remote, that Li had a second job testing the attitudes of foreigners to the regime.

It rained heavily during the night. We left Hotan on our return journey under overcast skies through a damp desert. About noon, we could see ahead a disorderly mass of cars, coaches and lorries faced in both directions and stopped at where the road had been completely washed away for roughly twenty metres. A horde of men were trying to fill the gaps with sand. Without earth-moving equipment apart from shovels, the job would require at least the rest of the day. The freshet responsible for the damage still stood about as surface water over a wide area on both sides of the road but had stopped flowing. The vehicle in front of us as we approached the jam was a local coach. We watched as the driver moved slowly forward towards a break in the road surface which looked as though it might be passable. The front coach wheels rolled into the sand and sank to the hubs. Carrying luggage and small animals, everyone climbed off the coach. We reversed the car and, using a brand-new towing strap, slowly pulled the coach back on to the solid pavement. Meanwhile, a group of Swiss tourists had left their coach and were making their way by foot away to the left in order to cross the stream. What they were going to do about their coach was unclear. To our right, one or two cars and some lorries set off to find solid ground and a ford across the stream. We followed and soon regained the road beyond the break.

Between Yarkant and Yengisar the next day, we came upon a second washout. This one was narrower, but the road surface was built up further from the desert floor. A lorry had ended radiator down in the great gap. The jeep sent to rescue it looked a little inadequate for the job. We would have done no better given the size and location of the lorry, but we were going the other way and did not have to test our strength or skill again. We forded the stream, now a placid brook, and continued on our way. There were occasional breaks like this north of the desert, but all of them seemed much older. Approaching breaks in the road surface might not be clearly marked in advance, but the detours were well-established tracks, often widely scattered to show where different vehicles had tried their luck. Traffic had to slow down, but traffic jams hereafter had causes other than flash floods.

# Chapter 10

# AKSU TO TURFAN
## ئاقسۇ قە تۇرپان

Just outside Kashgar heading north-east towards Aksu, we passed a cemetery without the rounded tops characteristic of Uigher gravestones. The variety in size and design of the stones suggested it could be Christian despite the apparent absence of the cross.

People were sweeping both sides of the road with besoms, raising clouds of dust in the early-morning sunshine. Thus began the final leg of our journey. To the left ran jagged red hills and to the right, flat gobi covered with white powder, evaporated mineral salts leached from the ground when the standing water from recent rains dried up. In the flats on the right a lake appeared in the distance, holding its place so it was not a mirage. Reeds grew near the shore, and the water looked very shallow. When the road rose a little, the view towards the south was a featureless sandy plain. To the north the mountains emerged suddenly in ranges so close that we could not see the highest snow-covered peaks behind them. Colours ran in bands, wide horizontal bands of red-brown in the nearer hills; two ranges of green-brown behind, and finally a much higher range which was red-brown again. On the right, we approached a second lake, somewhat larger than the first. From one of the rare houses along the road, a small boy emerged and walked towards the lake, carrying a string of fish.

We drove through Artux, Sugun, Akqi, all villages with small markets in small oases, before reaching Aksu, a regional capital important as a major stopping place along the northern Silk Road. Its bazaar was lively but smaller than the one in Karghalik. A new Friday Mosque had been finished recently on a dusty street lined by the stalls of meat sellers. The mosque reiterates the traditional floor plan of central Asia: an entrance iwan, fairly narrow but tall with decorative minarets built symmetrically on the top, leading into a tree-shaded garden. Opposite the entrance, a large porch approached up two steps was covered by a flat roof supported by rows of columns painted with flat bands of fruits and vegetables in bright colours. The entrance to the inner mosque was plain, and the mihrab had only a band of tiles across the top with words celebrating Allah. Benches scattered around the garden were for everyone. Two old ladies without headscarves shared mine. Three men knelt on the carpets covering the porch to pray.

There was plenty of time in Aksu for an interview with the hospital staff, first with those trained in Western medicine, and, separately, with a Uigher doctor and pharmacologist who practise traditional remedies. A man from the local health department acted as interpreter into *pu tong hua* for the latter two. These people were all eager to be helpful, but the time was too short and the questioning too inept to yield much more than their names and addresses. I decided in future to ask what we could do for them on our return that they might find useful. During later interviews, I asked the question regularly. A few people asked for Western literature, occasionally for specific books and articles. In Xi'an, the head of a department of immunology wanted addresses where she might be able to buy certain chemicals.

The local specialist in the archaeology of the region gave us directions about places of interest along the road to Kuqa. Several beacons, built when the western Han dynasty conquered this vast territory in the first century before Christ, still stand albeit as stumps which take a practised eye to identify. We passed at least one to the right of the road between Aksu and Kuqa, but the watch tower ten kilometres north of Kuqa is outstanding. It stands about ten metres high, lacking only its top platform, and the access doors at ground level can be seen. The construction, layers of mudbrick divided roughly every metre by a floor of willow trunks, some of which now stick out like a narrow ledge around the wall, must be very stable, like reinforced concrete. Defensive walls and even stupas and other shrines use the same techniques.

But if something could be seen of occasional beacons, only one of the caravanserais was identifiable. That stretched across the present road on top of the high west bank of a wide stream, a northern tributary of the Tarim River. To be honest, these foot-high walls might have been anything, but a caravanserai would be expected beside a ford over a river where a community of monks also lived.

The opposite bank was a red sandstone cliff perhaps fifty metres high. Rows of cave entrances could be seen at water level and ten metres up the cliff, but no means of access was visible. We walked down into the stream bed and even began to ford the shallow river but it deepened in the middle and no one felt like a swim. Even with binoculars, we could see nothing inside the caves, but our useful informant in Aksu said remains of Buddhist murals had been discovered in them.

There was also a modern village near the river. As in others we had passed during the day, a local market thrived. Always, these communities were surrounded by cultivated areas, oases that might interlink further south near the Tarim. Between the towns, people were moving on the same two- and four-wheeled flat bed carts pulled by a horse or donkey that we had seen in Kashgar. It was a Sunday and the first day of an annual Uigher holiday lasting a week. Unfortunately, we never found out exactly why, perhaps because people we asked thought even we ought to recognise a harvest festival.

Kuqa is smaller than Aksu, low and dusty. In the seventh century, it was the Chinese capital of the Tarim basin. There is evidence that during this period, Kuqa provided refuge for Iranians fleeing from the Arab conquest of their homeland.

The guest house was full, but the transport hotel had rooms for us. Built with pretensions, on a Russian model, the transport hotel looked as though it had seen better days. Dormitories used by local travellers and lorry drivers and some offices filled the first two floors and possibly the third. Bedrooms for foreigners were on the fourth. Running water extended no higher than the ground floor, and although we had electricity, it went off about nine o'clock, just as dusk settled. The hotel restaurant was no less spartan. Here was a very good example of a town where camping would have been more comfortable than a hotel had our Chinese hosts come prepared with the necessary equipment.

Stark though it was, I felt we could not complain about the accommodation because arrangements for us to stay in Kuqa had been made from Aksu after the archaeologist confirmed that the grottoes there ought not to be missed. Liu, our liaison officer, telephoned officials of the Kuqa Foreign Affairs Bureau to whom I am grateful.

Gratitude does not extend to the guide they assigned us, however. He met us at the transport hotel. Mercifully, I did not record his name. He was about eighteen and told us immediately that he usually led parties of Japanese. His English showed signs of having been translated from that language. Paul spoke to him in Chinese, of course, so that the profundity of his ignorance about the monuments could not be blamed on a language barrier. Although this embodiment of the tourist trap charged us for his services, his sole value was as a poor substitute for a map. My complaint is not about the money, a mere £7.50 which is hardly excessive for four hours of anybody's time, nor about the boy's inadequacies as such. He was assigned to us because the Foreign Affairs Bureaux and CITS offices all supplement their incomes by foisting poorly-trained and half-educated local guides and interpreters on travellers. I also object that although they had provided some medical support, our hosts had failed to lay on the kind of archaeological and historical advice made available to us in the Soviet Union. I should have built the Kuqa grottoes into our itinerary, and had Buddhist art history been my speciality, I would have, as I did with the much more famous grottoes at Dunhuang and Luoyang. But I had paid the Mountain Expedition Advisory Service a large sum of money to make up for our deficiencies. The services they supplied in return were patchy, to put it politely.

The Caves of a Thousand Buddhas, Ka Zi Er, are seventy-five kilometres west-north-west of Kuqa. It was an interesting road, the early trading route, running beside streams with regular supplies of water, in the spectacular foothills of the Tian Shan. The landscape was astonishingly grey, jagged and uncultivated, except for occasional small oases near rivers, like the one surrounding the grottoes. The road through the mountains towards Urumchi runs north from this alternative east-west connection with Aksu.

Six grottoes are now open for public viewing. There are about 230 altogether, either natural or manmade enlargements of natural caves in the sandstone or loess cliffs. Authorities see strong Iranian influences in these pictures, but to the untutored eye their inspiration is Indian. The murals celebrate Buddhist legends in colours made from minerals dissolved in water. Blue, both light and dark, green and an earth colour predominate, but yellow, red and probably black were also used. The murals are acts of worship, exactly like illuminated manuscripts and the Church art of the Middle Ages and Renaissance, designed to instruct as well as to enhance faith. The earliest probably date from the beginnings of Buddhism in the region during the third century, and new murals were painted sometimes in caves already decorated until the Arab conquest was confirmed by the spread of Islam amongst the local princes in the tenth and eleventh centuries. Then many of the murals were destroyed because they portrayed human figures. Destruction has gone on ever since. Thieves seeking valuables vandalised the murals. Western archaeologists cut chunks out of them for removal to Berlin or Stockholm. The Cultural Revolution disapproved of reactionary art. And through the ages, natural wear and tear has added to the damage. Styles of painting tended to change from a primitive linear outline filled by colour to baroque draperies and landscapes. Though the Kuqa murals were badly damaged, they were nevertheless an eye-opener, an appetiser for glories to come.

Ka Zi Er is a state enterprise, restoration being undertaken by the Xinjiang Ministry of Culture. Income from tourism must be small because the number of foreigners that can be accommodated in Kuqa is so limited. In fact, the city is technically closed, though, like Karghalik and Hotan, that status seems to mean only that there is no garish new tourist hotel. The grottoes at Ka Zi Er are directly under the care of a small community of Buddhist monks, however, judging by their costumes. They live in a new dormitory building constructed of logs, possibly from the surrounding woods stretching beside the stream. Whether their work on the grottoes is a part of their worship we did not learn, but their presence was unique; none of the other caves we visited were still the responsibility of a religious community.

When we arrived, the sky had been unexceptionally blue and sunny. Quite suddenly, it blackened. There was a flash of lightning, a clap of thunder out of *Siegfried*, and the rain belted down. It rained for half an hour until we began to wonder about the two streams we had to ford. Dr Zheng and Xiao Liu, the Toyota driver, had taken shelter on the wide wooden porch of the dormitory. The monks asked us to stay the night. With a sense of our own intrepidity, we declined. Within minutes, the sun came out. Though there was probably more water in the streams, the two fords proved manageable. Between them, a herd of camels, both bactrians and dromedaries, I thought, had moved up nearer the road where there was fresher grass.

A smaller complex of grottoes occupies dun-coloured cliffs beside a dried-up river bed about ten kilometres north of Kuqa quite near the well-preserved Tang beacon tower. Called Kizil Gaha, meaning Caves of the Girls Having a Rest, we were told, these grottoes are said to have been occupied for a much shorter time, from the eastern Han, about the first century AD, to the period of the Three Kingdoms in the sixth century. Very little remains of the murals in the four caves we were shown, and yet the vitality of the drawings that can be seen shows that the artists had a long tradition on which to build. Styles and colours were similar to those in the larger complex, as one would expect. In cave sixteen, on a relatively protected part of the wall near the back of the cave behind a platform on which a Buddha statue must once have stood, two small murals about a metre square seemed to concern the lives of the community of monks. One showed a laundry. The other was a bathhouse. Both were painted in light blue and tan with full figures, all men, outlined in black. The bathhouse scene was explicitly erotic, the only such depiction I saw in the Buddhist caves we visited. Incidentally, the damaged wall above these murals revealed clearly how the surface was prepared for them: a thin mixture of mud and straw was spread over the rough-hewn cave wall, trowelled smooth and allowed to dry.

Between the caves and the main road to Kuqa, we passed a modern Han

Chinese graveyard. Wooden structures mark the newer graves, many of which were littered with tins and bits of metal foil, the refuse from meals eaten in the vicinity as part of the funeral observances. These multifaceted cemeteries are documents of the cultures and religions that use them. In Istanbul, Ottoman cemeteries beside the great mosques such as the Süleymaniye have gravestones with the official head-dresses of their occupants carved on top to demonstrate their status for all time. At Ahlat in the great necropolis beside Lake Van, Seljuk and Ottoman turbes, or mausoleums, are dotted amongst the post-and-lintel gravestones, many still intact, containing carved inscriptions like those on Christian gravestones in English cemeteries. Many of the Kirgiz cemeteries are as new as the villages beside which they stand, and their gravestones and small domed pavilions reflect, in their simple lines, the Muslim inspiration. I have mentioned the Christian cemetery outside Kashgar, identifiable by the variety of its elaborately carved monuments rather than the cross, which was barely in evidence. Near Kumul, we saw a cemetery containing both Han and Uigher graves. Each nation had its sector. Uigher gravestones had a characteristic round protuberance carved on top of a plain rectangle of stone. Han graves were marked by a metre-high cone of small rectangular stones. Beside this graveyard stood an elaborate turbe in the Chinese style housing the tomb of an eighth-century Arab saint, one of three Muslim holy men invited to explain their doctrines to the Chinese Emperor, moved to this spot from the Xinjiang-Gansu border in 1945!

Before we left Kuqa, Paul recorded an interview with a party of Chinese who were planning to walk across the Taklimakan from Aksu to Hotan using two camels to carry equipment. The two men were students at the Aeronautical Institute in Beijing, the girl, who spoke English, a friend and reporter on the *Beijing Evening News*. A Uigher acquaintance of the two men was the fourth expedition member with the principal role of interpreter and camel driver.

"We want to see what the desert is really like, but camels are expensive, about 600 yuan (£100) each," explained the *Evening News* reporter, "and we were told that the price would be higher if we tried to negotiate in Chinese."

"How are you paying for the trip?" I asked.

"From our own savings, mainly, but the Xinjiang Academy of Sciences has lent us some camping equipment, a tent. We have also borrowed items from other institutions."

Paul suggested we give them one of our water filters now that we were using them only for our drinking water. Large, awkwardly-shaped blue plastic bottles, they defy easy storage, but there is no doubt about their efficacy. The Chinese party accepted with thanks.

"When are you actually leaving?"

"This week, but we have to go first to Aksu," she said. "We had expected to begin here, but there is a track from Aksu of course."

"Are there many informal exploration parties like yours these days?"

"We know of no others, but everyone has been most helpful and friendly to us."

Their adventure reflects the new economic era. Individual enterprise is encouraged, apparently even when it has no immediate financial objective. A small independent group like this arranging its own travel through dangerous terrain would not have been permitted five years ago. Self-reliance has always been a rare Chinese virtue. No doubt it is a double-edged virtue promoting self-interest ahead of honesty and plain-dealing, as we in the West have known even before Samuel Smiles, but it leads to enterprises exemplified by a trek across the Taklimakan (and the Marco Polo Expedition).

Normally adventures in China serve a purpose, as they do with us. A tall raffish Chinese wearing an American stetson joined us while we were chatting with the travellers. He had perfected his English during two years studying geology at the University of Michigan. Now, he was employed as a petro-geologist by the Ministry of Mines and Energy.

"I've just completed two years prospecting for oil in the northern Tarim basin," he said.

"Alone?"

"As part of a team. We had a surveyor and two men who could handle the test-drilling equipment. I was responsible for advising where to drill. We were not attempting to strike oil of course, but only to check the upper layers of sand."

"Can you say what results you have had?"

"Hopeful, I believe, but now it is necessary to try actual pilot wells, an expensive and time-consuming operation. I am going back to Urumchi to prepare my preliminary report to the Ministry. Then I shall be returning to Beijing. Perhaps you know that China is already self-sufficient in oil."

Like Aksu, Kuqa and Korla are on the northern edges of their respective oases. Not far away to the north are the Tian Shan, but the dried-up river basins are to the south. Perhaps the road ran closer to the mountains or even through them because there was water there, and the principal market places in the oases developed beside the road. Certainly, there was a highway along the route we were following before the Christian era. The edges of these northern oases are less sharply defined than in the south. You emerge from intermittent stretches of desert and trees into gobi, now lightly coated with green because of the recent rain.

Beside the road where the Korla oasis begins, a shrine consisted of tall poles bound together to lend mutual support with pieces of cloth tied to them, the visible signs of individual prayers. It looked like the grave marker we were shown beside an ancient walnut tree outside Hotan.

We passed people in a donkey cart with a dog, and behind them, a line of three donkey carts each with a covering of plastic tied to arched willow trunks like a sunbather's prairie schooner. Two of these had dogs tied to the back. I suspect the dogs were being delivered to market like sheep and for the same reason.

The road enters Korla from the north, along with the railway to Urumchi. Lacking any monuments of consequence, Korla is nevertheless a city with an unusually interesting history. Not only the railway but also an ancient highway link it to the northern half of Xinjiang, and of course the Silk Road ties it to East and West. In the 1770s, moreover, a remarkable Mongol tribe resettled in the vicinity of Korla. For 150 years, this tribe had lived on the banks of the Volga in southern Russian where it had migrated from a central Asian homeland. The tribe had retained its identity and in consequence had

The road to Kashgar on the Chinese side of the Turugart Pass.

Between Pingliang and Lanzhou, Gansu Province. ▶

Fishing near the Tomb of the Fragrant Concubine, Kashgar.

A roadside cafe near Aksu, Xinjiang.

suffered both legal and social discrimination from the Russians. The men were nevertheless conscripted into the Tsar's army and, to avoid service, decided to flee. Remembering their origins, the tribe migrated back along the route taken by their ancestors, pursued by the Russians. Today, almost 40,000 of their descendants live in Korla which has administrative autonomy as a Mongol district within the Uigher Autonomous Region. Street signs are in Uigher, Chinese and Mongolian.

Korla is also celebrated by some as the place where the last truly independent ruler of Xinjiang died. Yakub Beg was probably born at Pishkent near Leninabad in Fergana early in the nineteenth century. He survived by dancing for a living in the bazaar and probably in the homes of wealthy men. Some time before 1850, he fell into the ways of a soldier of fortune and eventually arrived in Kashgar. There, he acquired a following and declared himself the King of Kashgar about 1866. In the absence of any coherent opposition from the demoralised Chinese Empire, Yakub Beg and his motley "army" conquered Hotan in the south and the towns of the northern route along the Taklimakan until the Chinese finally rallied and defeated him near Korla in 1877. He died a few months later, probably of natural causes though it was rumoured that the deposed governor of Hotan poisoned him. Before the Second World War, a plain grave near the Tomb of the Fragrant Concubine outside Kashgar was said to be his, but Yakub Beg left almost no mark or memory in Xinjiang and certainly none in Korla. The local party official who masqueraded as an historian had never heard of him.

Whether it is because of the Mongols I cannot say, but Korla differs from all other Chinese cities I have visited. New buildings display a design sense, an adaptation to their function and setting that is unique. By and large, new buildings and new towns in China from Beijing to Kashgar are extremely ugly. Korla is different. On the way into the city, new housing blocks were under construction amidst old trees. They were horizontal buildings four storeys high with rows of simple, steel-framed windows set in tan stucco, interrupted by forward extensions in green stucco. White highlights set off the two prevailing colours of the landscape. Our hotel was white, combining the same simplicity of line and detail with Chinese elements in the red-tiled roof. It was set in a small park with a pavilion on a low artificial hill opposite the entrance and an unfinished pool between them. New office blocks in the town centre pleased the eye by not trying too hard. Proportions and colours were almost the sole elements of their design, except again for some Chinese quality of the roof line.

Korla looked prosperous. There seemed to be less dust, and the bazaar was as colourful and crowded as any other. We were told that the local paper-making industry supplies a significant part of China's requirements. Its raw material is primarily the reeds that grow in Lake Bosten to the north-east. The People's Hospital has recently doubled its capacity and now has 364 beds and 500 staff. There is also a Mongol Minorities Hospital in a nearby town. One of our local informants said that the railway would be extended to Kashgar in time, depending on when and where oil was found in the province. He had a clear vision of the role Korla would play when, as he explained, a new railway ran from Xining in Qinghai province to Korla and the whole western region of

China was linked by road to Pakistan and the Mediterranean. Happily, this man is in charge of planning for the city.

Although the road leaving the Korla oasis enters barren, eroded loess hills, the land immediately to the east is covered with lakes, the largest being Lake Bosten, Korla's main water supply. Naturally, this well-watered region is cultivated, and much more open and treeless than previous oases. On our left, the mountains had drifted into the desert, making way at Yanqi, a town closed to foreigners for unexplained reasons, for the main road north to Urumchi. We were told there were excavations nearby, but they too were closed. Because the highways have followed their present routes for centuries, Yanqi could hardly fail to be of historical interest. Official footdragging about opening Yanqi, Hotan, Karghalik and Kuqa seems to contradict the growing emphasis on tourism. Either the authorities have so far lacked funds to make sites available, for example, by providing safe access stairways, or they are embarrassed by the existing accommodation. Yet Yanqi is close enough to Korla with its handsome new hotel and on the main road to Urumchi. Perhaps the Xinjiang equivalent of the Ministry of Works is in conflict with the Ministry of Tourism and CITS. Indeed, neither explanation excludes the other.

Just south of the main road in the town centre, new, three-storey modern buildings indicate that Yanqi is more than an ordinary village. Perhaps it has some administrative significance for this fertile region. Opposite stood the old, single-storey workshops and shops. A new decorative arch led into the bazaar, relatively quiet on that Wednesday morning. There was a mosque beyond the market. The villages hereabout display one dominant feature, repeated in Yanqi: surmounting every house and shop, a willow or poplar trunk carrying a television aerial on top. They gave the town the appearance of a Thames marina in a desert.

Eastward, the crops were soon behind us. Across the flat desert to the north rose a new range of mountains, the Bogda Shan, with what looked at that distance like snow on the peaks. After a good lunch in a spotlessly-clean, privately-operated village restaurant run, our Chinese colleagues pointed out, by people of Han extraction, the road climbed once more through barren, eroded brown hills. In a few places, scrub plants struggled for life, but here there was no sign of water. We descended into a flat, absolutely barren desert covered with small rocks and extending south as far as one could see. To the north and east, the high mountains were perhaps 100 kilometres away. At a distance, I saw a lake beside the road, but this time, it was not there. It was much hotter as the road slowly descended from about 1,400 metres near Korla to below sea level at Turfan. You can see the depression as you become part of its landscape, a Brownian particle in a great brown bowl.

Turfan was a dusty oasis with paved streets. It was also the hottest place in the world, a perception confirmed for us by the aberrant weather conditions we had experienced since Samarkand almost a month before. New building in the centre, including half a dozen new mosques, was self-consciously Uigher Muslim. Turfan was a city on the make, a tourist centre with a posh new CITS hotel serving the worst food with the worst service we endured in China. The staff of attractive young men and women specialised in rudeness and chaos. When will the Chinese learn that for better or worse most tourists demand more than magnificent works of art and romantic ancient monuments?

Both of these attractions Turfan supplies in plenty. First, we drove east on the main road beside the Flaming Mountains, where the wind erosion has turned up unusually red loess in jagged scars on the hills, to the Flaming Mountain Commune. The village main street penetrated a tunnel of willow trees so dense that few of the mudbrick and newer baked brick buildings could be seen. Beyond was the great compound enclosing the ruins of Gaochang or Karakoja, the Uigher name by which Stein's contemporary the German archaeologist, Albert von le Coq, knew it. In the sixth and seventh centuries, long before Turfan existed, Gaochang was a provincial capital, the residence of local kings who paid tribute to the Chinese Emperor when he was strong enough to demand it. The Buddhist monk, Xuen Xiang, who travelled along the Silk Road and across the Karakoram to northern India and back, lectured on his travels to the King of Gaochang in a low round domed building that has alone been restored amidst the ancient ruins. The city survived until Mongol invaders destroyed it in the fourteenth century.

It must have housed some 50,000 people within its massive mudbrick walls, ten metres high and three or four metres thick at the base. Like defensible cities throughout central Asia, Gaochang had a citadel which included the principal Buddhist place of worship surrounded by a wall, an inner precinct, probably occupied by the monks, also inside its own wall, and beyond, in the remaining 80 per cent of the ground space, the city of tradespeople, artisans, scribes, soldiery, police, housewives and whores. The most identifiable structure is the Buddhist temple in the citadel. Four damaged murals remain, but with the colours and figures still dimly visible. In the centre of the area, a truncated tower has two rows of niches. In some, the remains of votive figures can still be seen.

The King's palace in Gaochang stands some distance from the temple towards the main gate. Two towers that marked its entrance have been partially reconstructed. Judging from the fact that its location breaks the standard city pattern, the palace may have been a later construction.

Looking at ruined mudbrick walls has limited appeal to the non-specialist even when the history is reasonably well known and laced with romantic incident. Just outside the mudbrick walls of the monastery, a camel driver with a mangy beast took advantage of the short attention span which we all displayed in the gathering heat. His camel rides cost 1 yuan and lasted almost exactly sixty seconds, but the camel's bells tinkled merrily in time with the lugubrious experience of being almost tipped on to the ground when the animal knelt to permit your more orderly descent. The main gate has remained through the centuries the entrance to the site where today tickets, a few postcards and soft drinks are sold. I sat down on the steps in the shade to wait for the others, but the man in charge evidently considered that my age and status demanded better. He very kindly brought me a folding chair.

Astana, the cemetery for the nobility of Gaochang, is a flat, dusty area just on the Turfan side of the Flaming Mountain Commune. There are said to be more than 200 graves dug into the rock, but they are unmarked by stupas or headstones. In my experience, one of Aurel Stein's major discoveries was a disappointment. A tall Uigher keeper, very bored by his job, unlocked each of the three tombs open to visitors and led us down the stone steps into the hand-hewn underground chamber. He switched on one or two light bulbs, hastily delivered a descriptive set speech without expression in monotones, allowed our local guide to translate them into a kind of English, and immediately used body language, words, darkness, everything but force to urge us out of that tomb into the next one.

Each chamber was roughly three metres square. In the first, the wall facing the entrance carried a mural depicting two Confucian legends. Across the upper part, framed by cloud patterns and pink pillars against a blue background, the four exemplary men are represented: Earth man, Metal man, Stone man and the Old man. Their story is complex, a parable of the need to mediate between conflicts of opposites. Thus, Metal man exemplifies the golden quality of words or action which should be used sparingly. Stone man is a non-Confucian answer, castigating insufficient involvement in issues. Earth man probably represents self-restraint and self-cultivation, both Confucian virtues.

Beneath these figures and to the left, you see a curiously-shaped container, an inverted bell. According to legend, Confucius was walking with his students when they came upon such an object.

"What is it?" asked the philosopher, who had seen nothing like it.

"Master, it is called a Qi," replied one of the students.

Confucius had read about a Qi. "We must test it," he urged.

The inverted bell stood before them slanting somewhat to the right. As they poured in water, it straightened up, but as the water reached the brim, the Qi slanted to the left and the water spilled out. The philosopher was much gratified: "He who becomes arrogant and conceited will certainly trip and fall," he said.

The style of the paintings is Tang, the figures vigorously drawn rather than merely allegorical. The messages are not something I would particularly wish to take with me into the hereafter, but the pictures comment wittily on life.

The mural in the second tomb presented a landscape filled by wild and domestic birds. Poultry, various kinds of duck and pheasant in beautiful detail inhabited the foreground. Behind them were stylised V-shaped mountains surrounded by clouds with swallows and other birds flying towards them. I assumed the people buried here looked at their world very differently from those in the first tomb.

On the burial platform the third tomb contained the mummified figures of a man and woman, said to have been found in situ. Certainly they looked as though the slightest touch would bring about immediate dissolution.

Of course, Stein and later explorers took away from Astana almost everything that was movable. The British Museum has wonderful painted silk wall hangings and funerary figures, and other artefacts can be seen in various museums, even at Turfan itself. Considering the state of the bodies in the third tomb, the argument that the archaeologists preserved what otherwise might have been lost lacks force, however well it might apply to other sites. Yet we soon saw worse.

Albert von le Coq admitted that he had been disappointed by his finds at Gaochang. He added disarmingly that he was more worried because the German Emperor, Wilhelm II, would be disappointed. He moved on a few

Portrait of a Uighur màn near Kashgar, Xinjiang.

A boy selling string beans in the Turfan bazaar, Xinjiang.

Portrait of a foreign affairs official, Pingliang, Gansu.

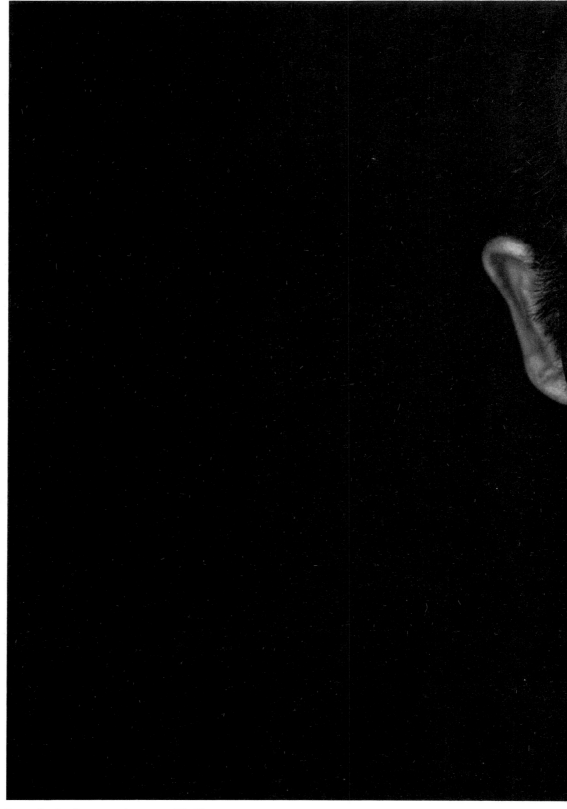
Portrait of a date-wood tuner at Bin Xian, en route to Xi'an, Shaanxi.

The chief doctor at Lanzhou Second People's Hospital, Gansu.

Street scene, Kashgar, Xinjiang.

After heavy rain in Hotan, Xinjiang.

Street scene in the old town of Kashgar, Xinjiang.

Restaurant doorway, Sha He, near Baoding, Hebei.

kilometres to the north where grottoes like those at Kuqa had been dug into a cliff above a stream that runs down through the Flaming Mountains. At Baziklik, von le Coq found both statues and murals rich enough to satisfy even his eminent paymaster. The statues, built up with mud and plaster on an armature of reeds and sticks and then painted, could be removed easily. Murals present more of a problem, but von le Coq had with him a specialist who had worked out the necessary techniques. In one grotto, we saw, just above head height, where work had begun on the removal of a metre-square section. The engineer drew pencil lines enclosing the desired morsel. He had drilled half-inch holes about two inches deep and about a half-inch apart along the pencil lines. For some reason, work on this segment had stopped at that point. What the next step would have been is made clear in von le Coq's book, *Buried Treasures of Chinese Turkestan*, where he describes procedures at Ka Zi Er near Kuqa.

> Next, a hole [or holes] must be made . . . to make space to use the fox-tail saw; in the excavated rock temples . . . this space often has to be made with hammer and chisel in the solid rock, which fortunately is generally soft.
>
> When the surface-layer is in a very bad condition, men are sometimes employed to keep boards covered with felt pressed firmly against the painting that is to be removed.
>
> Then this painting is sawn out.

Much larger segments of murals from Baziklik and other sites were sent back to Berlin by von le Coq where they were carefully mounted in what is now the Pergamon Museum in the eastern sector. Unfortunately, bombs and shells destroyed most of the central Asian wing. So much for preservation.

Despite Western depredations which had of course only followed those of invading armies and opportunistic thieves, Baziklik still contains wonderful works of art. They cover a shorter timespan than in other cave complexes, having been painted over 300 years from the fifth century through the early Tang period. The colours used also seem to be more limited. The largest cave we saw has been given the usual name, the Cave of a Thousand Buddhas, because of the rows and rows of tiny framed Buddhist saints or Bodhisattvas that fill the vault. Earth reds and dark greens have been used, but the major colours are dark and light blue, light green, a light reddish-brown and white filling black lines. The Bodhisattvas may each have different features but the forms used and the draperies are uniform. On the other hand, facing the entrance in cave thirty-nine, the faces and figures were so different that they must be portraits, perhaps of monks themselves. Most of the caves had large painted lotus-leaf sculptures against the walls or on raised altars. These were the pedestals for statues of Buddhas or other religious figures. In the four or five caves we were shown, the damage to faces was most extensive, suggesting the work of Muslims. But only after seeing the grottoes at Dunhuang can you realise what it means to have no statuary at all. Around the empty spaces above the lotus leaves and altars, the flame designs are often still in evidence at Baziklik. Like stylised mountains, lotus leaves or cloud patterns, the flame designs provided artists with opportunities for baroque self-expression, like the cross, or the trees at Gethsemane. Flame designs could be the inspiration behind the uniquely beautiful flying angels, the Fei Tian, of Dunhuang.

From the terrace in front of the grottoes, the river canyon stretched far below, green with cultivation, its fields counterpointing the red sand cliffs that soared above us on both sides. As we entered the canyon, we stopped to admire the wind sculpture in a conical mountain of red sand and gravel across the river and the raw sandstone towering 250 metres above it.

On the other side, south-west of Turfan, stand the ruins of the city of Jiaohe. Contemporary with Gaochang and for a time also a provincial capital, the remains of Jiaohe are more compressed by its geographical setting and much more spectacular. The city occupied a triangle of land formed by two rivers that have cut sheer cliffs to form green cultivated canyon floors on both sides. This highly defensible setting, completed by a wall across the narrow base of the triangle, was reminiscent of the Armenian capital at Ani, though Jiaohe is smaller, and certainly less wealthy, depending on a hinterland far more restricted by climate than the productive plains of Armenia.

The road enters Jiaohe at the apex of the triangle through walls ten metres high and five metres thick at the base. You are confronted by a jumble of red mudbrick walls, anonymous and featureless, but the road continues to the base of the triangle. Part of a round watch tower has been restored just before the entrance to the Buddhist temple-monastery. The monastery entrance wall has also been restored but no other buildings. About fifty metres from the monastery entrance towards the outer wall stands a square altar tower with niches above head height on all four sides, many of them containing small statues. Touches of colour are left as hints of what must have been. Again, as at Gaochang, the remains of apartments stand on both sides of the tower. The wall behind it encloses the temple area and is set at some distance from the defensive outer wall. At one point in the jumble of ruins in front of the temple complex, I came to the unmistakable intersection of two streets, both about two metres wide. Here, the construction techniques became clearer. House walls and defensive walls were made of layers of mudbrick but without the reinforcing willows found in the beacon towers. The surfaces appeared to have been smoothed with an extra layer of mud similar to the surfaces on which murals were painted in the grottoes. By wandering amidst the roofless walls, I realised that in this ancient city the compressed space had forced builders to add storeys, perhaps three or even four. Jiaohe may have been much more vertical than other ruined sites, adding to its visual impact. Although there were plenty of tourists and even a small chaikhana outside the walls, in the shade of trees above one of the streams, there was no camel to ride and perhaps no need for it at Jiaohe. A small enamelled sign in Chinese and English beside the entrance gate reads: "Please don't take the ruins of the old city away."

Because of the heat, we had visited Gaochang in the morning and Jiaohe late in the afternoon when the temperature was not more than about 37°C. A heat haze hung over the oasis and reached well into the desert most of the time we were in Turfan. You can actually see in this haze the water loss which far exceeds the total annual rainfall. For centuries, people who may not have understood this climatic imbalance were fully aware of its impact on their spartan lives. They had seen springs in oases that were not fed by rivers, and they recognised the existence of underground water. Throughout central Asia, from eastern Turkey to Turfan, they had learned to exploit these water sources for agriculture by building underground canals, often at depths up to 100 metres in their upper reaches, using artificial wells to maintain them. In Xinjiang, such a water course is called a kerez. Each of the maintenance wells is surrounded by a pile of the sand and rock dug out during its construction, and they form lines of warts across the desert. Where the kerez is deepest, furthest from the oasis, the piles of excavated sand and clay are the highest. Each winter when there is usually more water, the authorities assign people to the tasks of maintaining these ancient engineering wonders, following a strict rota. Not only is the work well paid, a young man from the village told us, but in the freezing winter deserts the water tunnels are warm and sheltered.

The water emerges from the kerez just before the oasis, near enough so that the trees can limit evaporation. While the others walked into the desert along the line of the maintenance excavations, I sat beside the stream under the trees watching two women washing clothes. They chatted together, apparently ignoring me as well as the three men loafing further upstream.

Everywhere in the countryside around Turfan you see new brick houses with a roofed second storey built with open work brick walls. We worked out that they were used for drying something, but did not guess that it was grapes. Much of the large local crop of seedless green grapes is converted to raisins.

The Turfan Museum is a dusty barn of a place with too little money to maintain its collection. Perhaps most noteworthy is a group of Tang tomb figures from Astana. The high-ceilinged rooms were too large to feel crowded, but local people alone or in small groups, sometimes a family, were having a look, perhaps taking advantage of the week-long Uigher holiday.

The bazaar was even busier. It had long since outgrown the fifty-year-old building with a rather handsome green and brown wooden entrance arch and stretched back through an unpaved open area another 100 metres. Fresh grapes were available everywhere, along with melons, especially watermelon and the smaller Hami melon. Otherwise, neither the food for sale nor the dress materials and manufactured goods was distinctive.

Paul and I sat on a disused table beneath the wooden arch and were approached by furtive young men who turned out to be money changers. I had not experienced a black market in China, but here they were offering 150 yuan in the national currency for 100 yuan in the notes sold to tourists for foreign exchange. Foreign Exchange Currency alone can be used to buy legal goods in the recently-established Free Economic Zones near Hong Kong or illegal smuggled merchandise in coastal towns. Such goods are imported to Turfan as well as dozens of other inland Chinese cities where they can be sold very profitably. The special Foreign Exchange Currency (FEC) can also serve in Friendship Stores selling primarily to foreigners where imported hi-fi equipment and TV sets cost much less in FEC than in RMB (Ren Min Bi, the national currency). The going exchange rate in Urumchi is 158 RMB for 100 FEC, we were told, and in Kashgar, 160. There were rumours in Beijing in September 1987 that the government intended to do away with the special tourist currency.

# Chapter 11

# KUMUL AND DUNHUANG
## 敦煌 قومۇل

We left Turfan by the Gaochang road under an overcast sky with the temperature already in the thirties. Just beyond the turning to Baziklik, the road began to climb out of the Turfan Depression following a green valley with high, barren, reddish sandhills on both sides. We passed a large crop of sorghum in the watered valley and saw evidence of more than one kerez running towards it. Men played a game of billiards on a dilapidated table by the roadside in one village. Further on, two women dressed in brilliant red and gold sat against a large water pipe beneath a tree. They expressed the whole of central Asia.

When the desert returned, all vegetation disappeared. Even the road was unmetalled, and the dust became fierce. We turned on the air-conditioning despite the increased risk of overheating. An oasis appeared in the distance on the right but could have been a mirage. To the left, the Bogda Shan supplied a jagged, real backdrop. To the hardy thousands who preceded us, riding on camels or walking across these arid wastes, distances must have seemed interminable. We drove easily from one oasis to the next, usually crossing several in a day. They had to go on for days with only the brackish water and moulding food they could carry. When they did finally reach the safety of a fresh water supply, there might be the threat of bandits. We had driven for thousands of kilometres along the Silk Road in peace and security. For us, the desert was dry, hot, samey space to be crossed with the near certainty of sleeping in comfort that night.

After miles of this, the longest stretch of absolutely barren desert we encountered, the road if not the scenery suddenly improved. Like the six or eight other vehicles we saw, we increased our speed on the macadam surface. A few scattered scrub plants had just appeared when we saw a group of vehicles in the road ahead and one yellow van on its side on the desert floor.

Our Toyota had been out of sight ahead of us for some time and was now stopped on the road near the accident. Our initial fear that they had somehow been involved quickly dissolved, but they had arrived very soon after the van had gone out of control and had tried to help. One of the two men was dead. The other was badly hurt and died later in hospital. Tom had comforted the two children, a girl about eight and a younger boy. They had cuts and bruises but were fortunately not badly hurt. Another van had taken the victims back to Kumul just before we arrived. Like our colleagues, the people in the other cars had not yet pulled themselves together to continue their journeys. One of the men, we also learned, had in fact been travelling in the van bed along with the plastic bags full of lentils and the containers of rape oil and petrol scattered about the site. A burst tyre, cause of the tragedy, lay by the roadside.

The Friday Mosque at Lanzhou, Gansu.

A stream formed by a kerez south-west of Turfan, Xinjiang.

The road from the Long March Memorial on Liupan Mountain.

It was the first of two accidents we saw that day. The second involved a lorry which had skewed across the road and shed its load of lead pipe. This too had happened on a stretch of well-paved highway following a long spell of rough, dusty, unmetalled road. As we drove east, the number of motor accidents grew. "Accident!" became a discouraging litany. In several, a one-stroke tricycle pulling a heavily-ladened two-wheeled cart had turned over. We came across one of these between Kumul and the Xinjiang–Gansu border. A young man was holding a bloody cloth to the forehead of an older companion. We stopped, but at the same time their neighbours arrived from a nearby village. Surely, not every driver had passed the examinations required of Liu and Shen. In too many villages and communes, the choice of driver seemed to fall on the man standing beside the vehicle door. I never saw a woman driver in rural China.

For hundreds of kilometres, there was only desert. Occasionally, we saw a few low bushes, even three trees together looking green and refreshing. But there was no oasis, no villages and no place for lunch until the early evening. San Dao Ling is a coal-mining village near the biggest mine in north-western China. The restaurant on the outskirts occupied the ground floor of a new brick two-storey hotel with a white-painted wooden balcony. The building was built and owned by a Han woman whose husband was the cook. Six more members of her own family worked there, assisted by six full- or part-time employees from the village. The owner raised the money herself from a co-operative bank and hired a co-operative building group established as part of a collective farm to do the work. At 6.00 p.m., we had the restaurant to ourselves; their principal customers are local people and the through lorry trade. The kitchen and the floor and tables were very clean and the food, fresh, well-served and delicious. Much of the information about the establishment came from snatches of conversation involving our Chinese colleagues and passed on later to us but, when we were about to leave, our hostess and host and their entire staff came with us into the forecourt to say goodbye. Each side wished the other good fortune. Each side thanked the other for good food and service and for honouring them by stopping there. Tom took pictures of two pretty local girls from the hired staff and of course of the owner herself. It was the kind of restaurant to which you would like to return because you would certainly be welcomed as a valued friend.

Kumul, the Uigher name of Hami, is the major settlement of the last oasis in Xinjiang – or the first after the Silk Road leaves Gansu. We reached the hotel in a small park just in time to hear the muezzin call unamplified from a mosque nearby. This industrial town has three formal attractions, but it was the informal and unexpected which gave it interest.

The museum displays some pretty pieces of eighteenth-century jewellery. Just outside the town itself stands the Sino–Arabic mausoleum built in 1945 to receive the tomb of a Tang dynasty Islamic saint that was moved from the provincial border. Beside it is the graveyard divided, unusually, into a Uigher and a Han section. Not far from these mortuary monuments stand the tombs of the Kings of Kumul. During the last two centuries of the Empire, the Uighers of Kumul had their own King, whereas the Han and other peoples in his kingdom were governed by the Emperor's prefect. The centrepiece amongst the tombs was a ten-metre square brick and stone construction with truncated minarets at the four corners. The entrance façade and minarets were once covered by blue and white Iznik-style tiles in vegetable designs. On the other three walls, the tiles were coloured light green and white. The remaining three pavilions were built of intricately-carved wood and were even more in need of care and restoration. Facing the complex stood the royal palace, a plain brick structure still used for offices and stables.

Returning from the tombs of the Kumul Kings, we heard drums and the skirl of horns. Beside the road but facing a large open area, a temporary structure of tree trunks supported a stage with a proscenium and roof decorated with red banners and flags. Today the Uigher holiday ended. Evidently, we had missed the wrestling, but a band of three wind instruments and two drums still held the stage. Paul asked them to play for us. Most of the crowd had gone, but an eight-year-old girl wearing a bright maroon shift and a square maroon Uigher felt hat began to dance to the music. Though at first she seemed quite unaware of watching eyes, her movements became more stylised as the knowledge grew upon her that she was the centre of attention. The remaining people stopped to listen and watch. For just five minutes, we had a local festival of our own.

The second unexpected event in Kumul arose because we disregarded the driving injunction. In our hotel dining room, we met two American zoologists who were studying a local desert rodent which appeared at dusk and far enough from the town not to be disturbed by it. I had begged off, but Tom and Paul wanted to see the animals and, as the zoologists had no transport, Tom volunteered to drive the four of them in our van. Unfortunately, just as they were leaving in our conspicuous vehicle, the local Foreign Affairs officer arrived to meet with our liaison officer, Liu, to whom he mentioned the departure. I believe Liu lost face because he had not been told of the adventure. In any event, he lectured us like children, very angrily. After we had made suitable apologies, in the presence of the Foreign Affairs officer of course, good humour was restored.

After leaving the oasis the next morning, the desert became absolutely barren again. To the left, the snow-clad peaks shrank to hills and abruptly disappeared, leaving us on a featureless, dry, brown, rolling gobi. Across this stretch of wasteland the Taklimakan joins the Gobi Desert itself, and the road deteriorated into a rough, dusty track that kept our speed to below 40 kph. At intervals of fifteen kilometres, we passed mudbrick shelters, about ten metres square, now roofless and disused. Once there was a group of buildings beside the shelter, possibly a caravanserai. The border between Xinjiang and Gansu, between the New Territory and China proper, consists of a line of eroded loess hills surmounted by a dozen or more ruined forts and watch towers.

First we made a short detour to the railway at Liuyuan to begin unloading our excess equipment, in this case the expensive sand tyres, unused because we had had to abandon the southern route. At Dunhuang, the Toyota would leave us, taking Dr Zheng, the journalist Hu, and Xiao Liu back to Urumchi. Then we would have to make room in our van, designed to seat no more than five, for the long-legged Deputy Liu, Shen and the four of us. So the three wheels in the roof rack were taken off and shipped by rail to Urumchi. When I asked why not the fourth sand tyre, on the bonnet, Liu said it was needed to hold the bonnet down. I suggested that was not its function and, in any case, the spare could be moved from the rear door if he felt it was safer, but only the space on the roof concerned him.

Dunhuang lies 120 kilometres south of the main Silk Road near the very end of the southern route. The road was newly resurfaced and ran across the same barren desert with distant hills to the south and west until we entered the Dunhuang oasis itself. First we passed an isolated house with two windmills in the farmyard. Nearby, an eagle sat by the roadside, apparently injured. Heron were hunting on our right. Then we passed two more houses each with a windmill on its roof. The first animals we encountered were a large herd of bactrian camels. At more than 1,100 metres, Dunhuang has a dry, hot climate which has made it the centre of a fertile zone inhabited since the second century BC when it became a pivot in the western border garrisons of the expanding Han state, most of them desert fortresses unable to support themselves. Great sand mountains extend almost to the edge of the town, another dusty frontier settlement with more new hotels than Las Vegas. Its attraction, the Mugao Grottoes, contains one of the art treasures of the world protected today by UNESCO as well as the Chinese government.

None of the new hotels was for us. Instead, we were first shunted into a Russian-style 1950s guest house twelve kilometres out of town in the opposite direction from the grottoes, which are themselves twenty-five kilometres from the centre. When I objected, Liu struggled with CITS, who run several of the new hotels, but came up with a noisy fourth-rate establishment where we had neither water nor electricity for two of our four nights. There was of course an excuse: we were two weeks late, and had changed our date of arrival twice. I pointed out that somehow our Soviet hosts had managed to find us rooms in first-class hotels despite even worse scheduling disorders. It did no good, but perhaps no harm. We ate our meals, such as they were, in the newest CITS hotel, 100 metres from our pit.

Dunhuang is one of several Chinese towns and cities where the Party believes that constant music and chat over public loudspeakers at street corners assures the mental and physical well-being of the populace. Inasmuch as the Japanese and European tourists probably outnumber the locals much of the year, this seems just a little arrogant, especially because the chat is naturally in Chinese. The racket added immeasurably to the discomfort of our hotel, situated on both the main street and the main plaza in front of the museum, library and civic centre.

Out of such tribulated darkness shone the brilliant light of the grottoes, which are themselves unilluminated. Everyone carries a torch. The effect is to focus your attention willy-nilly on the spot in the torch beam. It is that much harder to get an impression of a whole mural, and certainly of a whole cave, but the enforced attention to detail means that you cannot skip over the wit, social comment, aesthetic sophistication and immense beauty of the artist's individual images. You can see all of the Sistine Chapel at once, but apart from the juxtaposed fingers of God and Adam, what details can you recall?

A large parking area has been provided to accommodate the tourist coaches, probably the only parking place in the world dotted with half-ruined stupas, that peculiar Buddhist version of the tomb for the wealthy. Several more were scattered through sand hills beyond the ticket kiosks.

There are 460 caves at Mugao not counting additional caves at the Western Thousand Buddha Caves and other sites around Dunhuang. They were decorated by Buddhist artists between about AD 220, the end of the eastern Han, and the Five Dynasties in the mid-tenth century, although some work was done during later periods, especially on restoration. The styles are complex and, indeed, controversial because distinctions are not clear-cut. In addition to the wall paintings and sculpture, Mugao contained one of the great libraries of Buddhist manuscripts written in various central Asian languages as well as scroll paintings on silk. Because Dunhuang was inside the Imperial defensive area and neither invasions by the Arabs nor the Turkish tribes carried Islam that far, the grottoes escaped relatively undisturbed. As Albert von le Coq later wrote, it was only the sheerest accident that allowed Aurel Stein, with his archaeologically more modest interest in the easily removable library, to reach the grottoes before the German who specialised in the extraction of painted walls. I did see one or two places where pieces of the murals had been removed, and of course there may be others.

By the early years of this century, the whole cave complex was under the care of one ageing monk. The caves had been boarded up, and the library literally piled into two chambers where it was first discovered by Stein. Stein negotiated with the monk a fee of £50 in exchange for an agreed number of manuscripts and other items. In this way, the British Library acquired the oldest known printed book, the *Diamond Sutra*, to name but one of myriad treasures, many of them still unseen by the public.

Today, the grottoes are managed by a Research Station at the site. It reports to the Gansu Ministry of Culture, but ultimate responsibility rests with the National Bureau of Museums and Archaeological Data in Beijing. Forty caves are open to the public which is admitted only in groups with guides speaking Japanese, English, French, Italian or German. Like guides everywhere in China, they were young men and women recently out of university, but they knew the history and archaeology of the caves as well as the contents of the individual murals. The Mugao Grottoes, like most Buddhist cave complexes, occupy a series of cliffs above a stream which waters a small oasis. A high fence divides the cliff face from the oasis. Cameras must be checked on the oasis side in special huts. Anyone found with a camera may be ejected, and the camera may be confiscated. Permission to photograph can only be obtained from Beijing for large fees by scholars who must operate under rules which have not been published. However, the Gansu Ministry of Culture allowed Tom to take a few pictures inside the fence but outside the caves at a cost of £17 each!

Neither Liu nor his colleagues in the Mountain Scientific Expedition Advisory Service knew how or from whom to seek special authorisations for photography or for access without payment or to closed monuments as at Karghalik. While our hosts in Beijing were looking into the matter, something one might have thought they should have done in advance, Liu made an appointment for us to visit the Research Station where we were seen by the Deputy Director, Fan Jinshi. She could do nothing but consult her superiors in the Gansu Ministry of Culture by phone. That there was no fixed table of charges emerged from the delay of almost an hour during which Deputy Director Fan answered questions about the research work.

"Before we can do anything, certainly before the public can be admitted to a cave, we have to rebuild the ramps and stairs that lead from level to level across the face of the cliffs. They are in constant need of repair. This is also true of the murals themselves. After all these years, we are for ever faced with problems arising from different kinds of damage. For example, when the murals were painted, the basic stone was cut away and covered with a mud coating which could be smoothed. Now there is a tendency for the coating to pull away, lifting the entire mural off the cave wall."

"What causes this? Is it a process that seems to be getting worse because of visitors?"

"Basically, it is caused by the smooth surface required to paint the murals, but it has probably become worse. The caves are naturally extremely dry. No water seeps through the walls to break down the adhesion between the natural rock and the applied surface. Visitors add moisture to the air from their sweat and their breathing. We are going to try plastic sheets hung from bars held above head height on steel posts to separate visitors from the walls, a plastic screen."

"What about the paint itself?"

"Because it consists of mineral pigments suspended in water, moisture can make the paint flake, another aspect of the same problem."

"But surely your major problem is not just prevention but repairing damage already done?"

"Indeed yes. We are experimenting with a number of conservation techniques. They include glues that will resist moisture, glues both behind the mud surfaces and for reattachment of pigment flakes. We also try to repair some losses which means we have to try to reconstitute the original pigments, a study in itself. These are universal problems, however, and we welcome people from all over the world who can help us find solutions."

The Deputy Director may have been referring to an international meeting of conservationists and other art experts which was to take place in Dunhuang six weeks after our visit.

She added an interesting point about the sculpture. "The reason there are not many sculptures in the grottoes and on the walls is that the caves do not lend themselves to sculpture. The stone is soft and sandy. The sculptures that you see, especially the large Buddhas, are moulded on armatures of wood. Otherwise, the murals are a more suitable decoration on these walls."

In two days I managed to visit twenty-five caves, several more than once. Repetition allowed me to absorb much more than the usual very short visit permitted. Because individual inspection was not allowed, I attached myself once to a group of Italians who managed to enjoy a leisurely inspection despite the rules and regulations, unlike the German tourists who moved from one grotto to the next every four minutes. I took along a picnic lunch on the second day and ate it comfortably leaning against a large tree trunk. Hundreds of people were doing the same thing, but the tree- and flower-filled oasis is large enough to avoid the sense of crowding. Several kiosks sold food and soft drinks, so the picnic was really not essential. But because packaged foods are uncommon and because the Chinese have a well-developed sense of social obligation, the park stayed remarkably litter-free.

We began with the monumental caves: the thirty-three metre high Buddha built between 713 and 780 can be seen from three caves, one at the feet, one about halfway up the figure and one at the head. The brilliance of the reds and yellows, particularly in the halo, suggests more recent restoration. The huge reclining Buddha is also mid-Tang. Behind it are perhaps a hundred figures sculpted in the round but from the waist or chest, the remainder being hidden by the Buddha. The faces of these figures represent every race and nation so they must be an assembly of the faithful. Behind them, a huge mural depicting scenes from the life of Buddha covers the entire long wall. The cave has a vaulted ceiling running its length but is so dark that the murals covering the ceiling and the other three walls were very hard to examine. They contain hundreds of scenes and figures. Some are Bodhisattvas, particularly in painted niches high in the side walls, but other figures may be those of donors.

In many of the grottoes, the statues of Buddhas and their attendants, donors, Bodhisattvas or demons stand on, or just in front of, a stage surrounded by a proscenium arch. Like the theatrical curtain drawn in front of the altar in the Armenian cathedral at Echmiadzin, the proscenium underlines the role of religion as theatre. The arch itself is often decorated with flame designs or more elaborately with bas-relief trees, animals or human figures. One early cave from the northern Wei has a high-relief dragon, along with vegetation and animal figures on either side of the proscenium. Another, finished about a century later, has high-relief trees and lotus leaves intertwined around the entire arch. On either side of the Buddha stand threatening figures with horns and staring eyes, brightly coloured in blue and red with white and black markings. In another cave from the time of the northern Wei, great demons support each corner of the tent-like ceiling. Although many of the sculptures were damaged or missing from lotus pedestals, a surprising number remain. Almost without exception, their robes reflected the classical lines of Gandhara sculpture.

The ceilings are either tent-like or vaulted, often with cupolas carved upwards at the centre with elaborate bands of decoration separating each of the architectural elements, cupola, ceiling and walls. Many of the vaulted ceilings are covered with as many as two dozen rows of Bodhisattvas, each framed between lines or pillars. The colours vary, though backgrounds and frames in any one cave tend to remain the same. The former may be tan or light blue. The pillars are pink, blue or even black. I first noticed the Fei Tian, the flying figures surrounded by ribbons of colour, in a cupola, but they are also painted in the dividing bands and in wall murals, usually toward the tops. These rhythmic angels may be associated with musicians, for where they occur the instruments are very clearly delineated and sometimes surrounded by similar streamers of colour. On the ceilings of the passageway behind the proscenium stage in one cave dated from the early Tang, there are figures made with large circles into which features have been painted startlingly like Rouault's figures.

Although all of the murals are celebrations of Buddhism in one way or another, the content varies enormously. I have mentioned donors. Their life-size portraits often dominate a wall. In one cave a donor on horseback is identified as the King of Hotan. Donors are often accompanied by members of their families, especially their wives and concubines. The religious content may be direct, rows of Bodhisattvas in frames as on some of the ceilings, and painted or carved niches containing Buddhas or saints. Perhaps the most fantastic murals are the maps. One at least is said to be a map of Hebei province, but they are usually visualisations of terrain described in the Buddha's life. In a large tenth-century cave, all four walls are covered with an imaginary landscape. Different sections are divided by black vertical stripes about a foot in length and varying in width.

"And there are rivers and castles and farms and roads," say my notes. "Behind the main plinth where the Buddha stood is a painted Buddha of full height. The colours here on the back wall in the map are so vivid. They don't seem to have changed at all. Browns, blacks, reds, the base colour is tan, greens for the fields, blue rivers. The blue is a green blue, but there are blues in the mountains and the trees. It's beautiful. There's a house, a two-storey building here, probably a temple actually, and the door open . . . The mountains are multi-coloured and quite wavy. There's actually lettering on some of the red panels, probably the names of places. People on horses. People driving donkeys, and people just walking. Two look like monks, one in black, one in white . . . In the corner there's something that looks like a palace. You can see in these side panels that the method of the painter was fairly quick delineation. Faces, then, have been drawn in with a pen . . . Here's a cow that has horns and the body is outlined in pen or pencil but not filled in." Of course, the common people are often very busy. There were scenes of ploughing, hair-dressing, sewing and making clothes.

About a much later cave finished in the twelfth century I wrote: "So it's not a map; it's an account of the scripture about the transformation of the Buddha, and this of course is interesting because the cave itself is used now by couples who want a child, and there's a contributions box in it."

As Paul observed, perspective does not exist in the Western sense. The map-pictures tell a story if they are read from the bottom towards the top, area or incident following the one below it in space and time. Yet the particular scenes may be intensely realistic. Not only are people individuals, even to the faces of Bodhisattvas in rows of identical robes and frames, but so are the animals: a cow missing one horn, pigs with different patterns of spots. The structures that look like floating palaces in many of the murals are buildings or villages containing events, but they float because they are heavenly, not of this earth.

Towards the end of the second day, my legs felt somewhat leaden. I had also tried to see the contents of the Prado in two days and with very similar effects. But at Dunhuang, you face an additional problem: lack of familiarity with the stories, the techniques and the conventions of Buddhist art because, important though they are, little has been published about the grottoes. In the souvenir shop, you can buy a few slides but no postcards, and there is only one small, totally inadequate illustrated guide. Descriptions, often inaccurate, and illustrations have appeared in dozens of books since Aurel Stein and the French archaeologist, Pelliot, revealed the grottoes to the West eighty years ago, but they are available only to members of specialised libraries. One of the reasons for the photographic ban is the understandable Chinese desire to publish first, and in the 1980s at last, expensive volumes of colour reproductions have begun to appear.

You see the triangular frame construction indicating archaeological interest on several sites in Dunhuang. Nearby are the Western Caves of a Thousand Buddhas and, at greater distances, remains of garrisons that protected China's western boundary. Our limited time was largely devoted to Mugao, but there is a pretty bright blue lake, the Crescent Moon Lake, cupped by sand at the foot of a high sand hill. Most people seem drawn to filling their shoes by climbing the sand hill. Some even descend the other side to the lake and make the return journey. The sedentary or the lazy take advantage of the camels for rent at the entrance kiosk and make up a miniature camel train for the twenty-minute safari to the lake around the base of the sand hill.

Our last night was devoted to a farewell dinner for our Urumchi colleagues. By arranging for a private room in the Chinese dining room of the new CITS hotel, we were able to eat and drink together around one large table. It was a convivial and lengthy meal with toasts in English and Chinese, but by far the more memorable was the toast offered by Dr Zheng: "Up the bottoms."

# Chapter 12

# THROUGH THE GREAT WALL

## 長城內外

The last phase of our journey began on Friday, August 14th, when we left Dunhuang, starting late after taking two hours to repack the roof rack with all our luggage protected by a new tarpaulin. The back of the Land Rover had to be made comfortable for Liu with sleeping bags and mattresses strategically arranged. During the day, Liu graciously allowed Geoff, Paul and me to try out the new accommodation. Shen had to drive, and Tom rejected the offer on the ground that his job was to take pictures. It was remarkably restful, designed for sleeping because it was almost impossible to see outside.

An excellent road runs through desert with sand mountains on the right. At about eighty kilometres past Dunhuang, a small oasis contained the village of Nan Cha, and beside it in the desert stood the enormous mudbrick walls of another abandoned town. We knew nothing about the ruins until Paul found details in one of his Chinese guidebooks, but, attracted by their extent, we went to investigate. Called Liu Gong Pu, it turned out to have been built during the sixteenth century to resettle a tribe of about 9,000 people, the Ke Men He Je who had stood in the way of Qing dynasty expansion. The area inside the walls was almost as large as at Gaochang, but fewer buildings remained and these were unidentifiable. In the centre of a vast open area stood three structures looking much more recent. Two could have been wells. The third looked like an altar or ceremonial platform. The local people were either unable or unwilling to tell us anything about them.

Yet another Qing dynasty town stood beside the road fifty kilometres past Anxi near a roadside café where we had lunch. Much less of the mudbrick town had survived and with even fewer distinguishing characteristics.

As to the café, it was more typical of our luncheon stops than the large new restaurant before Kumul. This unostentatious establishment was also privately operated, but it occupied the two rooms of a single-storey whitewashed building. One room was the kitchen. Two lorry drivers had arrived before us. Two men and a boy did all the cooking and served. Though the menu was limited and the surroundings were not clean, the food was well cooked and served on crockery that was washed under Liu's inspection. We were brought a bucket of water, a piece of soap and a towel which were set beside the door so that we could wash our hands.

Now, our road had entered the Gansu corridor, a fertile valley varying in width from perhaps three kilometres at Lanzhou, the provincial capital, to fifty or more in the westerly region through which we were driving. Though it is often arid, the corridor is no longer desert and a series of oases. Cultivation is continuous. To the left rose the mountain barrier separating Gansu from the Gobi Desert and Mongolia. To the right, often at a considerable distance, were the higher ranges of Qinghai province. The fundamental nature of the landscape had changed to an altogether more familiar aspect.

A branch off the main road brought us through well-watered fields past sandy outcroppings at least one of which contained the remains of a small Buddhist cave complex. Ahead of us, a barren hill was topped by a pall of yellowish haze surrounding what looked like oil refineries. The town of Yumen, our destination that night, had wide streets and green trees that belied the first distant impression of an entrance to the Inferno. We spent the night in a comfortable guest house. The next morning, this factory town quickly supplied a welder capable of repairing one of the windscreen-frame attachments for the front struts supporting the heavy roof rack. The other support had been repaired in Kashgar.

Some twenty kilometres beyond Yumen, we crossed the line of the Great Wall just below the Western Gate which is on top of a hill at the outskirts of Jiayuguan. The present road enters the town 500 metres south of the old road, so we approached the gate from the wrong direction, unaware that it is easily reached by a street from the town side. All we could see of the gate was the outer wall surrounding the watch towers and other buildings which once housed a garrison. We took a side road up towards the wall and then walked around it. Below, between us and the main road, stretched a recreational lake with boats and a swimming area, the first of its kind we had come across in China.

The two main pagodas of the Western Gate, through which the Silk Road emerged into the desert, have been restored recently in all their nineteenth-century splendour, brightly painted in red, blue and green. A cobbled road neatly bordered with white cobbles still passes between them, but the main entrance through the outer pagoda has been blocked up. From the top of the crenellated wall below which we had walked there is a marvellous aerial view revealing the dual foundations of the wall that run towards the snow-capped mountains in the south. We had not noticed the twin construction when we drove across it.

Every traveller who left China to cross the Turkestan wilderness obliged with a description of Jiayuguan town and the Western Gate. One of the most revealing, I think, appears in the memoir of two intrepid British missionaries, Mildred Cable and Francesca French, *Through Jade Gate and Central Asia*. Jade Gate was the Western Gate, and in 1926 the town now called Jiayuguan was Yumen, the latter having been a village that was rechristened and enlarged to fulfil its industrial role "after liberation" in 1949. In 1926, there was only one "distinctive tower" in the gate. As to the "gay little town" it

was now looking its best, the opium fields were in bud, the wheat was green, while the freshness of early summer was still upon the foliage . . . a few changes had taken place since our last visit. The Mandarin . . . had left, and his successor had modernized the entrance to the Yamen . . . In place of the customary fresco of the tiger endeavouring to seize the sun in its jaws, which symbolizes the covetousness of the man who seeks to devour his neighbour's goods, the wall was frescoed with the "Map of China's Shame", showing China and her dependencies, with prominent scarlet patches indicating those portions which have been seized by foreign powers, and a similar map was exhibited in all the towns we visited in North-West China.

It was of course harvest time when we reached the Great Wall, and there is no sign of the yamen, or town hall as it then was. China's pride in its post-Revolutionary achievements, moreover, obviates the need for negative propaganda about the past. Foreigners are again welcomed fulsomely providing they serve the state either by working, for example, as teachers of English or eminent managers of multinational oil giants, or as tourists paying hard currency for every grain of rice. And why not? Europe and America exploited China for long enough.

Yet China is like the tiger endeavouring to seize the sun. In tourism and in its ordinary commercial dealings with foreigners, the Chinese forget that any transaction implies value for money. The Marco Polo Expedition paid the Chinese £11,500 in cash and added our fully equipped car, worth at least another £10,000. Our creature comforts were provided, but with the exception of Dr Zheng in Xinjiang, the purposes of our journey were ignored or misunderstood. Despite their academic connections, our hosts took more than they gave in return.

Arrogance and the need to obtain hard currency are only part of the explanation, I think. The Chinese are beset by an addiction to secrecy. Every citizen seems to operate on a "need to know" basis. In our case, the Institute of Geology knew how to get us across the border and arrange the formalities of our travel. They did not know and evidently considered they had no need to know how to identify less famous archaeological sites like the caves at Kuqa or what rules apply to photography at Dunhuang. Zheng Xilan said: "We did not know you wanted to take pictures."

"Our brochure told you that one of us is a professional photographer. Why should he accompany us other than to take pictures of important sites?"

"Your letters never specified that you would wish to take pictures."

"You knew Tom Ang was one of us. But you did not tell us there would be special fees for photography. You did not even *know* about such fees."

This is part of a conversation that took place after we had reached Beijing. If we assume that a military decision forced us to abandon the southern route, why were we refused an opportunity to see the order? Because it was secret. Secrecy underlies much of the corruption undermining the Chinese efforts at economic reform. It impales all attempts to make bureaucracy responsible for its actions on the thorns of privileged information. We British know all about this problem at home and are perhaps in a better position than others to recognise the intellectual and commercial impoverishment imposed by secrecy.

South-east from Jiayuguan, desert conditions returned. A very dry landscape covered with scrub stretched across a much narrower valley. The road runs closer to the southern mountains. To the north, two tiny trains marked the line of the railway. Railway and road had never been far apart since Anxi, but the visual relation is more marked when there is less vegetation to interrupt it.

Soon cultivation began again. Wheat and millet were being harvested. Sorghum and maize still stood in the small, carefully tilled fields. Suddenly, the windscreen in front of Shen shattered. A stone had been thrown up by a tyre, punching a hole. Fortunately, the glass stayed in place causing no injuries, but the windscreen had to be knocked out on the driver's side. That night in Zhangye, Paul went with Shen to replace the glass. They could obtain only ordinary window glass which had to be guarded with Scotch tape to prevent further accidents, but that got us through to Beijing.

Zhangye used to be called Ganzhou, the first (or last) of a series of garrison towns that protected the Gansu corridor against nomadic marauders from the northern desert like the Mongols, where Cable and French had spent a year assisting at the local mission. The next along our route was Jinquan, formerly Suzhou, followed by Wuwei which was Liangzhou, and finally, Lanzhou, now the provincial capital of Gansu. Zhangye still has an unrestored drum tower at its centre, a massive, two-storey wooden structure used as a platform from which to sound the alert in case of threatened invasion and, during quieter times, to issue orders to the citizenry. In all other respects, Zhangye looks like any other Chinese provincial city.

The signs of normal temperate agriculture continued to multiply. Just south of Zhangye, we passed beehives beside the road.

We were also seeing kilns in various states of repair, with two to four chimneys, their heights varying presumably according to the local wind conditions. Both kilns and chimneys were built of brick, and at first we thought they were brick kilns. Neither the shape nor the number of them fitted this theory, however, so someone suggested charcoal. At last, we noticed the drifts of white powdery ash beside the kiln mouths and guessed the truth. They are lime kilns, used to convert limestone into an ingredient of cement.

Below Zhangye, a new feature appeared in the landscape, a mudbrick wall running from north-west to south-east along the valley. Though it was in a poor state of repair with great gaps, there were also the clear remains of watch towers and battlements. The road had again approached more closely to the northern hills, now much lower and covered with scrubby vegetation. Evidently, the cultivated land lay to the south because the wall ran beside and parallel to the road. It consisted of only one line of masonry and must have been both narrower and far less elaborate than the Great Wall, a later addition designed to stop invasions by northern tribes who had managed to breach the natural mountain wall. This last-ditch defence was manned by the garrisons housed in the towns we were passing.

After lunch at a restaurant in Jinquan, a large, busy town, we heard music and saw a crowd on the other side of a main street. In its midst, two musicians, playing a stringed instrument and a kind of drum, sat on the pavement leaning against a wall. Two women and a man sang the songs being played as their voices were needed. Some of the music seemed to be traditional, possibly folk songs. Some was more formal, a part of the operatic repertoire. Paul found the verses extremely hard to understand and thought the singers were using a colloquial patois but not a distinct local dialect. The audience was rapt by the experience, as many as three dozen people, some of them seated on the pavement in a half circle. Though many were young, there were almost no children.

That night we stopped in the Liangzhou Hotel at Wuwei. Wuwei is the place near which a famous bronze horse statue of the Tang dynasty was found. Although the original has been left in the Palace Museum in Beijing since it was found in 1969, replicas in all sizes sit on the tops of lamp standards and public buildings throughout the city. Smaller varieties were offered for sale in the hotel gift shop.

The Liangzhou Hotel was without question the most comfortable of the many we used during six weeks in China. The rooms were large, old-fashioned and clean. Bathrooms had plenty of towels and toilet paper and, even more uniquely, hot water during most of the hours we were there. All the light fixtures had bulbs in them that worked. As soon as we arrived, cups of fresh green tea were brought to our rooms. The dining room could not rise to the standard of the bedrooms, but our meals were adequate.

Not only had the very young members of this hotel's staff been taught what might be expected of them by guests, like keeping toilet paper in stock, but they were required to attend English classes every night between 8.30 and 10.30. Paul was asked to speak to the class, and Tom and I went along. Although he was almost defeated by their extreme shyness, and the presence of their young teacher, he struggled to get the students-staff to reply to his Chinese questions in English. Then he hit on a stratagem. He invented a game. The students were to give Tom and me English words to translate into Chinese, and we gave them words in Chinese to translate into English. Our obvious inadequacy unsealed their lips, and the staff won with seven correct answers against three. I remember that two of their blockbusters were "banana" and "boiled potato", neither of which we could translate.

Beyond Wuwei, rice paddies began, indicating a significant change not only in the water supply but also the climate. Although temperatures well below zero Centigrade are common here during the winter, there is enough shelter and enough warmth for rice culture. The other crop, even more visible, is sunflowers, row upon row of huge yellow faces grown for the seeds which are eaten by the kilo. Years of practice are needed to get the knack of splitting the thin hull with your teeth to extract the minute green kernel. Farm animals now included long-haired cattle, white with black or brown markings or both.

Terracing had begun along the hillside. Higher up, it was not so easy to say whether the terraces were manmade or the result of weathering and erosion. Liu, a geologist, thought they were natural.

We stopped in a town called Gulang at the head of a very narrow valley cut by a small river. The purpose was to buy herbs from a herbal chemist for the Imperial Cancer Research Fund. In Ashkhabad, we had learned about a popular remedy for diverse complaints made of varying combinations of tar and ash called moumio or moumia. Although Geoff had obtained four samples in Uzbekistan street markets, all attempts to locate this allegedly universal home cure since then had failed. Nor was the chemist in Gulang an exception, well-stocked though the large shop seemed to be, with rows of bottles and jars, each bearing a label, lining shelves above head height. It was

Liu checks the bill at a lunch stop near Lanzhou, Gansu.

the smell in these shops as well as in hospital pharmacies we visited that impressed the uninitiated. Being a mixture, it is quite indescribable, but I think it would be recognisable anywhere.

From the van parked on the dusty village main street, there was time to study the hillsides too. As we left the town, we saw on one the stone containment walls that seemed to prove the case for manmade terraces, but despite the greenness of the hillside, there was nothing we could see planted in the terraces. Liu suggested they had been built for trees which had died. Possibly the containment walls exploited natural features of the landscape which were equally visible elsewhere but had not been terraced. Unfortunately, Liu could find no one who could settle the debate.

The hillsides were now covered with cultivated fields interspersed with uncultivated areas in an angular pattern like a Bukhara carpet. The fields were tan, tilled ready for planting the next crop; the uncultivated patches remained green.

The road had begun to climb through the hills, before it fell again into a valley. Here, at a sharp downward curve, was another accident – a lorry upside down in the middle of the road, but no sign of people, injured or safe.

As we descended through the pass we could see the spur of the Great Wall again on the other side of the valley. The green and brown field patterns continued beside the river interrupted by lines of poplar trees. Villages were mostly of brick. This river is a tributary of the great Huang He, the Yellow River, already surprisingly wide and swift where we crossed it about thirty kilometres before Lanzhou.

Chemical and petro-chemical plants soon brought the historically fertile

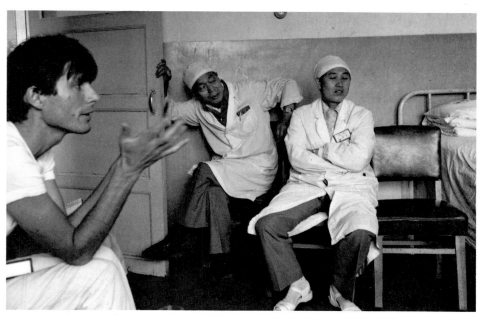

Paul interprets and translates for Geoff Clarke at Lanzhou Second People's Hospital, Gansu.

Gansu corridor to a full stop. Lanzhou is a city of more than two million. We had returned to modern civilisation with a vengeance. Lanzhou lies in the narrow valley of the Huang He, not more than five kilometres wide and at least four times that long. Over the city hangs a more or less permanent pall, a yellow smog. I had visited Lanzhou once before in January when the smog was much worse than in August, because most of the buildings burn coal for heat. Clear days are a rarity. High on the hillsides, pretty wooded parks have been built with an interesting temple in each. It may be impossible to see the river from the hillsides, but an attempt is being made to beautify the southern shore itself. Eventually, a park will run along the river through the length of the city. To me, the only notable building was the first bridge ever built across the Huang He, a cantilevered steel bridge constructed by a German company in 1909. It still carries two-way traffic, though there are now two other bridges.

The massive Friendship Hotel, 1950s Russian-style, stands across a main thoroughfare from the Gansu Provincial Museum of Art and History. Its treasures are to be found in the west wing on the first floor. I was fascinated by the lists of drugs and prescriptions on bamboo from the pre-Christian era. Just beyond them against the back wall of the gallery are small wall paintings from tombs near Jiayuguan dated between 220 and 316. The dates are significant because these murals, ranging in length from less than a metre to one and a half metres and proportionately in width, are from fifty to a hundred years earlier than those at Mugao. What is original and what restored or copied, I do not know, but the artists used line more extensively and colour more simply with less attempt to suggest shade or shadows. The drawing is flowing and very economical. Subjects include birds and animals, and the occupations of common people. Four related panels show servants carrying trays. At the bottom on stone, a man ploughs with a red plough, his robe also in red, and the oxen in black. There is humour in the pictures, like the black ewer being balanced by the ploughing man, and no religious symbolism at all that I could see. Either these tombs predate the arrival of Buddhism or, like those of Astana near Turfan, they housed unreconstructed Confucian dead.

Within a few feet of these displays stands a seventh-century stele about two metres high and twenty-five centimetres thick. Buddhist saints and human figures have been carved on all four sides and outlined in blue and azure. All of these displays are housed at the further end of the western gallery and are well worth the effort to find them.

During the morning after we arrived in Lanzhou, we were taken to the principal Minorities Hospital and then to the Number Two General Hospital, housed in a former Belgian mission in the narrow strip of land north of the river where most of the 200,000 Hui people live. The Hui are Muslims, but ethnically they are a mixture of early Persian and Arab invaders who inter-married with Han natives as well as the Uighers. There are two active mosques situated near to each other north of the river, both built since liberation, on sites historically devoted to the practice of Islam. One site may once have housed a madrasa. The muezzin calls regularly from the larger Friday Mosque. In these older sections of the minority city along narrow, muddy streets near the river and the cantilever bridge, decrepit, dark-stained wooden houses stand, their cornices and doors delicately carved more in the Arabic than the Chinese manner. The whole district looks as though the city officials had recently decided to halt discrimination against the Hui but had not yet advanced the money needed to integrate them into the rest of Lanzhou. Certainly, rapid industrial growth has created more urgent problems like traffic jams and pollution. To what extent, I wonder, is the apparent tardy recognition of minority needs also a direct result of local demand for labour?

We left Lanzhou in a thick smog which helped us to lose our way. We had now acquired a new passenger, the seventh occupant of a vehicle we soft Westerners believed would seat only five. Liu had produced his girlfriend, Wang. In Kashgar, he had first mentioned that she might meet him in Lanzhou. They intended to get married soon after the end of our journey. She was also in the travel business, employed by an organisation that provided facilities for mountain climbing by tourists rather than scientists. Xiao Wang, Little Wang as we were told to call her, was in her late twenties, and, like Liu, unusually tall and Westernised. He had formally asked me if she might travel with us to Beijing, and I had formally consulted my colleagues, but we all had the feeling that dissent would have been unhelpful to the smooth flow of our ten remaining days on the road. In fact, she was a pleasant quiet girl who even managed to dampen Liu's vocal explosions.

The country had now changed totally from semi-arid valley to intensely-cultivated, populous mountain terrain. August 19th was a sunny, clear day, but comfortably cool and dry. For the most part, our road followed the ridges, descending only occasionally to cross a valley and the river it contained. Villages dotted these valleys, and we drove through villages on the ridges too. Willows lined the road, some old and others newly planted, providing

A road in Kashgar, Xinjiang.

Turfan, the bazaar.

The Imperial City, Beijing.

continuous shade and a wind-break. Along some sections of this ancient highway, mud cliffs were pocked by cave openings directly on to the road. Most of these shelters were just large enough for a kang, the mudbrick platform with an opening for a fire to be built in the hollow beneath. The fire served both for cooking and to heat the platform on which the occupants slept. These caves may have housed shepherds, or they may have been used by travellers. The one we examined appeared to have been unused for a long time.

For hundreds of kilometres through these sharp, meandering hills, agriculture depended on terracing, beautiful to look at, but they must be hell to farm. In places, they climbed twenty high one above the other from the valley floor to the ridge, following the curve of the hill. Small, dirt farm roads ran up the insides of the bends connecting the terraces. Many had now been harvested and were tan or darker brown depending on whether they had been ploughed or harrowed. Others were still green with crops. The most common cereal still standing in this region was corn. There was a sense of permanence and stability about these terraces. They have certainly endured through good weather and bad, peace and war for generations.

We saw very little of the people through this fertile region. Occasionally, they would be threshing by hand on hard earth surfaces near the road. Now that we were nearing the end of the Silk Road proper, we had begun to collect grain samples after weeks of disregard. This meant stopping if it looked like wheat that was being threshed and asking to buy half a kilo. Only once or twice was there any objection. Usually, the hard-working farmer with his son or brother and their wives just looked at the Western faces and nodded, asking for about a penny. They were young, by and large, in their thirties and forties. Their children swept the threshed grain towards the centre. A few people cycled beside the road or drove farm carts, usually pulled by single-stroke tractors. But I had the impression that most people were elsewhere, repairing tools and machinery or damage to the irrigation channels.

About 325 kilometres from Lanzhou, the road entered the Liupan Mountains, higher and more rocky than the terraced hills but still green. At the top of the highest peak, also called Liupan, stands the shining white new pavilion built to commemorate the fiftieth anniversary of the completion of the Long March very near this place. In 1936, Mao Zedong (better known to the West by the old spelling, Mao Tse-Tung) and his lieutenants had successfully brought the Red Army from the far south to link up with Communist forces that had managed to hold on despite Guomindang and Japanese attacks in these north-western regions. For two decades or more, Mao's poem celebrating the Red Army crossing of this mountain had been the first classical style poem taught to primary school pupils, leaving an indelible impression.

We spent the night comfortably at a guest house in a small market town called Pingliang. To prove that harvest was nearing its climax, we saw corn on the cob for sale as an item of food. The landscape was obscured by haze the next morning, and the terraces were replaced by fields extending as far as the hills visible dimly in the distance. Much corn was still standing.

The Big Buddha Monastery (Da Fou Si) sits to the right of the road in a narrow valley about 135 kilometres past Pingliang. Like the familiar grottoes of the west, it had been dug into the side of the hill using natural caves in the soft limestone, but it is limited now to a central gallery and six side chambers. The Buddha in the central gallery is about twenty metres high and had been recently repainted in brilliant blue, green and red. The carving is also less subtle, possibly because it incorporates new work. The original figures are said to date from the Tang period, the oldest from AD 629. On either side of the Buddha stand two monumental female attendants, Bodhisattvas. Flame designs and halos are painted behind all three figures, and there are high relief carvings of animals and symbolic figures of greater subtlety and perhaps greater age. The caves on each side of the central gallery contained carved figures which were also less ostentatiously restored and more interesting. To the right of these large galleries are three smaller caves, containing rows of Bodhisattvas and other Buddhist figures, all carved in high relief.

The monastery is near a village called Bin Xian where one major industry is the supply of crafts, especially carved wood, to the row of stalls that lines the road opposite the caves. There are bowls, mortars and pestles and rolling pins in every conceivable size designed to manufacture the multiform dumplings that do for the cuisine of north China what bread and rolls do for us. We saw no other tourists between Lanzhou and Xi'an, but this part of the ancient highway must have had hidden traffic that we missed. All those stalls selling identical objects would cease to exist otherwise, nor can I believe that it was respect for art alone that caused the restoration of this out-of-the-way monastery and construction of a well-equipped ticket booth.

The road to Xi'an slowly deteriorated as the dust increased and industrial sites and new towns replaced fields. Because of the river basins surrounding the city, humidity soared as the weather got hotter and the traffic thicker. Plenty of slow farm vehicles and bicycles still travelled between the remaining farm villages amongst the disembodied limbs of this rich and well-watered agricultural region.

Xi'an with its immediate surroundings houses four million people. For 2,500 years, a city somewhere on the site of the present urban sprawl was the capital of either one of its major constituent states or of a unified China. From about 200 BC, the capital was called Chang'an, meaning everlasting peace. Under the Sui and the Tang the present inner walled city was built around the Imperial palace and the administrative departments. The outer town, following a grid pattern around the walled town, housed a million people even then. With the fall of the Tang dynasty, the capital was moved north to what is now Beijing. There is no evidence that Marco Polo ever visited Chang'an. He travelled further north to Kubilai Khan's summer palace, now disappeared, and to Beijing. But Xi'an continued to flourish because of its rich hinterlands. Even today, tourists are taken to see model communes in the neighbourhood.

It was at Chang'an during its administrative apogee where the Silk Road began and ended. Trade with the unknown, distant western regions and beyond began about the time of China's first unification when Emperor Qin shi Huang di, Huang di of the Qin dynasty, caused the construction of his personal memorial about fifty kilometres east of Xi'an. At the west end is his grave, still not wholly excavated, and beyond it, the astonishing terracotta army, row upon row of soldiers on foot and horseback, each face a portrait, extending for more than five kilometres from the tomb itself. The nation that could afford such a memorial, albeit one built by the Emperor in the image of his own massive ego, might be expected to send out priceless fabrics of silk in exchange for the raw materials of the undeveloped west. For centuries, China was like a great pump, ejecting rich goods of unbounded beauty and sucking in jewels, metals, animals and men along the great mountain-spanning highway.

In Xi'an we stayed in a Sports Hotel, inappropriately but comfortably. Paul and I shared an air-conditioned room that overlooked an inner courtyard partially filled by a great pile of coal. A building to the right appeared to house a dining room for young people, some of whom seemed to have rooms in another two-storey building on the far side of the courtyard. Perhaps the latter group were staff, and their non-resident colleagues were sports people attending a training course. Whatever the explanation, these young Chinese had to carry all their meals in a dish across the courtyard to the dormitory where the open windows indicated there was no trace of air-conditioning. I suppose second-class citizenship for the young breaches no civil right, but the juxtaposition of buildings and facilities seemed odd if not unfortunate. Beyond the courtyard towered the newest and poshest hotel in Xi'an, underlining the contrast between tourist luxury and the lot of citizens.

Xi'an, like Beijing, is too big to walk in comfortably even had the weather been cooler. The blocks are long, and about five kilometres separated our hotel, for example, from the Shanxi Provincial Museum. There are trolley buses but no route maps for the uninitiated. Bicycles, cheap to rent as in most Chinese towns, are also of limited value without maps.

As usual, we depended on the admirable Liu. He arranged the obligatory hospital visits for our second day. First, we visited the cancer unit of People's Hospital Number Two. Twelve members of the hospital staff made themselves available at short notice. The first questions concerned the tar-based remedy, moumio. Many of the doctors and pharmacologists, even those trained in traditional medicine, whom we questioned about the preparation in the Soviet Union as well as China, had never heard of it. In the Xi'an People's Hospital Number Two, the staff knew nothing about it. Geoff produced a sample. The chief pharmacologist smiled, and said she had never seen anything quite like it. Such can be the frustrations of science: the one previously unreported putative cause of oesophageal cancer we had uncovered was unfamiliar to many of the professionals who diagnosed and treated the disease along our route.

That afternoon, it was the turn of the Chinese Medicine Hospital, a large, well-staffed institution where we pursued the central role of diet and Chinese medicine and its possible relationship to oesophageal cancer. Earlier Chinese research had implicated methods of winter food storage as a possible source of cancer-causing substances. The traditional medicine doctors in Xi'an were aware of this work and had nothing to add, but pointed out that in Chinese medicine the food eaten is often a factor in diagnosis and diet is part of almost all therapeutic regimens. Appendix V deals at greater length with medical aspects of our work.

Paul and I had visited the excavations of the terracotta army a few years before and decided against repeating the journey. Once again, Tom was defeated by the no-photography regulations. We had tried through Liu to arrange a meeting with the Director of the installation, as we had done at

Mugao. This site is administered directly from Beijing, however, without a provincial intermediary. All arrangements had to begin in Beijing. So Tom took some pictures of the countryside, but otherwise observed the archaeological find of the century like any other tourist. Seeing the massed ranks of the clay army *in situ* is certainly a different experience from seeing two or three copies in the windows of Selfridge's. They are housed in a mammoth shed, roofed with corrugated blue plastic, which covers an acre or more. The shelter stands the same height above the ground as the excavations, revealing the warriors cut into it. Wooden walkways wide enough to admit four people abreast conduct the crowds on a one-way tour of the installation. Part of the excitement comes from the vast unexcavated area, twice as long as the present excavation, where thousands of troops still stand unrevealed.

Within the city there is a drum tower, two beautiful ancient pagodas and of course the city walls themselves. But the supreme sites in Xi'an are the Shanxi Provincial Museum and the Great Mosque. Strictly speaking, the Provincial Museum is part of the Historical Museum, but the entire complex is administered as a unit. It is housed in a former Confucian temple built beside a curious archive called the Bei lin or Forest of Steles. A gate in a corner opens into a large cobbled courtyard. There are shops built into the outer wall. A large inactive fountain stands in the centre of an artificial pond. Another decorative wall and gate lead to the main inner courtyard about 100 metres long containing a garden with walks and benches. Along the sides stretch the museum buildings proper. During our visit, there was a special exhibition of Shanxi archaeological relics, many of them from the Xi'an area and others from further afield.

Special hardly describes this small exhibition. First came the bronzes, the oldest known objects, dating from 1200 BC. The beauty of the half-dozen vessels surpasses even the early bronzes in the British Museum. There were chimes of bells with inscriptions dating them down the centuries and a superb ram's head. Towards the front of a case displaying various cast bronze and carved jade vessels stood a curved jade vase decorated with relief carvings picked out in gold leaf. It was about six inches high with a wasp waist dividing it into two roughly equal parts, and the overall proportions added as much to its solemn beauty as the decorations. Delicate cast bronze vessels in the shapes of animals had handles with stylised eyes and geometric designs. These were followed by carvings in bone, spearheads decorated with bifurcated serpents binding them to the wooden shaft. A small white-stone Buddha sitting on a lotus leaf still carried traces of colour including red on the robes. The porcelain was also superb: two Song dynasty bowls with oil-drop designs, the glaze containing small circles apparently of the same colour but reflecting light differently. Suddenly, my eye was caught by an oxhead cup carved from agate, perhaps one and a half inches in diameter, the carved oxhead bearing a gold plug in its mouth. It is said to have been a gift from Nepal to the Tang court, in the mid-Asia style, lustrous and still in perfect condition. By comparison with this special exhibition, the permanent displays almost lost their grandeur.

The Forest of Steles is the unique part of the permanent exhibition. Hundreds of carved black basalt columns in various shapes and sizes contained memorials to men or events, including the founding of a Christian chapel at Xi'an in 781. The earliest were fragments from about the time of Christ but the best were from the Tang period. One hundred and fourteen contain the texts of the twelve classics including the *I Qing*. In small courtyards between the pavilions containing the steles stood inscribed stones from many different sources such as mosques, churches and cemeteries. To study them properly would take years.

The Great Mosque is the largest still in use in Xi'an and probably the oldest. Not surprisingly, it stands in a district chiefly inhabited by Hui people. Founded in 742, the present buildings date from the late fourteenth century and have been much restored. During our visit, the mosque itself was undergoing a complete reconstruction. The three adjoining courtyards, divided by decorative walls, gave access to buildings such as the library. On the wall opposite the entrance door hung a woven silk map of the world showing Mecca at the centre with Xi'an in the middle distance above it. The names are Chinese transliterations of Arabic. Similarly, many of the gateways carry Qurânic quotations in Arabic transliterated into Chinese characters. The courtyards contained gardens, of course, and foreshadow the new mosque at Aksu with its restful garden courtyard. From the Topkapi to Xi'an's Great Mosque, the unity of Islam is nowhere more visible than in these gardens. In the entrance to the first courtyard where you buy your admission ticket, there is a souvenir kiosk, furthermore, which is the visible proof of the unity of modern Chinese tourism.

We left Xi'an before 8.00 a.m. on Sunday, 23rd August, in brilliant sunshine. The tassled heads of the maize looked ready for harvesting. Terraces covered only the lower flanks of the hills which were here too rugged to be farmed to the ridges. Fields across the valley floor were strips, long and narrow, perhaps a reversion due to the decentralisation of agricultural holdings. In almost every strip, bamboo frames covered by canvas or straw provided shelters against sun and rain. Many of the fields grew exotic crops such as lotus and sesame, and there were now many orchards, mostly apple. The villages often had new brick houses standing beside older mudbrick buildings, a sign of increasing prosperity, as were the ubiquitous TV aerials. Again, the people seem to be widely dispersed, a few of them threshing, many moving along the highway in carts or on bicycles.

One hundred and eighty kilometres past Xi'an, we glimpsed the Huang He to our left again, the first sight since Lanzhou. We had driven across the base of the great northerly curve of the river which is returning here to the heartland of ancient China. That night, we stopped at Sanmenxia, "Three Gates Gorges". A few kilometres north of the town, the Huang He is divided by hilly islands into three swift, unnavigable channels. During the Han expansion, a canal was built around them, remains of which can still be seen at least until completion of a hydro-electric project which will flood much of the river valley here.

Near the excellent guest house was a busy market with more variety of vegetables and fruits than household goods or clothing. Henan province is too far from Pakistan to benefit from imports in the same way as Xinjiang.

Just beyond the eastern boundary of the town stands a wonderful Song dynasty pagoda called Hama or Toad because it is surrounded by the marshy fields they populate. In Sanmenxia itself an effort has been made to display remains of a Neolithic culture unearthed by archaeologists since liberation. There is a tomb chamber beneath the ground level, and a pavilion containing artefacts though I suspect that the best items had been sent on to Beijing. If it seems strange to find so much of interest in a small provincial centre, I think the explanation lies in the role of the Huang He itself. Like the Nile, it has watered the rich valley, reaching east and north from Sanmenxia, assuring the survival of surplus-producing farmlands for millennia.

As in Egypt, furthermore, productive land depended on irrigation. Between Sanmenxia and Luoyang, we passed stone aqueducts at least some of which are still in use. One stretch near the town of Xin'an consisted of about twenty brick arches supporting a waterway more than a metre wide. Unharvested maize and the younger willow trees had taken a recent battering from hail storms.

For about 600 years from the beginning of the Christian era, Luoyang was the capital of dynasties that ruled parts of China. Under the Sui and Tang who reunified the nation, it shared that role with Chang'an, though the latter city was the principal residence of the Tang Emperors. Luoyang has continued to be an important administrative centre and the post-revolutionary addition of industry has caused a population explosion. Today, some three-quarters of a million people live in the long, narrow city on the banks of the small Luo River and its two tributaries, the Jian and the Chan.

My activities in Luoyang were largely restricted to the Second People's Hospital and the Friendship Hotel. I also visited the major local bookshop. Throughout China we encountered large, well-stocked bookshops. Two stand out, one in Karghalik and the second in Zhangye. It would be hard to match the variety these small-town shops offered just in dictionaries and atlases, reference books that even a foreigner with a limited reading ability could appreciate. There are two problems: sales clerks neither seemed to know nor care what stock they carried and, despite the choice, no two shops seem to have the same stock. In Zhangye, for example, Paul bought an excellent small atlas of China with various useful economic, historical and topographical maps of the provinces. When Tom saw it, he wanted a copy for himself. He looked at shops in Wuwei, Lanzhou, Xi'an, Luoyang and Anyang and had learned to appreciate his luck when he found one in the large bookshop near the Peking Hotel. Despite these faults, the riches on offer make me think seriously about persevering with the language – again.

At Luoyang, the most impressive ancient site is the Longmen Grottoes in cliffs on both sides of the Yi River just south of the city. These Buddhist caves are somewhat later than those at Dunhuang, having been decorated from the sixth to the twelfth centuries with the major work confined to the earlier years. They contain sculpture, much of it monumental, but no murals. Relief carving in many of the grottoes repeat figures such as the Fei Tian or flying angels so beautifully painted at Mugao as well as geometric and flame designs and many inscriptions. I deeply regretted my visit to the hospital prevented my seeing these works, especially since a few years before I had visited the caves near Datong, the first northern Wei capital, where the Emperor had also initiated a Buddhist complex. Tom partly shared my frustration because at Longmen, once more, he was unable to photograph and Paul was deprived of the grottoes because he came to the hospital to interpret for me!

From Luoyang, our route turned northwards across the flat north China plain. It was hot and so humid that haze obscured the land. Just north of Luoyang, we crossed the Huang He, now almost a kilometre wide, for the last time. At a place called Xinxiang, we joined the main north-south road connecting Beijing with Hong Kong and Guangzhou. Since Xi'an, the traffic has been notable for its slowness and the growing number of accidents, but on the main highway we discovered that worse was yet to come. Kilometre by kilometre, the build up continued all the way to Beijing. Work on a four-lane road has just begun. During that afternoon the weather broke; great dark clouds covered the sun. A few drops came down followed by a torrential downpour accompanied by thunder and lightning. The willows lining the road whipped and bowed before the storm. The sky had cleared again, and it was more comfortable by the time we reached Anyang.

Anyang is another of the ancient capitals of China, the most ancient of all. Two kilometres north-west of the town centre on the Huan River excavations during the 1930s revealed the city of Yin, founded about 1300 BC by an Emperor of the Shang dynasty, the earliest for which historical evidence exists. For short periods, Anyang again became the administrative centre of a separate Han state. After the Revolution, industry came to the city too and, like Luoyang, its population grew rapidly, reaching over half a million.

We had elected to spend a night in Anyang because of the Yin ruins and to see a newly-opened display showing tombs of various prominent figures in Chinese history associated with the town. As is so often the case, the most valuable artefacts from the Yin site had been removed either to museums abroad or to Beijing. Authorities in every country have only recently realised the importance of local collections. Small museums help to teach history to local students and their parents, and they also attract tourists away from the crowded major centres. In the case of Yin, this realisation came too late: the most significant discoveries had been oracle bones, the shoulder bones of sheep or tortoise shells on which prophecies were written before the bone was thrown into a fire which produced a pattern of cracks that priests read and interpreted. Oracle bones offer unique information about Chinese writing and data on the structure of the Shang state. The British Museum has half a dozen and examples can be found elsewhere in Europe and America. Those which had been collected in Beijing were spirited off to Taiwan by the Guomindang when the Nationalist government fled. The Yin ruins themselves are stark and not particularly informative.

On a rise of land a short distance beyond Yin stands a short, square Tang dynasty red brick pagoda with interesting carved Buddhist reliefs on its sides. Back in the city, the new display of tombs consisted of copies, many of them imaginary, of the graves of rulers suitably furnished with replicas. It was a waste of time and the entrance fee, but one aspect is worthy of note. The enterprise is a private venture. One of the owners told Paul they were aware of the shortcomings and hoped to improve the displays from their income!

Examples of private enterprise multiply. The next day we stopped at Sha He, a town about eighty kilometres north of Anyang where Xiao Wang, Liu's girlfriend, had grown up. She wanted us to have lunch in a restaurant opened in 1985 by a friend of hers. He owned the three-storey building and let out a ground-floor shop beside the restaurant. The upper floors were hotel rooms. Because he bought wholesale, the owner supplied part of the goods sold by the shop and sold vegetables and meat to nearby collectives. For a new enterprise, he seems to have a very large staff. The head cook had a second-class certificate on a scale from four up to Special and was paid about £60 a month. There were three more kitchen staff as well as several young waiters and waitresses some of whom probably worked part-time. We were served an excellent meal. A cousin of Wang's joined us. He was in his twenties. A year or two ago, he had bought a process for making rust-proof paint from a state enterprise. Now he sold to various state enterprises in the area, and to collective farms.

Our road went through Shijiazhuang, the administrative centre of Hebei province, a tree-lined city of no great distinction except that, after 1949, a memorial hospital was built there to a Canadian doctor, Norman Bethune. Bethune served in field hospitals in the Communist guerrilla areas nearby during the Japanese War (1938–39), gave unstinting medical help to the people and the Red Army and became one of the popular heroes of the Revolution.

We passed our last night on the road in a small city called Baoding. The guest house dining room had closed by the time we arrived, and we dined in a scruffy private-enterprise restaurant nearby. During the meal, I needed a toilet. One of the owners, a gruff and burly man, insisted on showing me the way. He held me by the arm as we walked around the side of the building to a privy that seemed to be in a separate compound. Nor was that enough. He remained with me throughout, holding the torch so that I should have no difficulties in the dark. Then he led me by the arm back to the restaurant and made me wait by the door while he fetched a basin of water so that I could rinse my hands!

The morning of Saturday, August 29th, was sunny and quite fresh. Once again, the lush agricultural land gave way to the incursions of urban development as we approached Beijing, and the traffic only got worse. Our road crossed a bridge about 500 metres from the Marco Polo Bridge, to which we would return. To our right, a new motorway bridge was under construction across the same, empty river. Meanwhile, the two-lane highway continued until at last it reached the south-east corner of the capital's new ring road. Xiao Wang left us near her flat off the southern ring. We would see her for one more moment at the airport.

When we arrived at the beautiful lakeside restaurant where lunch had been laid on for us, I knew we had come full circle. Paul and I had come to this lake by taxi in January 1986 when the Academy of Medical Sciences had agreed to sponsor the Marco Polo Expedition. Just across the road behind the restaurant was the Ministry of Public Health compound where we had an inconclusive interview with three representatives of the Bureau of Foreign Affairs. The lake had been frozen over, a few leafless trees standing like black skeletons under the leaden sky. I had not even noticed a restaurant. Now in the hot sunshine, cars parked everywhere and people strolling, we entered a glass front door into a low-ceilinged, air-conditioned room. Shen's mother, a partner in the Mountain Scientific Expedition Advisory Service, was there to greet us.

# Chapter 13

# END OF THE JOURNEY

Our agreement with the Chinese required that they house us for the first two nights in Beijing after which we would look after ourselves. Paul's parents had generously offered to accommodate Tom and me as well as their son. Geoff had arranged to work for a Chinese medical institution which would provide accommodation. By telephone from Yumen and points east, Paul had arranged with his brother in Beijing to book flights to London for the three of us on or about September 5th.

Our new and unremarkable hotel had been built about fifteen kilometres north of the city centre, outside the ring road but beside remains of a Yuan city wall. In Kashgar, we had been told to expect a banquet to celebrate our arrival in Beijing. We were to supply the names of people whom we wished to invite such as the President of the Chinese National Commission for UNESCO. By the time we reached Lanzhou, the banquet had become a reception. There was some doubt whether the Institute of Geology could find the telephone number for the National Commission. I asked the British Consul to pass it on. But when we arrived in Beijing, the reception had become a dinner party with members of the Institute of Geology and the former President of the Academy of Sciences, Lu Jiaxi. We dined in the restaurant by the lake the night after our arrival. The atmosphere was convivial, and we were made to feel very welcome over a fine meal. Nevertheless, who can doubt that "such maimed rites" reflected the status imposed on the expedition by my withholding payments and complaining about arrangements and accommodation.

A final interview with Zheng Xilan had been arranged to settle the matter of who was to pay for the excellent Dr Zheng. My early correspondence had made it clear that, much as we would welcome the company of a Chinese doctor, we could not afford to pay his way. However I wrote a cheque for £500 to reimburse their excess travel and accommodation necessitated by the late changes of our arrival date. But I also explained, with Paul's willing help, how disappointing and unsatisfactory had been their preparations, especially for photography. It took another three hours. Liu knew we appreciated his field efforts to fill the planning gaps day by day, and he tried to distance himself by staying away. In the event, he was present but said scarcely a word. I hope the Mountain Expedition Advisory Service and the Institute of Geology learned from their mistakes, and future expeditions will not be frustrated as we were.

On August 31st Liu and Shen collected us from Paul's parents' flat at 2.00 p.m. for the last episode of the Marco Polo Expedition. By the time we reached the Marco Polo Bridge, the sun had become quite hot. Built in 1912, the ornate white marble structure is now closed to motor traffic. It occupies a site on which there has been a bridge for centuries, but why Marco Polo, who approached the capital from the north with the Mongol court, should have entered the city from the south-west, I cannot imagine. Still, it has come to be known as the Marco Polo Bridge among Westerners in China, and it provided an appropriate venue for the formal presentation of our vehicle to our Chinese hosts. Two officials from the Institute of Geology joined Liu and Shen. Zheng Xilan had appointments elsewhere! The Consulate sent a representative. Mark Braine of the BBC interviewed us. A cameraman and sound man from the American NBC network filmed the proceedings.

For the last time, we all climbed into the car. Shen drove a hundred metres back from the bridge through a solid brick arch that must once have been part of a formal approach. He turned the vehicle and, on a signal from the NBC cameraman, began his approach. Just then, a coach appeared around a corner between the arch and the bridge, stopped to drop passengers and drove on around the next corner beside the dry river bed. Local people showed almost no interest in us. Shen returned to the side of the arch away from the bridge. At the signal, he drove slowly through the arch and on to the cobbled bridge approach itself. We all climbed out and exchanged greetings. When the papers had been passed to one of the Institute officials, we shared a case of soft drinks only slightly cooler than air temperature and drove back into the city.

From Lanzhou, I had asked the British Consulate to make an appointment for us to talk to the National Bureau of Museums and Archaeological Data which is in charge of the major monuments like the Mugao Grottoes and the terracotta army. Paul, Tom and I called on Mr Guo Zhan, Deputy Chief of the Cultural Relics Section the next afternoon. I asked him to explain the rules with regard to visiting and photographing such sites so that I could pass them on to UNESCO and as well as other interested people at home.

Mr Guo described how the Bureau had come into existence, and that it was now directly under the State Council although still administered by the Ministry of Culture. He said that at present, 243 places are under Bureau control and that the number will rise to about 500. At all of them, admission and photography, especially motion picture, are restricted. We learned that applicants for permission to photograph or film had to write to the Bureau and were required to complete a questionnaire, now being revised. No single set of rules had yet been agreed nor was there a schedule of fees. The Bureau would treat UNESCO like any other institution wishing to photograph or film relics, Mr Guo believed, but suggested that the international cultural organisation could approach the State Council directly. He was the soul of polite friendliness, but unable to provide much guidance because the Bureau still makes decisions on a strictly ad hoc basis.

Our remaining days in Beijing passed quickly. I allowed previous visits to make me blasé, and the warm weather made the huge swimming pool at the Friendship Hotel immensely inviting. Paul looked up old friends. Only Tom made some effort to explore the fabulous wealth of this great city. Even he stayed outdoors so none of us took advantage of the Imperial Museums or the baroque splendours of the Summer Palace.

Paul's brother was the office manager in Beijing of an American corporation with mining interests. Paul and I went to his office to pay for and collect the airline tickets he had booked for us. It was on the twenty-second floor of an office block beside the Friendship Store. Like London, Beijing now has a skyline dotted with high-rise buildings. There are fewer signs of poverty than a decade ago. People ride their bicycles wearing bright jackets and white trousers or even shorts. The narrow streets lined by single-storey houses with a privy at each intersection are disappearing rapidly. Hoardings advertise Coca-Cola. Beijing, more than other Chinese cities, displays the increasing homogenisation of world culture.

For better or worse, it is a trend the Marco Polo Expedition has furthered. We drove more than 20,000 kilometres along roads which are already choked with lorries. They carry goods within national boundaries, but there is no physical reason why they should not trade across borders. Stretches of road totalling perhaps 200 kilometres, about 1 per cent of the distance we travelled, are impassable for lorries, but to bring them up to a minimum standard would require quite small capital investments. The Silk Road, all the ancient international trading routes across central Asia can serve both trade and tourism any time governments decide they could be useful. We demonstrated that.

What else did we do? I can speak only for myself. I saw much that was beautiful, like water in the desert, mountain passes and the sophisticated art of civilisations much older than our own. I saw some things that are ugly like corruption and the threat of violence in Iran. Some of our Soviet colleagues have become good friends whom I hope to entertain at home in London. A field of learning, the history and archaeology of central Asia, has opened up to me. Even if I never see Andizhan again, the School of Oriental and African Studies library lets me continue the visit through the work of scholars and other travellers. I know what it is to be uncomfortable, sick, tired and bored when it is no one's fault but my own.

And I have a sense of achievement because my own planning, persistence and bloody-mindedness got me there. Happy is the person who can say that, and the joy of it is, you can too.

# APPENDICES

## APPENDIX I

## Letters to Mr M. S. Gorbachov

January 29th, 1986

Mr M. S. Gorbachov
First Secretary
Communist Party of the USSR
Moscow
USSR

Dear First Secretary,

The Marco Polo Expedition consists of a small team whose first objective is research into the causes of oesophageal cancer, a disease with a relatively high incidence along the ancient Silk Road connecting the Mediterranean Sea with China. Enclosed please find a brochure which describes the purposes and structure of the expedition.

The scientific research is being undertaken at the request of the Imperial Cancer Research Fund in London. Its results will be of use not only to the Imperial Cancer Research Fund but to all institutions studying cancer in the Soviet Union and in China. In fact, some of the theories being tested by our research were developed as a result of work done in north-eastern Iran and in north-western China by scientists from the Imperial Cancer Research Fund working in China with the Cancer Institute of Beijing.

Because of its research programme, the Marco Polo Expedition has received the support of the Royal Society. The Royal Society has written both to the Academy of Sciences of the USSR and to the Academy of Medical Sciences in Beijing requesting that these two organisations sponsor the planned travel of the Marco Polo Expedition through the Soviet Union and China, respectively. Sponsorship consists of official backing and the arrangement through local departments of health for hospitals and other health institutions to assist us with our research needs. The expedition is entirely self-supporting and is not requesting financial assistance from the sponsoring bodies.

The Academy of Medical Sciences has accorded us the sponsorship requested by the Royal Society. Although the letter from the Foreign Secretary of the Royal Society was sent to the Scientific Secretary of the Academy of Sciences of the USSR on October 17th, 1985, there has as yet been no reply. I have also written to the Scientific Secretary requesting sponsorship from the Academy of Sciences, and on December 15th, 1985, I cabled him asking permission to come to Moscow to discuss arrangements for our research and travel. We are aware, for example, that in both China and the Soviet Union, we wish to drive through areas normally closed to tourism. Apparently because of the nature of our proposed research, this is not proving to be a problem in China, and of course I hope it will be one that can be resolved with the help of the appropriate authorities in the Soviet Union. In any case, I cabled the Scientific Secretary of the Academy of Sciences a second time after my return from Beijing on January 22nd, 1986, in order to tell him about the favourable response of the Chinese Academy of Medical Sciences to our request for sponsorship and of the role being played by a branch of the Academia Sinica in arranging our actual travel permits. I also repeated my request that I be allowed to come to Moscow to discuss arrangements.

I would not take the unusual course of addressing this request for help to you were it not that time is growing very short. As you will see in the brochure, we hope to leave London about May 15th, 1986, and to cross the border from Iran into the Soviet Union about July 1st. There is much to be done before our departure date, as you can imagine. In the normal course of events, I am sure that the problems surrounding our unique journey could and would be resolved by the appropriate Soviet authorities, but such matters always take time, here as there, and we are very short of time. Can you possibly help us, please? It is our earnest belief that there will be real benefit to potential victims of this and similar cancers, whatever their nationalities, as a result of our proposed research.

Thank you.
Sincerely,
Richard B. Fisher
Expedition Leader


December 11th, 1986

Mr M. S. Gorbachov
First Secretary
Communist Party of the USSR
Moscow
USSR


Dear First Secretary,

Please accept my thanks and that of my colleagues for the help you have given us in the matter of obtaining permission for the Marco Polo Expedition to travel through the central Asian Soviet Republics. I have just returned from a useful and enjoyable week in Moscow and Leningrad as a guest of the Academy of Sciences. The Institute of Geography has offered the expedition the fullest co-operation in the organisation of our travel through the Soviet Union and with our research into the historical geography of the Silk Road. The individuals at the Institute involved in planning have been extremely helpful, and happily, will be accompanying us along the route. We are now planning to enter the USSR from Iran about June 15th, 1987, and to cross the Soviet-Chinese border about July 15th.

Because the Academy of Sciences is not itself involved in cancer research, we still have the problem of organising the medical side of our work within the Soviet Union. However, while I was in Moscow, the Institute of Geography kindly arranged for me to meet the Chief of Protocol at the Ministry of Health who is now aware of our plans and outlined some of the problems as he saw them. I was able to tell him that I had already written to the Director of the All-Union Oncological Institute of the Academy of Medical Sciences, and that we would again apply to the Director for technical advice and assistance.

The Institute of Geography was also able to arrange a meeting with the USSR Commission for UNESCO which is giving us their formal support. We will offer the Director General a report on the pleasures and problems of our journey to be used as part of UNESCO's preliminary planning for their proposed Silk Road project.

Again, thank you.

Sincerely,

Richard B. Fisher

Expedition Leader

# APPENDIX II

# Chronological List of Correspondence Relevant to Sponsorship in the USSR and China

USSR
19.11.83, Cultural Attaché, London
11.1.84, Union of Soviet Writers, Moscow
15.3.84, Union of Soviet Journalists, Moscow

10.4.84, Reply: Union of Soviet Journalists
20.6.84, Novosti Press Officer, London
7.8.84, Press Office, Ministry of Foreign Affairs, Moscow

23.8.84, British Council, London

China
19.12.83, Cultural Attaché, London

11.3.84, Dr Joseph Needham (asking advice concerning sponsorship)
19.3.84, National Academy of Social Sciences, Beijing
4.4.84, Reply: National Academy of Social Sciences

8.8.84, China Sports Service Co, Beijing
8.8.84, China National Tourist Office, London
22.8.84, Reply: China Sports

USSR

China

3.9.84, S. Klockov, USSR Commission for UNESCO, Moscow
26.10.84, Institute of Geography, USSR Academy of Sciences, Moscow
26.10.84, All-Union Geographical Society, Leningrad (three letters)
29.10.84, Chairman, East European Trade Council
5.11.84, Reply: Chairman, East European Trade Council
20.11.84, Royal Geographical Society to All-Union Geographical Society
26.11.84, Soviet TV, Moscow
23.12.84, Reply: Geographical Society
Undated, 84, Great Britain–USSR Association: Support
9.1.85, Reply: Soviet TV
11.1.85, Acknow: Soviet TV
14.1.85, Reply: Institute of Geography
5.2.85, Acknow: Institute of Geography
22.2.85, Soviet TV
22.2.85, Vice-Chairman, National Commission for UNESCO
22.2.85, Vice-President, Academy of Sciences
23.2.85, Klockov, UNESCO
25.4.85, Vice-Chairman, UNESCO

25.4.85, Vice-President, Academy of Sciences
28.5.85, Klockov, UNESCO
28.5.85, Institute of Geography
28.5.85, Soviet TV

22.1.85, China Central TV, Beijing

10.4.85, Chinese National Commission for UNESCO, Beijing

23.6.85, Reply: National Commission for UNESCO (to British National Commission, London)

3.8.85, Cultural Attaché, British Embassy, Moscow
15.8.85, Reply: Cultural Attaché

USSR

China

10.9.85, President, Chinese Academy of Medical Sciences, Beijing
10.9.85, Science Officer, British Embassy, Beijing
24.9.85, Central TV, Beijing
27.9.85, President, Chinese Academy of Sciences
27.9.85, President, Chinese Association for Science and Technology
4.10.85, Guangdong TV
4.10.85, Taiyuan TV
7.10.85, Reply: Science Office, British Embassy

11.85, Vice-President, National Commission for UNESCO
21.11.85, Foreign Secretary, USSR Academy of Sciences

19.12.85, President, Academy of Sciences (recommend Mountain Scientific Expedition Advisory Service)
15.1.86, Mountain Scientific Expedition Advisory Service
21.1.86, Ningxia TV

29.1.86, M. S. Gorbachov

27.1.86, Reply: Mountain Scientific Expedition Advisory Service (first of six negotiating letters)
1.3.86, Reply: Ningxia TV

10.4.86, Reply: British Council
22.10.86, Reply: Deputy-Director, Institute of Geography, Academy of Sciences
27.10.86, Deputy-Director, Institute of Geography (accepting basic suggestions)
30.12.86, Reply: USSR National Commission for UNESCO: Support

This listing omits cables and visits to Beijing (1.1.86–17.1.86) and Moscow (30.11.86–4.12.86 and 20.4.87–23.4.87)

# APPENDIX III

# The UNESCO Report

October 29th, 1987

To: Eiji Hattori, Executive Secretary, Task Force for the UNESCO Silk Road Project

From: Richard B. Fisher, Leader, Marco Polo Expedition

Report on
## PRACTICAL ASPECTS OF DRIVING ACROSS THE ANCIENT SILK ROAD

The Marco Polo Expedition left London on May 1st, 1987. We crossed from Dover to Ostend and travelled via Belgium, the German Federal Republic, Austria, Yugoslavia and Greece to Turkey. We reached Antakya, the official starting point of the expedition, on September 19th, entered Iran on June 1st, re-entered Turkey on June 13th, entered the Soviet Union at Leninakan on July 3rd, and China via the Turugart Pass on July 21st. We reached Beijing on August 29th. We returned to London by air.

Four of us drove through Turkey and Iran, but one (Don Baker) had arranged to leave the expedition on June 27th (when we had expected to be in Dushanbe). Though we were then still in Turkey, he was unable to change his plans. Similarly, Paul Crook flew to Samarkand as planned on June 22nd and was met by our Soviet hosts but joined us only when we linked up with the main Soviet group in Leninabad on July 13th. Four of us shared the driving with the occasional assistance of one Soviet driver. In China, we were forbidden to drive. None of us are trained motor mechanics, but, fortunately, the fact that the car was new plus good luck obviated the need for major repairs.

Although the expedition had the formal support of the Turkish, Iranian, Soviet and Chinese National Commissions for UNESCO, we were able to pay our respects only to the first two. In Ankara, the Secretary General, Mrs Guy Orimac, gave us what help she could. The Iranian National Commission had arranged our Iranian visas. When we reached Tehrān, Mr Saduq, the Director, and Mr Afkhani, the Acting Secretary, welcomed us warmly and helped us to arrange appointments including a guided tour of the superb Iran-Bostan Museum. They also made every effort to assist us before we were forced to leave Iran. Of course, the expedition went nowhere near Moscow. In Beijing, we telephoned the National Commission on the day we arrived, but unfortunately our call was returned only a matter of hours after our departure for London on September 5th.

1 *Roads.*    Our total journey covered about 22,500 kilometres. This total includes journeys in the vicinity of towns where we stopped as well as return journeys, both intended and otherwise; for example, we planned the delightful and instructive circumnavigation of Lake Van, but not the three-day retreat from Mashhad to the Turkish border. We used every means of transportation: we crossed the Amudar'ya by ferry boat, left Turkey and entered the Soviet Union by train, flew between Jerevan and Ashkhabad while our car was driven by two of our Soviet colleagues, and of course walked varying distances to explore monuments and natural wonders. But most of our journey was by car.

On the whole, roads were better than we had anticipated. For example, our four expensive sand tyres were never needed. We had taken them in anticipation of driving the southern route around the Taklimakan, but, at the last minute, the Chinese authorities refused us permission to drive any further than Hotan. On the other hand, we experienced the effects of unseasonable, heavy rain from the moment we entered China until we reached Korla. The details are listed in the following table. Nevertheless, all but perhaps 200 kilometres of the route we travelled are being used now by lorry traffic. The astonishing fact is that the ancient Silk Road could again become an international trade and tourist route with very little extra expenditure by the road-maintenance authorities.

The following shows towns through which we drove rather than route numbers, distances (in kilometres) and our observations of the state of the roads.

*Ostend–Köln–München–Salzburg–Klagenfurt* (1270): 4-lane motorway.

*Klagenfurt–Niš–Thessaloníki–Istanbul* (1880): mainly well-paved 2-lane highway, but with motorways around Ljubliana, Belgrade and Niš.

*Istanbul–Bosüyük–Kütahya–Konya–Adana–Antakya* (1195): good, 2-lane paved roads, excepting for 4-lane motorway the last 80 kms before Adana. Secondary roads often have less traffic and may be faster than main roads.

*Antakya–Fevzipaşa–Gaziantep–Urfa–Diyarbakir–Tatvan* (643): good, 2-lane paved roads, but the main road between Fevzipaşa and Diyarbakir is badly rutted and in need of repair, possibly because it was May and still early in the year.

*Tatvan–Van–Erçiş–Ağri* (381): good, 2-lane paved roads. Between Erçiş and Ağri parts of the surface are unmetalled, possibly due to frost damage. Spectacular views from hairpin curves through the mountains are unimpeded by protective barriers of any kind, a characteristic of all our later scenic drives!

*Erçiş–Tatvan* (150): an excellent, well-paved, 2-lane secondary road along the less-travelled north-western shore of Lake Van.

*Ağri–Bāzargān* (131): the main, east-west highway through Anatolia is 2-lane and often in a poor state of repair, but paved and very busy.

The next four entries were routes necessitated by our enforced departure from Iran:

*Ağri–Erzurum* (191): as above. I understand from Don Baker who travelled by coach to Ankara when he left Erzurum that the main road west of Erzurum is cobbled or unpaved for long stretches.

*Horasan–Kars* (141): excellent, 2-lane, paved road.

*Kars–Akyaka* (70): a wide, well-engineered highway in process of construction and unpaved. Almost no traffic. Population is small and scattered, and the border is closed to road traffic!

*Leninakan–Jerevan* (125): excellent, 2-lane, paved road, not too busy when we drove it in the early evening.

The next three entries are the original route plan, modified to reduce our time in Iran to a minimum:

*Bāzargān–Tabrīz–Takestān–Qazvīn–Tehrān* (925): excellent, 2-lane, paved road excepting that the 120 kms between Qazvīn and Tehrān is 4-lane motorway. From about 25 kms before Mīāneh to about 50 kms beyond that town, signs along the road in English and Turkish warn that foreign vehicles are not allowed to stop. Traffic builds steadily towards Tehrān, the city with the worst traffic problems that we experienced, including Istanbul. We understand that on Fridays and possibly other days, traffic from outside is barred from the city, but we do not know how this is accomplished.

*Tehrān–Āmol–Bābol–Bābol Sar* (188): 4-lane highway for the first 50 kms after Tehrān, but then 2-lane, paved road. For about 75 kms through the mountains, the road is badly pitted, especially in the tube-like tunnels that carry it around many of the cliffs. The terrible potholes are the more surprising because Iranian roads are on the whole the best we experienced. From Āmol, the problems end.

*Bābol–Sari–Gorgān–Gonbad-e-Kāvūs–Qūchān–Bājgirān* (652): excellent, 2-lane, paved road, excepting the last 60 kms between Qūchān and the border at Bājgirān. That road is narrow and unmetalled, but beautifully engineered through spectacular but difficult mountain terrain.

The next two entries were necessitated by our arrest at the Iran-Soviet border and return to the Turkish border:

*Bājgirān–Qūchān–Mashhad* (220): after Qūchān, 4-lane highway.

*Bābol Sar–Rasht–Qazvīn* (460): excellent, paved, 2-lane highway.

As noted above, the car was driven for us between Jerevan and Ashkhabad.

*Ashkhabad–Mary–Chardzhou–Bukhara* (710): good, 2-lane, paved road to the Amudar'ya. Though repairs and road improvements are being undertaken, the road surface deteriorates after entering the Uzbek SSR.

*Bukhara–Samarkand* (380): 2-lane, paved road, frequently with a badly-potholed surface. Traffic not heavy.

*Samarkand–Ayni–Leninabad* (220): 2-lane, paved road, as before to the Uzbek-Tadzhik frontier. In the Tadzhik SSR, the surface improves until Ayni. The pass over the mountains on the south is unmetalled but well-engineered; a paved surface is again available about 15 kms after the summit on the north side.

*Leninabad–Kokand–Andizhan–Osh* (350): excellent, 2-lane, paved road. Traffic through the Fergana Valley was generally light.

*Osh–Zhalalabad–Toktogul–Tanuk–Colpan–Naryn–Turugart* (960): with the exception of two sections – about 50 kms after the main road to Frunze branches off before Tanuk, and from Naryn to the border – this road is not only an excellent, 2-lane, paved highway, but spectacularly beautiful. The two unmetalled sections also traverse fine scenery and are well engineered.

*Turugart–Kashi* (130): this section included the worst road we encountered. It began about 20 kms below the pass and continued for about 60 kms. Heavy and unseasonable rains had entirely washed away short but frequent parts of what was otherwise a 2-lane, paved road, leaving the rocky debris of stream beds to be negotiated without puncturing tyres or breaking springs. Ironically, our Chinese hosts allowed us to drive this difficult section, insisting that we hand over permanently to our excellent Chinese driver only when the worst was over, at the first police checkpoint after the border. From the junction of the little-used Turugart road and the main road linking Kashi and Wuqia, the surface was excellent.

*Kashi–Shule–Yingchisha–Suoche–Yenchang–Hotan* (520): good, 2-lane, paved road, but the unseasonable rains continued, and sections of the road were sometimes awash, badly damaged or destroyed leaving unbridged gaps. Fortunately, the desert floor was sufficiently rocky so that it was possible for cars and lorries to ford the streams by detours. Roads within the oases were undamaged excepting where heavy traffic had pitted the surface. Here and elsewhere, the Chinese tend to fill potholes with tarred gravel which is quickly torn loose by lorry traffic.

Because permission to complete the southern route to Dunhuang was withdrawn, we returned to Kashi.

*Kashi–Aksu–Kuqa–Korla–Turfan–Hami* (1,620): good, 2-lane, paved road excepting for about 50 kms between Korla and Turfan and 100 kms between Turfan and Hami which are unmetalled. These unpaved sections are interspersed with well-paved sections where traffic speeds up. Between Turfan and Hami, we came upon the first of many serious accidents. In this one, involving a van that had gone out of control, two people were killed. Many later accidents were caused by differences in the speeds of the two vehicles involved: e.g., a two-stroke tractor and a lorry. The number of accidents rose as traffic increased towards the east, of course, sometimes numbering as many as six a day. Before Korla, unseasonable rains produced conditions similar to, but not as severe as, those to the south. Other comments about the southern route apply also to this section.

*Hami–Liuyuan–Dunhuang–Anxi–Yumen–Jiayuguan* (880): between Hami and Liuyuan, about 250 kms are unmetalled. Otherwise this section consists of 2-lane, paved road in much better state of repair than the previous sections. Traffic continued relatively light.

*Jiayuguan–Zhangye–Wuwei–Lanzhou* (710): good, 2-lane, paved road. Traffic becomes heavier as oases give way to more generally arable conditions.

*Lanzhou–Pingliang–Xi'an–Sanmenxia–Luoyang–Jiaozuo–Xinxiang–Anyang* (1,170): good, 2-lane, paved road, but although the road surface is now better than further west, traffic gets worse. Traffic consists primarily of farm vehicles and ranges from people pulling carts to lorries, with many buses. Between Xinxiang and Anyang, we had even a flock of sheep to cope with during the heaviest afternoon traffic.

*Anyang–Beijing* (470): as above, but new road works as well as taxis and cars add to the traffic chaos on the outskirts of Beijing.

2 *Customs.*    Our experiences as private travellers may not be relevant to the

UNESCO Silk Road Project. I outline them for what they are worth.

Our only significant problems arose in western Europe, more precisely in the EEC. Indeed, we were forced to return from Ostend to Dover on May 2nd because the freight agent used by the vendor of our car provided us with the wrong documentation, a T2L form instead of a T2 form! We had bought the car as an export vehicle and paid no VAT. In the event, the T2 was the only form we needed although we also bought a Carnet ATA during the delay in Dover. Our camera and recording equipment was either personal or on loan and was all returned to the United Kingdom. The fact that our car was to be exported to China, where it paid part of the charges imposed by our Chinese hosts for their services, meant that we could not use a Carnet du Passage, and the Carnet ATA was sold to us by a London agent on the theory that it would cover our entry into Turkey and Iran. It listed only the photographic and holographic equipment. In the event, Turkish Customs found the ATA more of a hindrance than a help, and Iranian Customs refused even to look at it. Excepting for cameras and film that we stated we required during our journey, Iranian Customs sealed all other photographic and holographic equipment. Of course, none of these forms is recognised in the Soviet Union and China.

Even the T2 was actually needed only at Ostend because, as an export vehicle, the car appeared on the ferry boat manifest. We found that if we stayed in the tourist lanes rather than the lorry lanes, only our passports would have been needed at all other European Customs points.

However, Turkish Customs at the Greek border required a fairly thorough examination of our equipment. On the other hand, Turkish Customs at the Iranian border, both departing and re-entering, inspected almost nothing but were much delayed by the Carnet ATA. Turkish Customs at the Soviet border, where we did not introduce the ATA, showed little interest in us.

Iranian Customs inspected our equipment and personal luggage but were interested primarily in the photographic and holographic equipment. On our return to the Turkish border, clearance was arranged without inspection by the Customs policeman who had travelled with us throughout Iran.

Soviet Customs were very thorough. Everything was removed from the car, but at Leninakan, the attentions of the inspectors seemed to be focused on printed matter. At Turugart, the inspection of our personal luggage was more thorough, but the examination of our car slightly more cursory. In both cases, Soviet Customs inspection required more time than any other.

Chinese Customs at Turugart made no inspection beyond the most cursory. The inspectors were more interested in the origin and intended fate of our vehicle. There was almost no baggage inspection at Beijing airport.

Customs officials were universally polite and helpful about shifting equipment and luggage.

3 *Availability of petrol and parts.* Petrol was never a problem, not least because our vehicle had been specially modified to carry a total of fifty-six gallons in the main tank and four supplementary tanks which could be pumped into the main tank while we were driving. Thus, we had a range of approximately 840 miles (1,400 kms). The vehicle was also capable of operating on very low octane petrol (in China, as low

as seventy-two, we were told) although at reduced efficiency, of course.

In Turkey and Iran, petrol stations are well distributed, especially along main roads and in small towns. Prices are somewhat lower than in western Europe. In Turkey, oil can be bought in automobile shops as well as petrol stations. We bought no oil in Iran.

In the areas through which we travelled, Soviet petrol stations are of two types: those which service state vehicles only and receive payment in an official script, and those which service the general public and accept payment in rubles. In the latter stations, which we used of course, it is necessary to tell the office how many litres you want and to pay for them in advance. Although at least one of each type is to be found in every town larger than approximately 5,000 people, they do not operate during the same hours. In fact, without local knowledge, it is impossible to know when petrol stations are open. For example, in Osh we went in search of petrol at about 8.00 p.m. We succeeded only at the fifth station we tried. Two were for state vehicles only, and two were closed. Along the Soviet route, we were able to obtain ninety-three octane petrol, but we did have to pass more than one station and go on to the next, perhaps 50 kms, in order to do so. Engine oil was not always available, but on the initiative of the Deputy Director of the Institute of Geography who led the Soviet party, one of the drivers in the Soviet party had brought five litres of engine oil from Moscow especially for our use.

Because driving in China was strictly the prerogative of a Chinese professional, servicing the car became his duty. Again, however, petrol stations were widely distributed, with new ones recently opened in several towns. As noted, the octane rating is pretty low. Engine oil was purchased once during our drive across China at a petrol station in Aksu. With one or two exceptions amongst the newer stations, payment is in advance as in the Soviet Union. Chinese petrol stations may also enforce a rule that only the driver can enter the compound where petrol is served; all passengers must wait outside the gates. However, this rule was not applied in stations that accepted payment after delivery.

Whereas petrol presented no problem, parts are a different matter. We required very few, partly because we brought with us a large number of items like oil filters, and partly because the vehicle was new when we left England. We bought a new horn in Doğubayazit, eastern Anatolia. One of the Soviet vehicles accompanying us required a new battery at Toktogul, a town beside a beautiful reservoir on the Naryn River in Kirgizia. No new battery seemed to be available, but one was supplied by the local police who cannibalised their own vehicle. Both rear shock-absorbers broke away from the springs, we discovered in Aksu, but could not be refitted or replaced on the road. On the other hand, our Chinese hosts used a Toyota Landcruiser to accompany us while we were in Xinjiang; parts for a Toyota were more widely available than parts for a Land Rover. We were told that a shock absorber for the Landcruiser cost about 96 yuan.

4 *Camping and accommodation.* We were able to camp in every country except China. We carried a tent that accommodated two, a second tent for one person, and two people could sleep in the car. We also had two single-burner

Optimus cookers and equipment for cooking and eating, as well as sleeping bags and air mattresses. We bought food locally, but we also carried a supply of dried food sufficient to feed five people for seven days.

In Turkey, most of the campsites we used were unofficial. The Turkish Tourist Office could not supply a list of official campsites, but we did use three, all of them privately operated.

The first was beside Lake Van at Akhtamar behind a roadside café. It had electricity and water with a toilet in the restaurant. There was room for about eight vehicles.

The second was above Doğubayazit at the Ishak Paşa Serai where we stayed both before leaving Turkey and just after re-entering the country. It is a small plateau just above the serai, with an outdoor privy. Water can be obtained from the serai. There is room for about six vehicles, depending on size of course. The view over the fairy-like palace, the mosque and ancient fortifications opposite and the valley below is among the most spectacular of the many we enjoyed.

The third was in a field about 6 kms west of Erzurum. During the stay there, I was in Ankara in order to arrange for revised Soviet visas, but I believe that all services were available.

In geographical order, other campsites in Turkey were on a hilltop above a reservoir about 50 kms before Kütahya, about 100 metres south of the highway behind a railway embankment some 150 kms east of Konya, in a pomegranate orchard west of Urfa, in a disused quarry on the banks of the Tigris 5 kms east of Diyarbakir, in the ruins of an early Ottoman caravanserai above the snow line in Beautiful Valley about 10 kms south-west of Tatvan, and about 40 kms north of Van on the shore of Lake Van beside a stream, a private orchard and an unoccupied house. This site we also used twice with the knowledge of the owner.

In Iran, we used one official campsite at Bujnurd west of Qūchān. It was a large park with water and toilets. Other campsites in Iran were beside a river about 30 kms before Mīāneh (just before the no-stopping zone began), in a quarry about 5 kms north of Qūchān and beside the highway about 25 kms south-west of Rasht.

Camping in the Soviet Union was a joint venture with the much larger Soviet contingent. Although we used our own sleeping facilities, cooking was done by them: in fact, by the two interpreters, both women, I'm ashamed to say, although when it was put to them that they were being exploited, one asserted her preference for her own cooking.

Three of the Soviet campsites which we shared were based on facilities belonging to towns (Kokand, Andizhan) or trade unions (Leninabad). The only other Soviet campsite was the last one, a high, treeless steppe beside a rushing stream about 90 kms north of Turugart. Like most of our earlier campsites, it was a matter of accepting the best available: we had planned to spend the night in the remains of a Kirgiz caravanserai about 15 kms further up the valley which was a tributary of the main route towards the pass. That afternoon, we had got within about 5 kms of the caravenserai only to find the track, hardly a road, closed by a mud slide. So we had turned round reluctantly to the steppe through which we had driven earlier.

I believe camping in China is possible, but our hosts had chosen to accommodate us in hotels or guest houses. The hotels ranged from brand-new (Beijing) to rundown and outmoded (Kuqa). From our standpoint, it would have been far more comfortable to camp in towns like Aksu, Kuqa, Dunhuang and arguably, Hotan. Hotels run by China International Travel Service (CITS: Kashgar, Korla, Turfan, Hami, Lanzhou, Xi'an, Luoyang, Anyang), moreover, offered facilities that worked occasionally, service ranging from passable to inexcusable and food ranging from adequate to inexcusable. Of the hotels, the most outstanding was the Liangzhou at Wuwei. Facilities worked, the hotel was clean, the staff took pride in helping and the food was good. We enjoyed the guest houses rather more than the hotels. Those at Yumen and Sanmenxia were very good indeed, and although the accommodation was old-fashioned, the food at the Karghalik guest house was by common consent the best we had in China.

In the Soviet Union, we stayed in hotels in Jerevan, Ashkhabad, Bukhara and Samarkand. All of them are relatively new, and of course all of them are operated by Intourist. The best was the hotel at Bukhara: more facilities worked more of the time, and it was cleaner. I believe that on balance the dining room in Bukhara had available more of the dishes we wanted from the imaginative (because most of the dishes are "off") Intourist menu which seems to be universally used throughout central Asia. I will politely refrain from comment on Intourist service because our Soviet hosts deserve nothing but thanks from us.

We stayed one night at the Repetek Desert research station belonging to the Institute of Geography of the USSR Academy of Sciences, our Soviet hosts, and were extremely comfortable. In Osh, we spent two nights at the excellent municipal guest house.

In Iran, we used hotels in Bāzargān on our first night, Tehrān, Bābol Sar and Mashhad. Although it was a fortunate choice, the hotel in Tehrān was the third we asked for accommodation. The first two said they had no rooms, it seemed to us because they did not want Western customers. Customs officials in Mashhad had offered us hotel accommodation when they told us we would have to spend the night in that city. Because we had no Iranian riyals, having expected to leave the country that day, the Mashhad Customs office had offered to pay for our rooms. In the event, they denied this, and we paid with Eurocheques, not legally cashable in Iran.

In Turkey, we stayed in a well-situated small hotel in central Istanbul called the Hotel Klodfarer. It is cheap and comfortable if a little primitive. We spent one night when our tents would have been preferable in a hotel on the beach at the curiously stillborn seaside town of Samandaği, 19 kms from Antakya. In order to be near a phone, I used a hotel in Doğubayazit which was by Turkish standards expensive and pretentious. In Ankara, the Hotel Hanecioglu is cheap, very clean and comfortable and highly recommended.

5 *Special problems: Turkey.*  It is not possible to drive out of Turkey at Akyaka, north-east of Kars, into the Soviet Union. Cars must be put on a train at Kars which will carry them into the Soviet Union. These trains leave Kars on Tuesday and Friday at about 10.30 a.m. and arrive on the Soviet side of the

border at about 3.00 p.m. Passengers may of course travel by the same train but may not ride in their cars. At Leninakan, I drove our car off the train and into the town, about 4 kms, to the railway station where Customs inspection takes place. Information about this procedure was not available to the Turkish officials whom we asked. At the border, moreover, Turkish Customs officials insisted that we remove all objects from our roof rack and place them inside the car because, they said, Soviet Customs would allow nothing to enter their country unless it was locked inside. This is not true.

*Iran*. We discovered that there were two problems with travel in Iran: the legal rate of exchange between pounds sterling and riyals, and Customs refusal to allow us to leave Iran at the previously-agreed point. At the Bāzargān entry point, we exchanged pounds sterling at the legal rate of 117 riyals to the pound. In practical terms, this rate of exchange makes a loaf of bread in Iran cost about £3 and a meal consisting of kebab, rice and salad at a roadside café, about £10. In other words, it is fixed as a tax on tourism.

I had been told by travellers in London that in order for us to drive across Iran on our own, we would have to travel with a guard. This advice was confirmed by the Director of Customs at the Bāzargān border post who authorised assignment of a Customs policeman to us and told me that the fee would be about £100. However, the bill presented to me by the Customs police for payment in advance amounted to 90,000 riyals or more than £800. The Customs police apologised and suggested we should exchange money on the black market where the rate would be about 900 riyals for £1. I objected that because we were working for UNESCO, that avenue was closed to us. Returning to the Director of Customs in the company of our assigned guard, I complained that we were being charged more than eight times the fee he had named to me. He expressed considerable surprise: surely, I had realised, he said, that the fee of £100 was based on exchanging currency at the black market rate. He strongly advised us to do so.

We were confronted with similar illegal propositions on two further occasions: in the presence of his staff, the manager of the Bank of Iran branch in Bābol offered to exchange a US dollar travellers' cheque for one of us at the black market rate. When my colleague refused and asked for the exchange to be made at the legal rate, the manager refused because he said it was necessary that he send the travellers' cheque to Tehrān so that the cash could be made available there. I have already referred to the second occasion: because we had no riyals, the hotel in Mashhad accepted Eurocheques in payment of our bill. The Eurocheques were made out at the legal rate of exchange, about 117 riyals to a £1.

Our second problem in Iran arose when we were refused permission to leave the country at Bājgirān. We were arrested by Customs police there, in the presence of our guard who accompanied us throughout, taken at gunpoint to Customs headquarters for Khorāsan province in Mashhad and then told to leave the country either by entering the Soviet Union at Astara (which our Soviet visas did not allow) or by re-entering Turkey at Bāzargān.

I first applied to the Iranian Consulate in London informally in December 1984. At that time, the Consulate informed me that I could travel through Iran on a two-week transit visa, and that I could enter the Soviet Union at any crossing agreed by the Soviet authorities. At that time, nothing was said about any Iranian crossing point being closed.

On February 10th, 1987, I applied formally for Iranian visas, completing the visa application forms and paying the £10 fee for four people. The Consulate told me that the Soviet border was closed but offered to make special application for us to the Ministry of Foreign Affairs. Nothing had been heard from Tehrān by May 1st when we left London. Meanwhile, however, the Permanent Delegate to UNESCO from Iran, Dr Feiz, had kindly taken an interest in the expedition. Through his intervention, the Iranian National Commission for UNESCO in Tehrān had applied on our behalf to the Ministry of Foreign Affairs. Therefore, the London Consulate suggested that we reapply for visas in Istanbul. This I did, on May 11th. Not only did I pay the visa fees a second time, but I also filled in the application forms again. *Both sets of visa applications indicated that we wished to leave Iran at Bājgirān.* I had also written to Dr Feiz that we wished to enter the Soviet Union from Bājgirān. The visas were issued at Istanbul on May 17th.

We have been given no explanation other than that the border was closed. Customs at Bāzargān had told us the border was closed at Bājgirān but accepted that our visas were issued in terms of the route we proposed to follow across Iran. Customs at Bājgirān told us the crossing point was closed and ordered us to consult their superiors in Mashhad. In Mashhad, we were told that the border had been closed for eleven years, that it was closed "by law" and that we could not cross. We believe that the clear contradiction between the behaviour of the Ministry of Foreign Affairs who issued our visas in response to applications which twice stated that Bājgirān was our intended exit, and of the Ministry of the Interior under which Customs operates, can be explained only by a ministerial conflict at some higher level.

Our second problem was complicated by another fact which we discovered only in Mashhad. For some reason, my Iranian visa was good for two weeks from June 1st, 1987, whereas those of my three colleagues were good for four weeks. We reached Mashhad during the night of June 9th. The Iranian National Commission for UNESCO advised me by telephone the next day to apply to the police for an extension of my visa, but the Customs officials in Mashhad said no extension would be granted. Thus, I had three full days at most to get back to the Turkish border and out of Iran.

*USSR*. The only special problems arose as a result of the delay caused by events in Iran, and they were made worse by the fact that our Chinese visas expired on July 22nd. The party of eleven people organised by the Institute of Geography of the USSR Academy of Sciences was waiting for us at the Bājgirān crossing on June 9th. It was at least four days before they learned what had happened to us, and at least a week before they knew that I was applying through the Soviet Embassy in Ankara for visas that would allow us to enter the Soviet Union at Leninakan. Meanwhile, the Institute of Geography had arranged with the Turkmen, Uzbek, Tadzhik and Kirgiz Academies of Science to provide experts to accompany us and had co-ordinated our travel with officials in the towns and regions through which we would be driving based on the schedule we had agreed. In the event, we entered the Soviet Union on July 3rd instead of June 9th and finally caught up with our

Soviet hosts on July 13th. Any special problems in the Soviet Union confronted them, not us.

*China*. Our hosts in China were the Mountain Scientific Expedition Advisory Service, a commercial subsidiary within the Institute of Geology of the Academia Sinica. They made it possible for us to drive across China, although the route we had requested was changed at the very last minute because of the military authorities. They also arranged our accommodation, food, petrol and motor maintenance. During our stay in Xinjiang, they provided a physician with training in cancer epidemiology to travel with us. In every stopping place, they arranged our excursions through the local foreign affairs department or CITS branch which overlapped in some towns, the manager of one acting also as the manager of the other.

We confronted three special problems: 1 Although we all had International Driving Licences, and there are precedents, we were forbidden to drive. We strongly advise the UNESCO Task Force that this may be a problem for them too.

2 Despite our specific request, we were not allowed to camp in China although the accommodation provided was sometimes distinctly inferior. Again, this may be a problem for UNESCO.

3 By far the most important problem, however, arose because neither our hosts nor we understood the costly complexities involved in locating, visiting and photographing the sites that interested us. Our hosts failed to take into account our interest in the historical geography of the Silk Road. They provided no expert local guidance but depended on the usually very inadequate knowledge of the local foreign affairs department or CITS branch guides. They made no attempt to arrange in advance for us to visit the excavations at Karghalik, which we were unable to see, or to enter major monuments such as the Mugao Grottoes at Dunhuang. Even more serious, they disregarded the fact that one of us is a professional photographer and made no attempt until after we had reached Dunhuang to find out how to obtain permission for us to photograph major national sites and relics, let alone to arrange for us to do so. In the event, we were unable to photograph the Buddhist grottoes at Qucha, Dunhuang and Luoyang or the terracotta army at Xi'an, and major Chinese museums, unlike those in Turkey, Iran and the Soviet Union, were out of bounds for photography and holography. Even small museums required the payment of fees; for example, the museum in Hotan charged 20 yuan for a photograph, but even this institution refused us permission to make a hologram of one museum piece. The failure by the Mountain Scientific Expedition Advisory Service to deal with these vital subjects reduced the usefulness of our journey in China.

With the help of the British Consulate in Beijing, we arranged to meet with representatives of the Chinese National Bureau of Museums and Archaeological Data on September 1st. The Deputy Chief of the Cultural Relics Section, Mr Guo Zhan, explained the general principles by which sites of national interest were designated and fees are set for visits and photography. It is essential that UNESCO make arrangements in advance with the National Bureau and probably with the Ministry of Culture which administers the Bureau.

# APPENDIX IV

# Note on the Holography and Photography by Tom Ang

*Holography*

There is nothing noteworthy about an expedition that sets out to photograph whatever chance and fortune have to offer it. Almost any expedition of any scale, whether it plans a day trip to the seaside or a scientific survey throughout an Arctic winter, will regard the making of a photographic record as one of the essential tasks of the venture, not very far behind the need to keep its socks dry.

While the Marco Polo Expedition was no exception in this regard, we did hope to pioneer the making of a wholly modern and radically different kind of visual record.

Holography, we wished to demonstrate, could travel. It could leave its usual and comfortable haunt in the optics laboratory and take its place on the dusty trail, alongside photography, cinematography and television, as an invaluable means of recording in the field.

What is holography? It is similar to photography in that a flat piece of light-sensitive film (the holographic film) is exposed to make a record (the hologram) of the points of varying brightness on an object. However, a hologram is exposed or taken in a different way from photographs. For one thing, the light that is used must be a very pure colour or "monochromatic" and it must be highly organised or "coherent": lasers are the usual source of light.

Holograms are also processed quite differently from photographs. The entire procedure ensures that holograms record information about the *directions* from which each point of light has come as well the brightness. Thus the hologram stores details about how the object had occupied space. In contrast, a photograph is only a point-by-point record of *brightness* in the object.

When the resulting hologram is correctly illuminated or "replayed", it projects back the light-wave that came from the object: thus we have a fully three-dimensional image, one which appears to occupy space. Indeed, by moving your head around, you will be able to see more of the object than if you had looked at it from only one position. For example, looking at a hologram of a face from the left you will see the right side of the face; move over to the right and you'll be able to see the left side which was previously hidden. What's more, the original holographic image is *exactly* the same size – to a high level of precision – as the object. All from a flat piece of film.

There are several kinds of hologram. For the expedition, we chose to make Denisyuk holograms, named after the Soviet scientist who invented the technique. Denisyuk holograms combine two important virtues. They are relatively easy to produce as the optical components needed are quite minimal. Then, they are easy to "replay" as they can reflect an image even when illuminated with ordinary light. Denisyuks were thus the ideal candidates for taking on the expedition.

We used the Holocam holographic camera, produced by Holofax Ltd. The Holocam is essentially a rigid metal frame which holds the laser and main optical components in alignment and it also contains the electrical parts. The laser was fitted up to be powered by a car battery. We also took the film and all the processing chemicals needed.

The most bulky part of the equipment was the camera which took up the whole of a steel box measuring about $680 \times 360 \times 450$ mm. The accessories and materials took up two boxes, each about the size of a typical car battery. The Holocam worked faultlessly despite a rough ride in the back of the Land Rover. (Fuller practical and technical details are given in 'Holocam in the USSR', *British Journal of Photography*, pp. 1424–5, Vol. 134, no. 6642, November 26th 1987.)

To make holograms it was only necessary to remove the Holocam, take out a car battery, find or set up a darkroom and find suitable objects to holograph. Clearly, the technique is ideal for making a record of small and precious artefacts which could not be removed, such as museum exhibits. As we could make only same-sized images, the maximum size of the object is fixed by the film size which was in this case $5 \times 4$ inches.

By the end of the expedition we had succeeded in making only nineteen holograms, in two museums in Soviet central Asia. Many of these were given to the museum authorities, some of the others now form part of a travelling photography exhibition.

It is worth noting that we took only about eight hours in total to make these holograms – this time includes the scramble needed to turn offices into impromptu darkrooms and to unpack all the equipment. There is, however, no virtue in taking such a short time to do holography unless it is to take a he-man pride in proving the possibility: rather it merely reflects the fact that the main obstacles to holography were not technical. In the USSR, there was the pressure of a hasty schedule. After that, we could make no holograms at all, thanks to the way the expedition was administered while in China. We were also equipped to turn the Land Rover into a darkroom but had no opportunity to put that to the test.

Nevertheless, we think we have shown that it is not only possible, but also relatively straightforward, to make holograms under expedition conditions. Indeed, with advances in laser technology as well as in optics, the next attempt at holography under expedition conditions should be even easier.

*Photography*
For all the importance of the holography, common-or-garden travel photography was also attempted.

All photographs for this book were taken on Leica equipment. For the official expedition photography, we took a Leica R5, Leica R4sII, Leica R4 and Leica R4s with one each of the 21 mm, 28 mm f/2.8, 35 mm f/2, 50 mm f/2, 60 mm f/2.8, 135 mm f/2.8, 70–210 mm f/4 and 350 mm f/4.8 lenses. We also took a Leica M6 with the 35 mm f/2 lens supplemented by the 50 mm f/2 and 90 mm f/2.8 lenses.

While the Leica R cameras were not totally reliable, all the lenses performed very well indeed. The 21 mm and 60 mm lenses were particularly outstanding and the 70–210 mm lens was also used a great deal. The Leica M6 with its 35 mm lens was found to be perfect for street scenes and portraits.

For the expedition colour photography, we used Ilford Ilfochrome 50 and for most of the black and white, we used Ilford XP1. Both films turned in excellent results and survived periods of extreme heat without any apparent distress. Many rolls of film were developed as much as three months after a blasting in desert sun but they also showed no obvious sign of distress.

A Polaroid Image camera was taken along: predictably, it proved popular for giving instant memorabilia to dignitaries we met on the way. Film was too valuable to give to just anyone who happened to be passing. Besides, we did not approve of making friends through hand-outs. Polaroid Polachrome and Polapan were also used to perform camera checks and, in one instance, to provide pictures for the Soviet team to use in publicising the expedition.

Essential accessories which were taken along included a case custom-made by Camera Care System for a Minolta Flashmeter III, a Cullman Titan tripod and a Novoflex shoulder pod.

Another accessory, essential for some countries,* was an ATA Carnet: this was a pile of paperwork covering the photographic equipment. Like much paperwork it never seems worth the trouble and expense needed to obtain and administer it because when you do possess it you don't ever seem to suffer any trouble or expense. The Carnet streamlines the temporary import and export of valuable goods across borders of most signatory countries.

As with the holography, the main obstacles to photography were not technical nor were they due to any unfriendliness from the people we met. Indeed, we almost always enjoyed very friendly and welcoming encounters wherever we travelled. To those transient friends who readily gave us their smiles and trust, we owe a great debt in the photographs they allowed us to obtain. Without the cheery welcome and friendliness from passers-by, the expedition would have been for me a pale experience – for all that we saw wonderful sights.

---

* Author's note: The T2L sufficed for EEC countries, Austria and Jugoslavia. Turkey, a signatory, accepted the Carnet ATA after long delays but partially inspected the cameras on only one of four opportunities. Iran, previously a signatory, refused to accept the Carnet. USSR and China are not signatories. According to the Chamber of Commerce and the Road Haulage Association, the Carnet ATA is essential for commercial goods passing through one non-EEC country for disposal in another, unnecessary for personal equipment intended for return to the country of origin with the owner, but each situation should be checked with these authorities.

# APPENDIX V

# Medical Research Protocol and Final Report by Geoff Clarke

*Medical Research Protocol, prepared 1986*

The main medical aim of the Marco Polo Expedition is investigation of the high incidence of carcinoma of the oesophagus and stomach known to occur in many regions along the ancient Silk Road. Before we complete our plans, we would like to have advice and suggestions from medical experts working along the route and cancer specialists in Turkey, Iran, the Soviet Union and China. In particular, we need advice on where to find the materials we wish to collect. These fall into three categories:

1   Information about demographic data and the diet, working arrangements and medical history of the people living in the places we visit. Apart from local written records, the best source of such information will undoubtedly be discussions with local nutritionists and doctors, especially those interested in cancer epidemiology.

2   Samples of anything regularly swallowed by the local people, both food and medicines. We will wish to take ourselves several representative samples (5 ml in volume) from a number of randomly-selected batches of flour, cereals, sauces and vinegars. Of medicines, we particularly want samples (5 ml in volume) of herbal remedies given regularly, especially for sore throat or pain in swallowing. If talc, zeolites or tabashir are given by mouth, samples (5 ml) are desired because the fibrous minerals have been shown elsewhere to be tumour promoters. Of course, tabashir is an exudate of bamboo which is probably not grown anywhere along our route, but it may be a source of silica fibres and is given by mouth in other parts of China.

3   We recognise that there may be difficulties in obtaining tissue samples from patients along the whole of the Silk Road because autopsies are infrequent. Nevertheless, we hope to collect samples (2 to 4 ml) of tissues from growing and necrotic regions of tumours and from any normal tissue removed with them. These should be thoroughly washed with normal saline to remove contaminating food particles before fixation in formalin. Where operations are performed just before or during our visits, we also wish to fix material (2 to 4 ml) in glutaraldehyde which we will bring with us. These samples can be used for electron microscopic and x-ray analysis. Suitable samples will be made available to any institute wishing to conduct similar investigations, and of course our own analyses will be shared with them.

Abridged final section of Report to the Imperial Cancer Research Fund, April 1988:

*Oesophageal cancer, General*

In Soviet Central Asia we had discussions with groups of doctors in Ashkabad, Samarkand (from Tashkent) and Leninabad; another planned for Dushanbe was cancelled because a landslide stopped us from driving there. In China we met groups of doctors trained in Western medicine at Kargalik, Hotan, Aksu, Korla, Kumul, Lanzhou, Xian and Anyang; also others trained in Uigher traditional medicine at Kashgar, Hotan and Korla. We met doctors trained in Chinese traditional medicine at Kumul, Lanzhou, Xi'an and Anyang. Groups varied from three to thirteen. In Anyang we met two doctors from Zhengzhou: Professor Zhang Tanmu and Dr Ge Ming. Dr Charles O'Neill [of the Imperial Cancer Research Fund] and I met them in Henan in 1981. During the month I spent at the Institute of Basic Medical Sciences (Military) in Beijing after the Expedition, I travelled to Zhengzhou for further talks with Dr Ge Ming.

At meetings we first heard a brief history of the hospital and a description of its present concerns, the nature of the catchment area including the life-style and diet of its patients. We quickly moved on to cancer and oesophageal cancer (o.c.) in particular. Gastric cancer and o.c. were generally the two commonest malignancies followed by liver, breast and lung cancers. The incidence of tumours of the mouth and tongue were variable in position and possibly associated with the chewing of naas (a local tobacco-based stimulant varying in composition). Along the Silk Road it usually consisted of wood ash (often cotton), tobacco sometimes in sesame oil and lime. Like opium use, it is a difficult subject for discussion. In China naas is banned and in Soviet Central Asia, "only used by old men and never by Russians". Incidentally, I remember seeing no local woman smoking between Istanbul and Beijing. As far as alcohol is concerned, a rapid change is taking place in China, large stocks being visible in shops even in small towns, but I doubt if either alcohol or tobacco is relevant to the high incidence of o.c. today (cf. Shanghai and Guangzhou where the incidence is low). The male/female ratio is said to be around 1:5, similar to that in Britain; in Karghalik it was said to be less than 1:0. This compares with over 20 in the Calvados area in north-west France where impressive reports incriminate alcoholic beverages and tobacco. This area has the highest incidence in Europe, about six times that in Britain but only about one tenth that in some places on or near the Silk Road.

*Silica fibres*

Though rice and noodles are eaten in Xinjiang, bread is a staple along Soviet parts of the Silk Road. Turkmenia is very dry, and we travelled largely through stony desert with some sand and loess. In damper areas cotton was the main crop. Wheat was variously said to come from Kazakhstan, Canada and the USA. Further east we saw fields of ripening, long-eared wheat with only short European weeds. Owing to our enforced haste in order to catch up with the Soviet party, I decided to collect wheat samples from town markets. I was given considerable help in this by an historian from the Uzbekistan Academy of Sciences, but it was hard to find because harvesting was near, we were told. Eventually, we found two end-of-season samples which, perhaps for that reason, had a heavy contamination with oats and non-grass seeds. Even the bread shops had no flour.

Xinjiang is a sparsely-populated desert province but with large oases in which the main food crops were vegetables and oil seeds. From the end of the desert east through the highest incidence area of o.c. near Lin Xian and to the lower incidence areas around Beijing, we collected eighteen samples of wheat from harvesting in fields, threshing on the road by passing vehicles, flour mills and stores issuing seed wheat for autumn sowing. Most were extremely clean, sometimes with no non-wheat seeds in samples of 500–800 ml. I could not determine how long the grain had been so clean. Since we only saw harvesting by hand, roguing is perhaps practised. I had seen wheat spread on the road for harvesting in other parts of China, but a doctor told me that the practice was discouraged by the authorities because of the fear that the flour would have become carcinogenic. The non-wheat seeds from my samples were sorted out at leisure and irradiated to avoid problems with British Customs.

I gave ampoules of glutaraldehyde to Dr Zheng of Urumchi and to Professor Zhang (Zhengzhou) for fixation of tumour tissues taken during operations. ICRF can examine these samples by transmission electron microscopy for silica fibres. Because of local religious customs, it is almost impossible to obtain autopsy specimens along the Silk Road.

### Nitrosamines and aflatoxins

Most of the medical people we met thought nitrosamines are the main carcinogens or initiators of o.c. They have been found in pickled vegetables and those stored during the long, dry, cold winters. In Lin Xian in particular such pickles, made without vinegar, are covered with a thick pellicle of mould which is considered a delicacy. In large areas of northern China such pickles are consumed in winter in vegetable quantities and are the main source of vitamin C. Recently suggestions have been made that there is little difference in the nitrosamine content of the food between high and much lower incidence areas. However, this ignores the amount that may be derived from the interaction of nitrite from food and water with secondary amines in the stomach, particularly an achlorhydric stomach. Vitamin C inhibits this interaction (see below).

Aflatoxin was often spoken of as a contaminant of grain stored in the damp, especially the B1 form. Its relevance to o.c. is unclear.

### Vitamin C deficiency

This was the most common deficiency referred to en route as well as in the literature. In both Soviet central Asia and China we were told of areas in which a more than twofold incidence was attributable solely to vitamin deficiency compared to the vitamin intake in neighbouring areas. Nomadic Kazakh herdsmen are often on diets entirely lacking fresh fruit and vegetables. Trial dietary supplementation of 0.3 and 1.0 g per day, respectively, are underway. A three-year trial with vitamins A, B-complex and C in Lin Xian has recently been discontinued because 30 per cent of those initially in the trial sample had left the area. With the exception of bleeding gums, there were no reports of scurvy symptoms. The inhibitory action of vitamin C on nitrosamine formation may be relevant, and it is possible that deterioration of the basement membranes in the oesophagus due to unhealthy collagen allows unhealthy growth of premalignant cells.

### Tannins

Dr Julia Morton has emphasised the "tannin" aspect of "hot tea" (*J. Env. Sci. Hlth.*, 1980, C4, 203; *Rec. Adv. Phytochem.*, 1986). Since in leather making, tannins are used to denature collagen, they may be considered suspect on chemical as well as epidemiological grounds. However there is a considerable difference between the concentrations taken by mouth and those used to treat hides. This may be balanced to some extent by considerations of daily frequency, years of use and temperature. Tannins occur in all alcoholic beverages and their astringency is, apparently, so appreciated that whisky is matured in oak casks for years to extract them. Because they are present in highest concentration in seeds, twigs and skin, beverages made from small fruit have the highest tannin concentration.

Morton has stated that the amount of milk added to tea is sufficient to precipitate all the tannins and thus protect the oesophagus from their effects. A Chinese doctor stated with confidence, though without details, that the milk precipitates only half the tannins in tea. His remarks do suggest that tannins are now under investigation in China. The brick tea drunk in Xinjiang comes from Hunan in south-east China, though it is said not to be drunk there nor in any of the richer areas. The samples I have collected for Dr Morton certainly contained a lot of twigs. It is harvested green and at once made into bricks; not surprisingly, since it is allowed to mature for a year before use, it is said to contain undesirable mould products. The tea we drank at lunch times in transport cafés along the route was made and served in kettles, having been boiled. Dr Zheng said it was drunk much stronger in the countryside, especially by the Kazakh herdsmen in the Ili river area of high o.c. incidence, though they add milk.

I can find no report of tannins by mouth causing tumours. One would like to see results of tannins given by mouth to animals initiated with nitrosamines.

### *Mumiya* (Arabic and Uigher), *Moumio* (Soviet Central Asia), *Mumia* (Latin)

As a result of a question about folk remedies used regularly in the home without medical consultation, doctors in Ashkabad at our first interview mentioned *mumio* or pitch. It was said to be found in pools above oil-bearing rock. It had apparently been an old remedy for a number of ailments. It is applied locally and also given by mouth in hot milk. We raised this subject with all subsequent groups of doctors, and *mumio* was known and used as a folk remedy as far east as Lanzhou. A doctor from Tashkent said that a controlled trial showed that it had halved the time of the healing of fractures and was found to stimulate the proliferation of bone cells. When I asked if it was considered to be carcinogenic, he would only say that it did not contain benzpyrene. Pitch is said to be used along the route to Lanzhou for vaginal discharge after childbirth, impotence and other sexual problems, for digestive complaints and as a tonic. Plant gums and resins in forms resembling pitch are also used.

I was unable to trace samples of *mumio* anywhere in China in street markets or private or hospital pharmacies. At the People's Hospital in Korla where all the out-patients to be seen had arms or legs in splints, the pharmacist told me that *moumio* was not available locally because it had to come from Iran and was now very expensive, but it was used in Urumchi.

Another folk remedy in China for minor gastric complaints is to heat a lump of coal to redness, plunge it into a mug of water until the water boils, add salt and drink as hot as possible.

### Treatment of oesophageal cancer

Even where there is no routine screening, the public awareness of early symptoms such as swallowing pain is such that many cases present earlier than in a low incidence area. The results of treatment, therefore, may be expected to be better in a high incidence area.

In Samarkand a surgeon from Tashkent said that hyperthermia combined with X-irradiation following resection gave good results. Treatment was 30–60 min at 45–50°C before X-irradiation daily for 2–4 weeks. Results were:

| | |
|---|---|
| Surgery only, for stages 1 and 2 | 5-year survival: 5–15% |
| Surgery and X-irradiation for stages 1–4 | 5-year survival: 10% |
| Surgery, X-irradiation and hyperthermia for stages 1–4 | 5-year survival: 18% |

These results were presented recently in Hungary.

Precancerous lesions, particularly leukoplakia, are treated in Soviet Central Asia by local electrothermal heat via endoscopy. A reduction of three-fold in the incidence of o.c. within 20 years is expected. In Uzbekistan a yearly certificate of screening by fluorography is necessary before anyone can use the state GP service.

For two years Dr Ge Ming at the Henan Tumour Hospital has been collecting spleens, thymuses and livers from aborted foetuses over a wide area around Zhengzhou for intravenous injection of cells into cancer patients with easily measurable tumours. Up to twenty foetuses per patient my be used. He has published nine papers in China and gave me four unpublished English versions. He reports a significant decrease in tumour size within a short time in some cases. He assured me that records of previous and subsequent treatments and the long-term state of the patient are being kept.

### Reflections

There is a general agreement that o.c. along the Silk Road is not attributable to alcoholic beverages and tobacco but to diet. Its aetiology is generally considered to be multifactorial; nitrosamines are considered to be the major initiator. Of course there is a difficulty in relating the concentrations to which the oesophagus is exposed and those necessary for successful animal experiments.

Silica fibres of the type found in flour from Iran a decade ago have not been found in Putian or Lin Xian.

Vitamin C deficiency has not been reported clinically.

Tannins are certainly the most widespread of the purported causative agents. However, Morton's enthusiasm has not been very infectious, though her view has received support recently from Uruguay (Vassallo, A. et al., *J. Natl. Cancer Inst.*, 1985, 75, 1005) and from Brazil (Victoria, C. G. et al., unpublished). In both of these investigations there was an association of the use of hot maté, a tea from *Ilex paraguarensis* sucked through a tube, and o.c. incidence. The method of consumption is said to deliver the tea at a very high temperature to the lower oesophagus.

It seems strange that, throughout the world, hot food and drinks are mentioned as possible causes of o.c. In Lin Xian this seems to be the case: Dr Ge Ming tells me that he has measured gruel being eaten quickly at over 80°C. Along the Silk Road it was suggested that the habit arose due to the very cold winters. However, similar reports emanate from Japan, Singapore, Uruguay and Brazil. I questioned medics in China on whether they thought hot foods and drinks cause o.c. or a premalignant condition. All said they thought it to be a cause. One doctor added, "there is no doubt that those about to get o.c. do take their food hotter", implying that in the area of high incidence, the habit is not universal. Some recent research in this country has established that food temperature is less important to the lower oesophagus than the unit volume taken.

# APPENDIX VI

# Commercial Sponsors and their Products or Services

The Marco Polo Expedition is grateful to the following companies:
Camera Care Systems, CCS Centre, Vale Lane, Bedminster, Bristol BS3 5RU, for photographic accessories; E. S. Tenten BV, 's-Gravelandseweg 28–30, 1211 BS Hilversum, Holland, for tent and camping equipment; Fairey Industrial Ceramics Ltd, Filleybrooks, Stone, Staffs ST15 OPU, for ceramic water filters; Giffard Newton & Sons Ltd, Townsend Rd, Chesham, Bucks HP5 2AD for boots; Haldane Foods Ltd, Unit 25, Hayhill Industrial Estate, Sileby Rd, Barrow-upon-Soar, Leics LE12 8LD, for dehydrated food; Holofax Ltd, Netherwood Rd, Rotherwas, Hereford HR2 6JZ, for the portable holographic camera; Ilford Ltd, for photographic film; E. Leitz (Instruments) Ltd, 48 Park St, Luton LV1 3HP., for cameras; A. B. Optimus Ltd, Sanders Lodge Estate, Rushden, Northants NN10 9BQ, for a field stove and cookery equipment; Polisox Ltd, Park Rd, Blaby, Leicester LE8 3ED, for socks; Silva (UK) Ltd, 15 Bolney Way, Feltham, Middx TW13 6DB, for compasses; Tilley International, 33 High St, Frimley, Surrey GU16 5JD, for gas mantle lamps; Vitramon Inc, Bridgeport, Conn. 06601, USA, for a Universal watch; Zamana Gallery, 1 Cromwell Gardens, London SW7 2SL for holding the photographic exhibition of the expedition.

# An Outline of Chinese Dynasties

2200?–1766? BC: Xia (unverified)
1766?–1122? BC: Shang. Capital near Anyang
1122?–256 BC: Chou. Capitals at Xi'an and Luoyang
221–207 BC: Qin. Capital at Xi'an (terracotta army; origin of name, China)
202 BC–AD 9: Han (also, western Han). Capital at Changan
AD 9–23 Xin. Capital at Changan
AD 25–220: Han (also, later or eastern Han). Capital at Luoyang
AD 220–280: Three Kingdoms
266–316: Qin (also, western Qin). Capital at Luoyang, then Changan
317–589: Northern and Southern Dynasties

Northern (386–581)         Southern (317–589)
  Northern Wei (386–534)     Eastern Qin (317–420)
  Eastern Wei (534–550)      Liu (Song) (420–479)
  Western Wei (534–557)      Southern Qi (479–502)
  Northern Qi (550–577)      Liang (502–557)
  Northern Chou (557–581)    Chen (557–589)

581–618: Sui. Capital at Changan
618–907: Tang. Capital at Changan
907–960: Five Dynasties
960–1127: Song. Capital at Kaifeng
Northern Conquest Dynasties (916–1234; Inner Mongolia and Manchuria, Beijing from 1127)
1127–1279: Southern Song. Capital at Hanzhou
1264–1368: Yuan. Capital at Beijing. First Emperor: Kubilai Khan
1368–1644: Ming. Capital at Nanjing, then Beijing
1644–1912: Qing. Capital at Beijing
1912–1949: Republic of China
1949–     People's Republic of China

# Glossary

ark: the citadel, the best defended area of an ancient town, often centrally placed with its own wall and a water supply. This word is used by Soviet archaeologists.

Bodhisattva: a Buddhist saint destined to become a Buddha.

cami (Turkish transliterated from Arabic): mosque

caravanserai: a kind of inn usually with a large central courtyard along trade routes in Asia and in African and Asian cities where merchants, drivers and pilgrims stayed for varying periods. Animals could be exchanged, food and water bought and goods traded. In Islamic regions, usually included a mosque. *See also* han.

chador: cloak or veil covering the head and upper body worn by Muslim women.

chaikhana: tea house or restaurant. Used both in Soviet central Asia and Xinjiang. *See also* han.

dastar khan (Turkic): meal consisting of tea, fresh fruit, cakes and possibly other local dishes served at no fixed time by servants of a local dignitary at the side of the road or in the reception room of a local official to honour a traveller. Although the phrase is rarely heard today, observance of the custom ranges from full meals (at mealtimes) to tea and fruit in offices and factories.

Gandhara: a style of Indian Buddhist painting and sculpture influenced by the classical Greek tradition. It was first identified in the Gandhara region of Afghanistan. The Greek influence reflects the conquests of Alexander the Great.

gobi: an extremely arid region in which the surface consists of sand mixed with rock. Also a desert in northern China.

han (Turkish): caravanserai. Sometimes preferred for those located in cities.

Han (Chinese): the name of a Chinese dynasty (see Outline, p. 229) adopted by the Chinese as a designation for the majority ethnic Chinese population.

iwan: roofed or vaulted hall open at one end, but a smaller door at the other end may afford entrance to a mosque.

kang (Chinese): raised platform, usually of mudbrick, inside a shelter under which a fire could be lit and on which the occupants slept.

kerez (Uigher): underground water channel which utilised an existing aquafer but was kept clear and often extended by means of holes dug from the surface.

kolkhoz (Russian): a collective farm on which the land is owned by the state.

Kufic: a rectalinear Arabic script often used on buildings.

kümbet: mausoleum.

madrasa: literally: place of study. An Islamic institution for the teaching of religion including scripture and the laws. A collegiate mosque.

mihrab: niche indicating the qibla or direction of prayer.

mimbar: pulpit.

moumio (Soviet central Asia), mumiya (Arabic and Uigher), mumia (Latin): pitch or plant gums and resins resembling pitch; a folk-remedy reported in Iran, Soviet central Asia and Xinjiang.

Ottoman: the ruling dynasty of Anatolia from 1281 to 1413. Later conquests gave them control of south-eastern Europe as far as Vienna and of other Arab lands. The Ottomans were overthrown in 1922, but by that time they controlled only Turkey within its present boundaries. Also, Osmanlis after Osman, the Turkish name for 'Uthman who founded the dynasty.

plof (Soviet central Asia): pilaff, pilau

pu tong hua: literally, common tongue. The Chinese national dialect, previously called Mandarin and more accurately, Han.

Qarakhanid: the name given by European scholars to the ruling dynasty of Transoxania (that is, territory north of the Oxus or Amudar'ya including Merv, Bukhara and Samarkand) and eastern Turkestan (including Fergana and Kashgar) from about 998 to 1211. The name means black Khans.

Qara Qoyunlu: a confederation of Turkmen rulers who ruled Azerbaijan, eastern Anatolia, western Iran and Iraq between 1380 and 1468. For a time, their capital was Tabrīz. The name means black sheep.

qibla: the direction toward which Muslims turn in prayer; i.e. Mecca. Indicated in a mosque by the location of the mihrab.

registan: literally place of sand. Market place or bazaar.

Samanid: a dynasty that ruled in Transoxania (territory north of the Oxus or Amudar'ya) and Khorāsan (north-eastern Iran and north-western Afghanistan) from 819 to 1005. The founder was named Saman-Khuda. Succeeded in Transoxania by the Qarakhanids.

Selcuk: the ruling family of eastern Anatolia, Iraq and Persia between 1038 and 1194 and for shorter periods, Syria and parts of Afghanistan. The original chieftains were Turkish nomads from the same central Asian region north of China that later produced the Mongols. This spelling is Turkish, pronounced Seljuq.

serai: palace.

Shia: the branch of Islam (*see also* Sunni) whose adherents are known as the "Party" of 'Ali, the Prophet Muhamad's cousin and son-in-law. They include those Muslims who uphold the rights of 'Ali and his descendants to leadership of the community of believers.

Song: a Chinese dynasty (see Outline, p. 229).

squinch: an arch-shaped element spanning a corner, forming one part of the octagonal base of a circular dome.

stupa: a Buddhist tomb or mausoleum with a characteristic bulbous shape.

Sunni: the branch of Islam (*see also* Shia) whose adherents are known as "People of the Sunna", customs sanctioned by tradition based on the practice and authority of the Prophet and his companions.

Tang: a Chinese dynasty (see Outline, p. 229).

tekke (Turkish): monastery. Hospice. Arabic: takkiyya.

Timur: customary transliteration of Tamer or Tambur. He was lame, and thus, Timur the Lame; Tamerlane. He was supreme ruler in Samarkand and established his empire between 1370 and his death in 1405. The dynasty he founded is called Timurid. It survived until 1500 and in Khorāsan, north-eastern Iran, until 1506.

turbe (Turkish): mausoleum. Literally: dust.

Uigher: a Turkish tribe which entered what is now Xinjiang province, western China, from the north in the tenth century. It is the largest minority in Xinjiang.

ulu cami (Turkish): great mosque. Friday Mosque.

Urartu: a kingdom around Lake Van in eastern Anatolia with its capital at Van, 840 to 590 BC. The Urartians were defeated by the Medes.

Wei: a Chinese dynasty (see Outline, p. 229).

yamen: official residence and office of local magistrate or commanding officer in western China.

yurt (Turkic): a tent of felt or skins stretched over a rigid frame of sticks used by nomadic peoples throughout central Asia. In Mongolian: gur.

# ACKNOWLEDGMENTS

In addition to the people and organisations whose help has been acknowledged in the introduction, "Marco Polo and Other Preliminaries", and in Appendices II and VI, I wish to thank the Imperial Cancer Research Fund for its financial as well as its research support.

Ken Slavin of K. and J. Slavin (Quest 8os) Ltd gave me good advice about the purchase of a vehicle, and I am grateful for his support during the crisis of the EEC export forms at Dover. Despite their original sin in the matter of these forms, moreover, P. Foley Land Rovers Ltd agreed to guarantee financially the correct export document and incidentally supplied a vehicle that performed well. In this context, I also acknowledge the serious consideration given by Daimler-Benz AG, Stuttgart, builders of Mercedes-Benz cars, to our request for sponsorship, withheld in the end because we could not make room for one of their engineers to travel with us. Their positive attitude contrasted starkly with that of the only British manufacturer of a suitable vehicle.

Our insurance was written at the last minute but with professional know-how by Campbell Irvine Ltd. Finally, I am grateful to the Expedition Advisory Centre of the Royal Geographical Society for their practical advice and informal support during the preparatory years.

The librarians and their assistants at the Royal Geographical Society and the Great Britain–USSR Association have gone out of their way to assist my reading in preparation for the expedition. I am also grateful to Dr Shirin Akiner, Lecturer at the School of Oriental and African Studies, University of London, because she has been a fount of good advice and stimulating ideas and has become a good friend. My editor, Margaret Body, has used wit and sensitivity in addition to meticulous care and has immensely improved the finished product.

The calligraphic chapter headings in Farsi are the work of M. Zoshki; those in Russian have been written by H. Yen; in Uigher, by M. Hakhim; and in Chinese, by V. Shui. My thanks to all four for adding to the quality of the book.

My colleagues, Don Baker and Paul Crook, have suggested useful books and provided insights into the understanding of Islam and China, respectively. They have also read and corrected the manuscript, though it goes without saying that any remaining errors of omission or commission are mine alone.

Finally, I acknowledge with thanks the work of our brilliant expedition photographer, Tom Ang. The reader will already have appreciated the significance of his contribution to the book, and I hope the text conveys some sense of his contribution to the preparations and the pleasures and achievements of the journey itself.

RBF
London, May 1988

# BIBLIOGRAPHY

The books listed are a personal selection from the vast literature of central Asia.

Akiner, Shirin, *Islamic Peoples of the Soviet Union*, Kegan Paul International, London, 1983. An essential reference book.

Becker, Seymour, *Russia's Protectorates in Central Asia: Bukhara and Khiva, 1865–1924*, Harvard University Press, Cambridge, Mass, 1968. Scholarly but readable.

Blunt, Wilfred, *The Golden Road to Samarkand*, Hamish Hamilton, London, 1973. Enjoyable, illustrated travel writing.

Boulger, Demetrius Charles, *The Life of Yakoob Beg; Athalik Ghazi and Badauket: Ameer of Kashgar*, W. H. Allen, London, 1878. Almost the only biography of the swashbuckling conqueror of Xinjiang, much filleted but fascinating.

Boulnois, L., *The Silk Road*, George Allen and Unwin, London, 1966. Useful history of the trade route through Bukhara and Samarkand.

Byron, Robert, *The Road to Oxiana*, Picador, London, 1983. Persia and Afghanistan in 1936, a true classic.

Cable, Mildred and Francesca French, *Through Jade Gate and Central Asia: An Account of Journeys in Kansu, Turkenstan and the Gobi Desert*, Hodder and Stoughton, London, 1947. An important travel book about the region.

Clavijo, *Embassy to Tamerlane, 1403–1406*, translated by Guy Le Strange, George Routledge, London, 1928. The mission covered the year of Timur's death, and the books give a contemporary account of Samarkand.

*Complete Collection of Chinese Art*, Volumes 14 and 15, *Paintings Section: Dunhuang Volumes*, State Publishing House, Beijing, 1987 (in Chinese).

Conolly, Violet, *Beyond the Urals: Economic Developments in Soviet Asia*, Oxford University Press, London, 1967. Dated but essential background.

Curzon, George Nathaniel, *Curzon's Persia*, edited by Peter King, Sidgwick and Jackson, London, 1986. Whets the appetite for the unabridged version.

Danziger, Nick, *Danziger's Travels: Beyond Forbidden Frontiers*, Grafton, London, 1987. Solo travel through Iran, Afghanistan and Xinjiang.

Dunhuang Institute for Cultural Relics, editor, *Art Treasures of Dunhuang*, Joint Publishing Co., Hongkong, 1983. Good colour prints.

Fleming, Peter, *News from Tartary*, Futura, London, 1980. Brilliantly readable classic from 1936.

Gordon, Lt Col. T. E., *The Roof of the World, Being the Narrative of a Journey over the High Plateau of Tibet to the Russian Frontier and the Oxus Sources on Pamir*, Edmonston and Douglas, Edinburgh, 1876. Marred but good exploration literature.

Haidar, Dughlat, Mirza Muhammad, *The Tarikh-i-Rashidi of . . . , A History of the Moghuls of Central Asia*, N. Elias, editor, E. Denison Ross, translator, Sampson Low, Marston, London, 1895. Post-Timurid history by a relative of Babur, the Moghul conqueror of India.

Hedin, Sven, *The Silk Road*, George Routledge, London, 1938. Swedish archaeologist and explorer of Xinjiang dominated more than usually by European arrogance.

Hedin, Sven, *Through Asia* (2 volumes), Methuen, London, 1898. Records of his journals and digs.

Hopkirk, Peter, *Foreign Devils on the Silk Road*. John Murray, London, 1980. Highly readable account of early archaeological discoveries in Xinjiang.

Ibn Battuta, *Travels in Asia and Africa, 1352–1354*, H. A. R. Gibbs, translator and editor, Routledge and Kegan Paul, London, 1963. Iran and Uzbekistan.

Keddie, Nikki R., *Roots of Revolution: An Interpretive History of Modern Iran*, Yale University Press, New Haven and London, 1981. Good background to help understand Khomeini's regime.

Kinross, Lord (Patrick Balfour), *Within the Taurus: A Journey in Asiatic Turkey*, John Murray, London, 1954. Literate and enjoyable.

Knoblock, Edgar, *Beyond the Oxus: Archaeology, Art and Architecture of Central Asia*, Benn, London, 1972. Very good and well illustrated despite its inability to live up to its subtitle.

Komroff, Manuel, editor, *Contemporaries of Marco Polo: William of Rubruck, John of Pian Carpini, Friar Odoric, Rabbi Benjamin of Tudela*, Boni and Liveright, New York, 1928. Practically the only English translations of these journals.

Kwanten, Luc, *Imperial Nomads: A History of Central Asia 500-1500*, Leicester University Press, Leicester, 1979. Superficial but readable.

Lattimore, Owen, *Pivot of Asia: Sinkiang and the Inner Asian Frontier of China and Russia*, Little, Brown, Boston, 1950. Current history by an important early scholar of the region.

Le Coq, Albert von, *Buried Treasure of Chinese Turkestan: an Account of the Activities and Adventures of the Second and Third German Turfan Expeditions*, Allen and Unwin, London, 1928. Quoted in Chapter 10.

Lynch, H. F. B., *Armenia: Travels and Studies*, Volume II: *The Turkish Provinces*, Khayats, Beirut, 1965. Scholarly and detailed.

Macartney, Lady, *An English Lady in Chinese Turkestan*, Oxford University Press, Hongkong and Oxford, 1985. Marvellously naïve and sympathetic record of life in Kashgar by the wife of the first British Consul, published in 1931.

Maclean, Fitzroy, *Eastern Approaches*, Cape, London, 1949. Experiences in Soviet Russia.

Maillart, Ella K., *Forbidden Journey: from Peking to Kashmir*, Heinemann, London, 1937. Somewhat carping account, by Peter Fleming's unnamed companion.

Morgan, David, *The Mongols*, Blackwell, Oxford, 1986. Excellent illustrated history of the tribe of Genghis Khan.

Polo, Marco, *The Travels*, Ronald Latham, translator, Penguin, Harmondsworth, 1980. Good introduction and very readable translation.

Reitlinger, Gerald, *A Tower of Skulls: a Journey through Persia and Turkish*

*Armenia*, Duckworth, London, 1932. Good travel writing by a great art collector.

Rice, Tamara Talbot, *Ancient Arts of Central Asia*, Thames and Hudson, London, 1965. Outmoded scholarship, but full of matter.

Ross, Sir E. Denison, *The Persians*, Clarendon, Oxford, 1931. The standard history, as was.

Ruthven, Malise, *Islam in the World*, Penguin, Harmondsworth, 1984. Excellent introduction.

Saunders, J. J., *The History of the Mongol Conquests*, Routledge and Kegan Paul, London, 1971. Scholarly but heavy going.

Schuyler, Eugene, *Turkistan: Notes of a Journey in Russian Turkistan, Kokand, Bukhara and Kuldja*, Geoffrey Wheeler, editor, Routledge and Kegan Paul, London, 1966. Perceptive and lively, by the American Consul in St Petersburg about 1875.

Severin, Tim, *Tracking Marco Polo*, Arrow, London, 1984. Only as far as Afghanistan, in 1964.

Shaw, Robert, *Visits to High Tartary, Yarkand, and Kashgar and Return Journey over the Karakorum Pass*, John Murray, London, 1871. And walking all the way.

Sinclair, T. A., *Eastern Turkey: An Architectural and Archaeological Survey*, Volume I, Pindar Press, London, 1987. The author generously allowed me to use relevant sections of Volumes II and III (publication: 1988) and IV (publication: 1989).

Skrine, C. P., *Chinese Central Asia*, Methuen, London, 1926. Standard history.

Skrine, F. H. and Edward Denison Ross, *The Heart of Asia. A History of Russian Turkestan and the Central Asian Khanates from the Earliest Times*, Methuen, London, 1899. Still very informative.

Stein, Sir Aurel, *Innermost Asia: Detailed Report of Explorations in Central Asia, Kan-su and Eastern Iran*, 3 volumes, Clarendon, Oxford, 1928. Late summary volumes by the great master of central Asian archaeology.

Stein, Sir Aurel, *On Ancient Central-Asian Tracks*, Macmillan, London, 1933. A popular summary of his immensely readable research reports.

Stein, M. Aurel, *Sand-buried Ruins of Khotan*, T. Fisher Unwin, London, 1903. One of his earliest research reports.

Stewart, John Massey, *Across the Russias*, Harvill, London, 1969. Travel by public transportation from west to east.

Sykes, Ella and Brigadier-General Sir Percy Sykes, *Through Deserts and Oases of Central Asia*, Macmillan, London, 1920. The first part by Miss Sykes is a readable and sympathetic memoir of her two years as Consular hostess in Kashgar. The Brigadier, her brother, and the Consul at the beginning of the First World War, contributes to geography, economics and boredom.

Waley, Arthur, *The Secret History of the Mongols and Other Pieces*, Allen and Unwin, London, 1963. Almost the only translation of the one Mongol primary source dealing with the rise of Genghis Khan.

Younghusband, Captain Frank E., *The Heart of a Continent*, John Murray, London, 1896. British military arrogance, but still one of the earliest accounts of a trip from Peking to Kashgar across the Gobi Desert.

# INDEX